T0330583

BOKO HARAM

BOKO HARAM

Security Considerations and the Rise of an Insurgency

Ona Ekhomu

CRC Press
Taylor & Francis Group
Boca Raton London New York

CRC Press is an imprint of the
Taylor & Francis Group, an **informa** business

CRC Press
Taylor & Francis Group
6000 Broken Sound Parkway NW, Suite 300
Boca Raton, FL 33487-2742

International Standard Book Number-13: 978-1-138-56136-6 (Hardback)

Library of Congress Cataloging-in-Publication Data
Names: Ekhomu, Ona, author.
Title: Boko Haram : security considerations and the rise of an insurgency / Ona Ekhomu.
Description: Boca Raton, FL : CRC Press, Taylor & Francis Group, 2019. | Includes index. | Summary: "Boko Haram analyzes the activities and atrocities of Nigeria's Jihadi terrorist group, Boko Haram in the context of global religious fundamentalism and extremism. The book traces the early beginnings of the religious sect, the conversion of its leader to radical Islam in 2002, and the group's campaign of violence beginning in 2009 and continuing to the present. The group's attacks against a variety of targets are examined in detail as are their general tactics and strategies. The Nigerian government response is also examined in order to provide critical lessons to counter-terrorism planners, officials and scholars. The initial military response was hampered by capability and legislative constraints including lack of arms and ammunitions, lack of modern counter-terrorism equipment, training gap, leadership issues, intelligence gap, politicization of the conflict, and limited support for the Nigerian Military by the international community. The book looks at the work that has been done thus far, and what work needs to continue, to make gains to combat, marginalize, and ultimately defeat Boko Haram and resolve the conflict facing Nigeria."—Provided by publisher.
Identifiers: LCCN 2019020895 (print) | LCCN 2019981544 (ebook) | ISBN 9781138561366 (hardback : alk. paper) | ISBN 9780203710838 (ebook)
Subjects: LCSH: Boko Haram—History. | Terrorist organizations—Nigeria—History--21st century. | Terrorism—Prevention—Government policy—Nigeria. | Social conflict—Nigeria--Religious aspects. | Insurgency—Nigeria.
Classification: LCC HV6433.N62 B6524 2019 (print) | LCC HV6433.N62 (ebook) | DDC 363.32509669—dc23
LC record available at https://lccn.loc.gov/2019020895
LC ebook record available at https://lccn.loc.gov/2019981544

Visit the Taylor & Francis Web site at
http://www.taylorandfrancis.com

and the CRC Press Web site at
http://www.crcpress.com

This book is dedicated to the memory of the Nigerian service members who lost their lives in the war against the Boko Haram insurgency. May their supreme sacrifices not be in vain. Amen.

CONTENTS

PART THREE   *Combating Insurgency*

ACKNOWLEDGEMENTS

This author is exceedingly grateful to editor Mark Listewnik for ensuring that the book was completed and published. I also owe a profound debt of gratitude to Mrs. Jennifer Abbott who first asked me to consider writing a book on Boko Haram after she attended my presentation in October 2014.

My gratitude also goes to my wife, Victoria, who nudged me daily to complete this book. Aside from encouraging and cheering, Vicky also sometimes assisted me with research. My daughter, Dr. Omonigho Ekhomu, served as the project manager for this book project. She set deadlines and followed up with me on meeting those commitments. My other daughter, Miss Edowaye Ekhomu, also kept me focused on completing this with her gentle but persistent nudging.

I am also grateful to my former secretary, Mrs. Joke Shittu, Vicky's former secretary, Mrs. Shakirat Omowunmi, my research assistant, Mr. Chigozie Onyemachi, and my personal assistant, Ms. Tope Adesuyi, for assisting me in numerous ways in the delivery of this product.

My greatest thanks go to Almighty God – my enabler and the source of my knowledge. I give all praise to God and God alone.

PREFACE

This book grew out of my research since 2010 on the Boko Haram phenomenon in Nigeria. I was quite agitated that a group of criminals would kill with impunity in a modern democratic state. I gave lectures at several fora on the subject including the ASIS African Security Conference 2011, Nigerian Institute of International Affairs Brainstorming Session 2011, Association of Industrial Security and Safety Operators of Nigeria (AISSON) Annual Conference. At the ASIS annual seminar and exhibits this author presented papers on Boko Haram over a six-year period.

The vision for this book is to provide a factual narrative of the Boko Haram insurgency and what the future holds. This author realized quite early on that top government officials in Nigeria did not understand Boko Haramism and the deadly Islamist sect. They did not know the history or what the organization stood for. This book is intended to fill that knowledge gap. The book also dissects major attacks, exposing vulnerabilities that facilitated the attacks and the countermeasures that might have mitigated the losses from the terrorist attacks. The author adopts a storytelling approach in the book, narrating and analyzing incidents.

This book is intended as a resource and companion for policy makers, researchers, counterterrorism (CT) officials, multinational and international officials and other stakeholders in understanding Boko Haram and indeed any such local jihadi group.

The author believes that given the growing popularity of social media and easy access to illicit weapons, more jihad groups will soon spring up in Sub-Saharan Africa. This book provides a guide on how to deal with the threat. It is hoped that government officials, CT professionals and researchers will pay close attention to the issues raised.

The book is organized in three parts. The first part is a narration of the history of the Islamist group. This part also considers its funding sources. The second part examines the choice of targets as a way of understanding Boko Haram's motivation and mission. The third part deals with ways to mitigate the threats of insurgency. These include military solutions, negotiation, international assistance and creative solutions.

It is hoped that with greater and deeper understanding of the threat that Boko Haram poses to Nigeria, its immediate neighbors and the West, there will be the political will to do the right thing and overcome the jihadi threat.

THE AUTHOR

Dr. Ona Ekhomu, CFE, CPP, CSP, PCI, CPOI was born in Irrua, Nigeria. A Certified Fraud Examiner (CFE) and Certified Protection Professional (CPP), Dr. Ekhomu obtained a BA (History) Summa Cum Laude (First Class Honors) from Voorhees College, Denmark, South Carolina, USA (1977); an MA (Political Science) from the Iowa State University, Ames, Iowa (1979); and a PhD (Public and International Affairs – Policy Management) from the University of Pittsburgh, USA (1985). He attended the Security Officer Training Academy of Allegheny County in Pennsylvania, USA (1986). He also obtained the Commonwealth of Pennsylvania Act 235 Lethal Weapons Licence in 1986. A management consultant, policy analyst and corporate security consultant, Dr. Ekhomu is the Chairman of Trans-World Security Systems Ltd. (Lagos, Nigeria) and Chairman of the School of Management and Security Ltd. (Lagos, Nigeria). He is also President of Trans-World Security Systems Inc. of Chicago, Illinois, USA. He is a lecturer in the Sociology Department of the University of Lagos, Nigeria. He is also a part-time lecturer in the Nigeria Police Force Intelligence School, Enugu. Dr. Ekhomu has written two highly acclaimed books on security awareness: *Effective Personal & Corporate Security* (2009) and *Kidnap: Face to Face with Death* (2014). He is President of the Association of Industrial Security and Safety Operators of Nigeria (AISSON) and the Africa Representative of the International Foundation for Protection Officers (IFPO). From 2001 to 2007 he served as the Regional Vice President (West and Central Africa) of ASIS International. Dr. Ekhomu is also the co-author of the following books: *Contemporary Social Problems in Nigeria* (2017), *National Security: Intelligence and Community Partnership* (2013), *The Professional Protection Officer: Practical Security Strategies and Emerging Trends* (2010), *Crime and Policing in Nigeria: Challenges & Options* (2004), among others.

PROLOGUE

The Boko Haram insurgency in August 2016 metamorphosed from domestic terror into international jihad. The dreaded jihadi brand ISIS effectively established regional operations in Nigeria's North East region when it named a new *Emir* (leader) for the group.

The Boko Haram radical Islamist ideology was imported from Talibanism in Afghanistan, and the group had received funding from the founder of the Al Qaeda Network (AQN), Osama Bin Ladin. Upon the emergence of Imam Abubakar Shekau as the leader of Boko Haram in April 2010, he expressed admiration for the Al Qaeda Network with which his group was ideologically aligned. Boko Haram was the recipient of significant assistance from AQN affiliates following the crackdown by Nigerian security forces in July 2009. Jihadi groups such as Al Qaeda in the Islamic Maghreb (AQIM) and Al Shabbab, among others provided refuge, training, finance and treatment for Boko Haram fighters.

ISIS was founded in 1999. However, it became a household name in 2014 when it captured important Iraqi cities like Fallujah and Mosul. The terrorists controlled vast swathes of real estate in Syria and Iraq – from the Mediterranean coast to the south of Baghdad. The image and reality of ISIS in July 2014 was that of a seductive, rich, powerful jihadi group. It was an overnight sensation with proven military prowess. In March 2015, Shekau pledged *bayat* (loyalty) to ISIS. The oath of fealty was accepted by Sheikh Abubakar El-Baghdadi.

In August 2016, ISIS appointed a leader for the Nigerian terror group who immediately issued a clear mission statement of Islamism, extremism and hate.

Since July 2018, Nigeria's military facilities have come under intense, repeated, brazen attacks by the Boko Haram insurgents. The intentional targeting of hardened military bases was the first indication that profound tactical, operational and strategic changes were occurring in the terror franchise.

Suspicions of ISIS operations in Nigeria have since given way to evidence of ISIS operations in Nigeria and West Africa. The Nigerian government on February 17th, 2019 announced formally that

The Boko Haram has aligned with the global terror group ISIS, to form the Islamic State of West Africa Province (ISWAP). ISIS now has a strong foothold in West Africa, with Nigeria in the forefront of the battle against them.[1]

Nigeria's Information Minister, Alhaji Lai Mohammed, lamented that the Nigerian military was fighting a global insurgency without commensurate external assistance from the United States which had combated ISIS in Syria and Iraq.[2] The Nigerian government argued that the Boko Haram threat had mutated from the "rag tag Army of 2009 to highly sophisticated terrorists."[3]

The Nigerian official was merely stating what had become common knowledge and existential reality since March 2015 when the leader of Boko Haram, Imam Abubakar Shekau, pledged *bayat* (loyalty) to the Islamic State. The leader of ISIS, Sheikh Ibrahim El-Baghdadi accepted the oath of fealty and renamed Boko Haram the Islamic State of the West African Province (ISWAP). In August 2016, the ISIS leader made an executive leadership change in Boko Haram/ISWAP. He appointed Abu Musab Al-Barnawi, the son of the deceased leader of Boko Haram, Sheikh Mohammed Yusuf, as the new leader of the group.[4] Boko Haram leader Shekau refused to relinquish leadership, and this led to factionalization. The jihadi group now exists in two forms – Boko Haram led by Shekau, and the ISWAP led by Abu Musab Al-Barnawi.

STRATEGIC BLUNDER

The Nigerian authorities apparently misunderstood the implication of the decision by ISIS to appoint the former spokesman of Boko Haram as the new leader of the insurgency. In August 2016, the Minister of Information, Alhaji Lai Mohammed, urged Nigerians to ignore the ISIS action. His words were: "Don't believe the cheap propaganda by the global terrorist group ISIS. Our gallant military has put Boko Haram on the run and nothing will bring back the terrorists, not even the wishful thinking by ISIS."[5]

This author was very disturbed by the leadership change of Boko Haram. He described it as a dangerous development in the ongoing war on terror. He advised the Federal Government to consider ISIS as a credible threat, and to be proactive by placing intelligence agencies, the military, law enforcement and citizens on full alert to avert terror attacks. In August 2016, he wrote: "If ISIS gets to appoint senior leadership for Boko Haram, then they are probably running the terror group as a local franchise. Strategic decisions, such as leadership appointments are made by the spiritual leader of a terrorist group."[6]

It is unfortunate that this advice went unheeded and in February 2019 the government had an epiphany that ISIS and its local branch Boko Haram/ISWAP was a terror monstrosity, requiring international help and citizen cooperation for combating. On February 17th, 2019, the Minister of Information publicly presented a campaign in support of the war against Boko Haram and ISIS. The stated purpose of the campaign was to tell Nigerians that Boko Haram had grown beyond homegrown insurgency. Another purpose was to boost the morale of troops who were making the supreme sacrifice.[7]

EVIDENCE OF A NEW TERROR WAR

ISIS has been decimated and is in retreat in Syria, Iraq and Libya, due mostly to determined local fighters and foreign coalition assistance usually led by the USA. However, ISIS is more about Islamist jihad than territorial control. So establishing a franchise in West Africa called the Islamist State of the West African province was well known within the global terror group's operational mandate.

Subsequent to his appointment as the leader of ISIS in West Africa, Abu Musab Al-Barnawi declared:

1. That the Christians in Nigeria will be the new target of the sect's attacks.
2. That the ISWAP will kill all Christians and "blow up every church that we are able to reach."
3. That the group's activities in Nigeria will be a war fought by Muslims against "apostates" and "crusaders."
4. That BH/ISWAP is unhappy that the West has been trying to Christianize Africa. Charities are assisting the West in spreading Christianity.
5. That victims of insurgency were being kept in internally displaced persons (IDPs) camps, fed and sheltered for the purpose of turning their children into Christians.
6. That the ISWAP will continue fighting West African governments.[8]

The words of Abu Musab Al-Barnawi clearly constituted a mission statement. They spelt out what the terror group intended to achieve in West Africa. And they have largely stayed with the scripted mission.

ATTACKS ON THE MILITARY

As from July 2018, the insurgents intensified attacks on military targets in the North East. The 81 Division (Nigerian Army) Forward Brigade troops were attacked at Jilli Village, Geidam Local Government Area (LGA) in Yobe State. Although the base had 734 troops, the insurgents overran it after fierce fire fights. The insurgents were said to have driven from their base in Lake Chad through Gubio to conduct the audacious attack.

Kumuya military barracks in Borno State also came under insurgent attacks. Military reinforcements from Buni Yadi, Yobe State, were called in to repel the attacks. The insurgents did not take control of the military facility.

In September 2018, Senator Ali Ndume, representing the war-ravaged Borno South senatorial district decried the resurgence of Boko Haram attacks. He said:

> I am worried about the sudden resurgence of Boko Haram on the North East. Some weeks ago, it was alleged that 48 soldiers were killed. There was attack sometime ago in Jilli where many soldiers were killed. Another came in Zari and there was another one in Njimtilo and Bama axis.[9]

Metele Attacks

On November 18th, 2018, insurgents attacked the 157 Task Force Battalion at Metele, Borno State.[10] The Battalion Commander Lt. Col. Sakaba, his deputy and several senior officers were killed in the fierce armed conflict. The insurgents overran the military facility. In a secondary attack, first responders who were sent to rescue military personnel were ambushed by the insurgents causing more fatalities. Eyewitnesses placed the casualty figure at over 100 dead. However, the military authorities confirmed that only 23 soldiers were killed in action (KIA)

Reacting to the Metele Attacks

On November 28th, 2018, Nigeria's President Muhammadu Buhari ordered the military to eliminate all threats of Boko Haram declaring that the war against insurgency is "**a must win**."[11] He tasked the military with "eliminating Boko Haram from the surface of the earth."[12] The President promised to empower the troops by "**providing all necessary equipment, force multipliers and enablers**."[13]

Analyzing the Metele attacks, former head of the Nigerian Spy Agency (Department of State Service) Mr. A. Gadzama wrote:

> The authorities must also not overlook reports from diverse sources that other deficiencies have contributed to the upsurge in attacks by the insurgents. The most noticeable are lapses and gaps in intelligence sourcing and application. The incidents without doubt are suggestive of serious intelligence failure. Something definitely needs to be done to strengthen the intelligence components of the counter insurgency operations. If current intelligence is anything to go by, Islamic State of the West Africa Province (ISWAP) is consolidating its stronghold in these countries (Nigeria, Chad, Cameroon and Niger). The country (Nigeria) should not be in denial that the Islamic state of West Africa Province has taken over the leadership of Boko Haram and has gained footholds in the North East especially on the shores of the Lake Chad.[14]

The Metele attacks compelled fresh attention to the ongoing war on insurgency, some new features of which include:

a. The insurgents may soon deploy drones in their operations.[15]
b. BH has changed its *modus operandi* with its fighters now fiercer and bloodthirsty.[16]
c. BH factions have adopted unique survival methods, membership recruitment and attacks.[17]
d. BH factions are no longer interested in conquering large territories that they cannot permanently control, so they concentrate their strength in few places.[18]
e. The Nigerian military is handicapped in terms of equipment, arms and ammunition. However, President Buhari has promised to remedy the equipment gap to give the Nigerian troops the winning edge.

PERFORMANCE MEASUREMENT

The attacks on military bases are intended to intimidate and overawe the troops. Fortunately, the psychological operation is not having the intended effect on the Nigerian military. The fighting spirit is high and the troops are certain of victory.

The scary mission statement that the ISWAP leader made in August 2016 deserves urgent analysis. Does the insurgency have mission focus, and how can the Nigerian government and global partners disrupt the mission of terror? The mission objectives as set out by Abu Musab Al-Barnawi included:

a. Targeting of Christians and churches
b. Attacks on charities
c. Attacks on IDP camps
d. Attacks on West African governments.

Christians and Churches

Although the ISWAP leader threatened to kill Christians and blow up churches, the terrorists have not killed a large number of Christians since 2016. Many years of targeted violence against Christians in the North East, particularly under Shekau's leadership, had sent many Christians packing from the area. This objective has not been met by the insurgents.

When attacks on churches became persistent and deadly prior to August 2016, churches were target-hardened by the parishioners as a survival mechanism. With effective security countermeasures in place, BH/ISWAP has not been able to bomb churches as planned. However, continued vigilance is urged at churches as the enemy is a patient one, bidding its time before striking.

Charitable Organizations

BH/ISWAP has accused charitable organizations including the United Nations, the International Committee of the Red Cross (ICRC) of being Christian organizations subtly trying to convert Muslims to Christianity through their help to affected populations. This is very inaccurate as the charities employ Muslims and locals to serve the affected populations. This objective must have informed the attack on Rann IDP Camp (Borno State) and the seizure of three female aid workers, two of whom were later executed in September and October 2018. The fate of the third aid worker Alice Loksha is still unknown. In September 2018, Saifura Khorsa, a mid-wife employed by the ICRC and kidnapped in March 2018, was executed by the ISWAP after the ICRC and the Federal Government of Nigeria failed to pay ransom for her release. On October 15th, 2018, Hauwa Liman, the second of the three abducted Rann IDP Camp aid workers, was executed by the ISWAP. She was only 24 years old.

Justifying the murder of Hauwa Liman, BH released a video which argued that "Liman deserved to be killed because she had abandoned Islam by working for the ICRC."[19]

Reacting to an upsurge in insurgent attacks, in January 2019 the United Nations announced the withdrawal of 260 aid workers from Monguno, Kala/Balge and Kukawa Local Government Areas (LGAs) where intense armed clashes had been occurring since November 2018. On December 28th, 2018, BH/ISWAP overran the naval base in Baga, Kakuwa LGA, and this triggered a migration of 20,000 people to IDP camps in Maiduguri.[20]

Attacks on IDP Camps

In November 2018, BH killed eight people in an attack on an IDP camp in Maiduguri. The terrorists attacked the Dalori camp and four neighboring communities – Kofa, Mallumti, Ngomari and Gozari. The villages are all located on Bama Road, close to Sambisa Forest.[21]

A female suicide bomber (SB) hit Bakassi IDP camp in Maiduguri on October 29th, 2016 killing five people. The bombing occurred at 6:00 AM in front of the camp as scores of people were coming out to begin a new day.[22]

Eight IDPs were killed and 14 injured when two female suicide bombers attacked an IDP housing complex in Dikwa, Borno State, on July 29th, 2017. The attack took place at 9:30 PM.[23]

On August 15th, 2018, Kondugha, Borno State, was the scene of a coordinated bombing attack which claimed over 30 lives. Three female suicide bombers worked in tandem to produce high fatalities. One SB detonated herself at the entrance of the IDP camp. When a crowd gathered the others detonated their explosive payload, killing a large number of people.[24]

Seven people were killed when Boko Haram insurgents fired rocket-propelled grenades (RPGs) into an IDP camp in Ngala, Borno State. An eyewitness, Umar Kachalla, said that the insurgents were operating in two trucks when they attacked the camp – home to about 80,000 people.

West African Governments

Abu Musab Al-Barnawi's mission statement included targeting West African governments. This strategic goal derived from the geographic area allocated to the group by the ISIS leader, Sheikh Abu Bakr El-Baghdadi. The appointment was to be the leader of ISIS in West Africa and not ISIS in Nigeria. Although the insurgency is located in Nigeria's North East, it is designed as a regional terror network.

Long before Al-Barnawi became the head of the ISWAP, BH had been making cross-border raids into the Niger Republic, Chad Republic and Cameroon. The inclusion of West African governments in the target list was merely a confirmation of this operational reality.

The ISWAP is based in the Lake Chad basin area. Lake Chad has been described as an unpoliced lake with an expanse of land, dense forests and mountains in the remote parts of the Sahel region.[25]

CONCLUSION

The Boko Haram insurgency has factionalized into Shekau's faction and the ISWAP. While Shekau continues to attack civilian and military targets in central and Southern Borno and the Northern Adamawa State, the ISWAP faction holds sway in Northern Borno, Yobe State, and is based in the Lake Chad area.

The ISWAP faction has been repeatedly targeting military bases, keeping the Nigerian military on the defensive. The ISWAP is also implementing a strategy of benign jihad where Muslim civilians are not harmed or molested. This has endeared the local populace to ISWAP fighters, raising the probability that the ISWAP might win the support and acquiescence of civilians in the struggle.[26]

The Boko Haram insurgency is a minimalized insurgency, particularly in the West (USA, Europe, Canada, etc.). However, it has the potential of becoming a large regional security threat. Understanding the threat that the insurgency poses to Nigeria and West Africa is important in putting in place strategies and countermeasures for containing the threat and preventing the rise of similar insurgencies in the future.

NOTES

1. Iyobosa Uwugiaren. "Our Soldiers Fighting Sophisticated Terrorists, Say FG, Defence HQ" *This Day* (February 8th, 2019): Page 50.
2. Igho Akeregha and Nkechi Onyedika-Ugoeze. "Military Fighting Global Terrorism Without Commensurate External Coalition's Help, Says Govt" *The Guardian* (February 8th, 2019): Page 4.
3. Olusola Fabiyi. "Military Fighting Tested Boko Haram Fighters, Says FG" *The Punch* (February 8th, 2019): Page 17.
4. Yinka Ajayi. "What We Know About Boko Haram's New Leader, Abu Musab Al-Barnawi" *Vanguard* (August 7th, 2016). https://www.vanguardngr.com/2016/08/know-boko-harams-new-leader-abu-musab-al-barnawi/

5. Ibid.
6. Ibid.
7. Yusuf Ali and Yomi Odunuga. "Fed Govt Launches Campaign Against Boko Haram, ISIS" ***The Nation*** (February 8th, 2019): Page 6.
8. Yinka Ajayi. Op cit.
9. "Ndume Expresses Concern Over Escalation of Attacks in North East" ***The Guardian*** (September 8th, 2018): Page 7.
10. Editorial. "The Brazen Metele Attack: A Call to Arms" ***This Day*** (November 29th, 2018): Page 9.
11. Ismail Mudasir. "Boko Haram: Buhari, Deby, 4 Leaders Meet in Chad Today" ***Daily Trust*** (November 29th, 2018): Page 18.
12. Ibid.
13. Ibid.
14. AA Gadazama. "Still on the Massacre at Metele" ***Daily Trust*** (November 29th, 2018): Page 43.
15. Jide Babalola. "Watch Out for Boko Haram Drones, US Intelligence Warns" ***The Nation*** (November 18th, 2018): Page 8.
16. Hamza Idris. "How Metele Attack Reignited War on Boko Haram" ***Daily Trust*** (December 1st, 2018): Page 4.
17. Ibid.
18. Ibid.
19. Jason Burke. "Nigeria: Boko Haram Militants Kill Kidnapped Aid Worker" ***The Guardian*** (October 16th, 2018): Page 4.
20. John Alechenu and Kayode Idowu. "UN Laments Upsurge in Boko Haram Attacks, Withdraw 260 Aid Workers" ***The Punch*** (January 10th, 2019): Page 3. In a statement, the Spokesperson of the UN to Nigeria said: "The impact of the recent fighting on innocent civilians is devastating and has created a humanitarian tragedy."
21. Success Nwogu and Michael Olugbode. "Boko Haram Attacks Borno IDP Camp, Kills Eight" ***The Punch*** (November 2nd, 2018).
22. "Female Suicide Bombers Behind Maiduguri Attacks" ***The Punch*** (October 29th, 2016).
23. "8 Killed, 14 Others Wounded in Suicide Bomb Attack in Dikwa, Borno" ***The Guardian*** (July 29th, 2017).
24. "Boko Haram Militants Kill Seven in Borno IDP Camp" ***The Nation*** (September 9th, 2017).
25. Guy Fineman. "Nigeria's Boko Haram and Its Security Dynamics in the West Africa Sub-region" ***Journal of Language, Technology and Entrepreneurship in Africa*** Vol. 9 No. 1 (2018): Pages 102–131.
26. Omar S. Mahmood. "The Lake Chad Region Is Being Terrorized by Two Groups, One of Which Poses a Long-Term Threat" ***ISS Today*** (July 12th, 2018) (Addis Abba).

Part One

Historical Background

1

History of Boko Haram

Since 2009, Nigeria has faced a determined and deadly Islamist fundamentalist insurgency. The Islamist group known as *Jama'atu Ahlus-Sunnah Lidda'Awati Wal Jihad*, better known by its nickname "Boko Haram," was founded in 1995 as a Sunni Salafist organization preaching Islam and providing services to the poor, to widows and to vagrant children (*almajiris*). The group, then known as the Sahaba, was led by a Muslim cleric, Malam Lawan Abubakar. In 2002, Malam Lawan relocated from Nigeria to Saudi Arabia for further studies at the University of Medina.[1]

Subsequent to the departure of Malam Lawan, older clerics in the Sahaba group chose a charismatic, intelligent, diplomatic, gifted, young versatile preacher named Mohammed Yusuf to succeed him.[2] The choice of a younger and more energetic leader was aimed at injecting youthful energy and drive into the religious organization. It was hoped that with a younger leader the group would increase its appeal to the youth and thereby increase its membership. The strategy succeeded as the group experienced a significant increase in membership and it became very influential among religious organizations in Northern Nigeria.

The new leader of the Sahaba Group, Mohammed Yusuf, had high school education but was not able to gain admission into the University of Maiduguri to further his education. He served in the Yobe State civil service. An ethnic Kanuri from Girair Village in Yobe State, Yusuf was a fiery and gifted preacher. He received high-quality religious education under the Kano-based Izala cleric, Sheikh Ja'afar Mahmud Adam. Malam

Figure 1.1　Photo of Mohammed Yusuf.

Yusuf, a precocious and intelligent scholar, was praised by his revered teacher Sheikh Adam as "the leader of young people."

According to a prominent Zaria-based Salafi imam, the new leader of the Sahaba had also been mentored by the leader of the Islamic Movement of Nigeria (IMN), Sheikh Ibrahim el-Zakzaky. The IMN is the umbrella organization of the Shiites sect in Nigeria, which is different from the Sunni sect that Yusuf represented. Yusuf later became the Borno State amir (leader) of *Jama'atu al-Tajdid al-Islami* (JTI) which translates into Movement for the Revival of Islam. The group JTI was a Kano-based IMN breakaway group founded in 1994 that continued Sheikh Ibrahim el-Zakzaky's confrontational stance toward the government but through Salafist doctrine. The members of JTI are suspected of having carried out the beheading of Mr. Gideon Akaluka, a Christian Ibo trader in Kano accused of desecrating the Holy Koran. In 2002, Yusuf became the Borno State representative on the Supreme Council for Sharia in Nigeria (Figure 1.1).

THE CONVERSION

The trajectory of the Sahaba group changed from service and preaching to extremism when in 2002 Malam Mohammed Yusuf met a radical, fanatical cleric named Mohammed Alli. Mohammed Alli indoctrinated

Yusuf into the Taliban extremist ideology of strict Wahabism. Coming under the doctrinal influence of Mohammed Alli became a turning point for Yusuf as a person and the organization that he led.

Alli was a devout fundamentalist who believed in jihad. The Taliban came into prominence in Afghanistan in 1994 led by Mullah Mohammed Omar, a puritanical cleric. He recruited members from Koranic schools hence the name "Taliban" which means "student." The Talibans, whose fundamentalist doctrine did not favor anything Western, took over political control of Afghanistan from 1996 to 2001 and implemented strict Islamic Sharia code with stonings, amputations, public executions and harsh treatment of women.

The Muslim coalition that defeated the Soviets was united by their fundamentalism – Wahabism and Sunni Salafism. The Talibans began a process of converting Muslims to their extremist ideology in order to reduce the "pollutant" effects of Western civilization on pure Islam. Based upon the Taliban radical ideology, Yusuf regarded secular governance as morally bankrupt and Western education as antithetical to pure Islam.

Alli proselytized to Yusuf that Western education only led to Westernization and secularization. He posited that Western education brought greater dependence on income. He condemned the lifestyle, opulence, ego and vanity of Western-educated elites (*Yan Boko*). Alli argued that governance was ineffective in the hands of *Yan Boko* and that it merely led to growth in white collar crime, collapse of societal values, debauchery and other social vices. To the traditionalist Taliban mindset this was appalling and horrific. Alli urged Yusuf to change society beginning with his group by becoming a true jihadist.

The conversion of Yusuf changed the doctrine of the Sahaba group to a Taliban-style traditional orthodoxy that considered Westernization as aberrant, abhorrent and unIslamic. The teaching was that Western education pollutes and dilutes Islam. It maintained that Western institutions were infidel and must be avoided by Muslims.

BOKO HARAM

With radicalization came new realities and changes. Sahaba group leader Mohammed Yusuf concluded that although Western education (*Boko* or Book) significantly improved material well-being, it did not lead to wholesale conversion to Islam. Ironically, "*Boko*" or sorcerers (the educated elite) were respected in the Muslim North. "*Book* school" taught Islam more effectively than the local Islamiyya school which is also known as "*Makaranta Alo*." It was known that *Yan Boko* had deeper knowledge of Islam than *almajiri*. However, the *Boko* version of Islam was impure. The Yusufiyyas (meaning the followers of Yusuf) then concluded that Western education (*Boko*) is sinful or forbidden (*Haram*).

Basic Religious Beliefs

The Boko Haram sect does not believe in banking, taxation or jurisprudence in the country. It considers those economic and legal practices to be *haram*. The zealots argue that Western education is unIslamic as it practices things that Allah and the Holy Prophet reject. Some of these practices include the mixing of boys and girls under the same shade, and the teaching of evolution theory and rotation of the earth.

Boko Haram members removed themselves from contact with other city dwellers in places like Maiduguri, Bauchi, Damaturu and Kano and built their own communities where they could interact with fellow sect members only. They strategically located their communes on the outskirts of town, apparently in order to escape Western vices.

The Taliban doctrine teacher Mohammed Alli convinced Yusuf to avoid democracy, civil service and Western education. Yusuf subsequently resigned from the Yobe State government as counseled by Alli.

With Mohammed Yusuf's conversion, *Ja'amatu Ahlus-Sunna Lidda Awatil Wal Jihad* became a radicalized Muslim sect at the Ndimi Mosque in Maiduguri. The religious sect viewed Nigerian society as extremely corrupt. It also considered the Borno State Government led by Alh. Mala Kachalla an epitome of corrupt governance. Yusuf's aversion to Gov. Kachalla's alleged corruption informed his decision to work for the victory of the All Nigeria Peoples Party (ANPP) in the 2003 gubernatorial election. Senator Ali Modu Sheriff was the ANPP candidate for governor in the 2003 election.

As a pre-condition for supporting Senator Sheriff, Mohammed Yusuf was promised the implementation of strict Sharia code in Borno State. The charismatic preacher, pleased with this pledge, urged his followers to support the candidacy and eventual election of the ANPP candidate.

Senator Ali Modu Sheriff's political career included serving as the Senator representing Borno Central Senatorial Zone on the platform of the United Nigeria Congress Party (UNCP) during General Sani Abacha's military regime. Senator Sheriff ran again for the senate in 1999 on the platform of the ANPP and won the election.

It was the gubernatorial candidature of Senator Ali Modu Sheriff that brought him into close contact with Mohammed Yusuf and the Yusufiyya movement. Instead of implementing the strict Sharia code which he had promised as a pre-condition for Yusuf's electoral support, Senator Sheriff created a Ministry of Religious Affairs and appointed the national secretary of the Yusufiyya movement, Alhaji Buji Foi, as the Commissioner of Religious Affairs.

Mohammed Yusuf and his group were disappointed that the strict Sharia code which Governor Sheriff had promised them was not implemented. It was a betrayal of trust and further reinforced the radical Islamic ideology that his group should have nothing to do with government. Realizing that he had been cheated by the governor of Borno State, Yusuf resigned his appointment with the government as did Alhaji Buji Foi, the State Commissioner for Religious Affairs.

THE HIJRA

The fundamentalist cleric Mohammed Alli did a good job indoctrinating the charismatic Yusuf, who accepted almost all the tenets of radical Islam except one – *hijra* (migration from a bad place to a better place).[3] Alli tried to persuade Yusuf to migrate with him from Maiduguri to Yobe State in a *hijra*, Yusuf declined.[4] He saw his calling as service to the less privileged and preaching the true Islamic faith.

THE NIGERIAN TALIBAN

The terminology "Nigerian Taliban" was first used by US government officials to describe the small radical Islamic group that migrated in October 2003 from Maiduguri to Yobe State, camping at a small desert village named Zagi-Biriri in Tarmuwa Local Government Area. Zagi-Biriri Village is 70 km north of Damaturu, the Yobe State capital.

The sect, which styled itself "Talibans of Yobe," comprised university undergraduates, ex-military personnel and professionals, among others.[5] Consistent with their religious beliefs, they maintained a Spartan dress code and wore a long beard – similar to that of the Talibans in Afghanistan. The Yobe Taliban group named itself *Ali Sunnah Wal Jamma* ("Followers of Prophet Mohammed's Teachings").

The choice of the remote desert location was to insulate the Yobe Talibans from what they perceived as the corrupt Nigerian system and to

7

effectively dedicate themselves to a life of prayer and study of the Holy Koran. Their seclusion was also preparatory to a revolution that would overturn the corrupt administration at all levels of governance in Nigeria. The Yobe Talibans planned to replace the corrupt incumbent administration in Nigeria with a "holier" government founded purely on the teachings of the Holy Koran and the Hadith.[6]

Nigerian intelligence officials reported to the government that the Yobe Talibans were conducting military training in their commune. However, neither the Yobe State government led by Alhaji Abba Ibrahim nor the federal government presided over by Chief Olusegun Obasanjo (a former military ruler, retired general and civil war hero) paid attention to the growing threat. Perhaps it was assumed that if the threat was ignored, it would fizzle out on its own. Initially, there was considerable confusion about the true identity, origin and purpose of the Yobe Talibans. While some thought they were a rump of the Maitatsine religious sect that perpetrated large-scale violence in Kano, Maiduguri and Yola in the early 1980s,[7] others thought that they were members of the Al Qaeda network who were hiding in Nigeria attempting to escape the wrath of the United States government which was attacked in the US homeland on September 11th, 2001, claiming about 3,000 lives.

The Yobe Talibans were vocal in their criticism of the state governments in Northern Nigeria for their failure to implement "true Sharia" or strict Islamic code in the 12 Northern states that had passed the Sharia law. Although Nigeria is a secular state, 12 Northern states had passed and operated the Sharia code as of 2003 (Figure 1.2). The first state to legislate Sharia in Nigeria was Zamfara State.

The Fish Pond Incident

A middle-aged, married woman reportedly challenged the right of the Yobe Talibans to fish in the local pond in Zagi-Biriri Village. She told them that since they did not own any portion of the pond, they had no right whatsoever to fish in the stream.[8] Using a creation argument, the sectarians said that the pond was created by Allah and the fish therein. They told the woman that no mortal could lay claim to any section of the pond, nor decide who should fish in it. In the ensuing argument over fishing rights, the woman was badly beaten for daring to challenge them.[9]

The villagers promptly notified the police of the presence of the sect members in Zagi-Biriri. In a swift reaction to police reports about criminal activities of the sect, the Yobe State government issued a three-day

Figure 1.2 Map of Nigeria showing Sharia states.

ultimatum to the sect members to leave Zagi-Biriri. On Sunday December 21st, 2003, in obedience of the expulsion order, the group relocated east of Zagi-Biriri to Kananma Village in Yunusari Local Government Area (LGA) of Yobe State. In December 2003, Kananma was a homogeneous community of about 3,000 inhabitants situated only 7 km from the border of Nigeria and the Niger Republic. The remote location of Kananma conferred several advantages on the Yobe Talibans:

1. They escaped the attention of the Nigerian authorities.
2. They continued with their hermetic meditations on the teachings of Islam.

9

3. They continued their military training undisturbed.
4. They recruited other like-minded individuals from the border communities.
5. The porous borders provided a conduit for illegal arms and ammunitions.

On Wednesday December 24th, 2003, the Talibans attacked Kananma burning down the police station, the local government secretariat, the Palace of the District Head and the residences of the LGA Chairman and the Divisional Police Officer. The residence of the community leader was also razed because he was seen as the representative of the government in the village. In addition, a young police recruit was murdered by the holy warriors.

The attack on various targets in Kananma followed a warning issued by the jihadists one day earlier (December 23rd) that they wanted to see the District Head of Kananma. Upon being told by townsfolk that the government official was not immediately available, the Yobe Taliban members left a chilling message that they would be back the next day to kill him. The Divisional Police Officer (DPO) immediately sent a message to the Yobe State Police Command headquarters in Damaturu reporting the death threat.

The militants abducted 30 villagers from Kananma and forced them to dig trenches around their camp to maintain a defensive stance. The tactical knowledge of former military and law enforcement personnel in their fold became useful. The hostages were also forced to pray with the jihadists.

A contingent of Police Mobile Force personnel dispatched to dislodge and arrest the Yobe Talibans retreated from the camp when they encountered superior fire-power from the militants. The trenches dug by the abducted villagers also conferred tactical advantage on the Talibans. Armed soldiers were subsequently sent in by the government to quell the rebellion. The soldiers engaged in fierce gun battles for over seven days before defeating the jihadists in January 2004. The town of Kananma was under Yobe Taliban control for about one week.

The enclave set up by the Yobe Taliban was nicknamed "Afghanistan" in apparent reference to the birthplace of Talibanism. Due to the proximity of Kananma to the Niger Republic border, many nationals of neighboring West African countries joined the Taliban movement. The Salafist-jihadi message appealed to them.

After their defeat in Kananma, some of the jihadists continued the assault on the Nigerian state. In September 2004, about 60 Talibans attacked a police station in Gwoza, Borno State, killing two police personnel and torching cars in the police station. The jihadists then invaded the neighboring city of Bama in Borno State and killed an Assistant Commissioner of Police – the Area Commander for Bama. Seventeen people were injured in the attacks which Borno State Police Commissioner, Mr. Ade Ajakaiye, blamed on the Talibans.[10] The choice of police targets was informed by two factors: (1) to seize arms and ammunitions and (2) to show contempt for law enforcement officers.

While the Talibans were engaging the security forces in violence in Yobe State and the southern part of Borno State, the charismatic Malam, Sheikh Mohammed Yusuf, continued to grow his Yusufiyya movement out of his Ungwar Doki Compound in Maiduguri. For purposes of historical accuracy, this author maintains that Yusuf who was more diplomatic than violent was not part of the Taliban violence that wracked Yobe and Borno States under Mohammed Alli. When Alli was killed later in 2004, his adherents dispersed and some of them rejoined Boko Haram for spiritual and perhaps material sustenance.

This clarification is important as some writers have erroneously placed Mohammed Yusuf in Kananma as part of the *hijra*. His religious mentor migrated from Ungwar Doki to Kananma frustrated by the liberalism of Mohammed Yusuf. However, the leader of Boko Haram Mohammed Yusuf did not go. He concentrated on institution building and was vocal in the defense of his increasingly radical religious viewpoints.

In 2015, the governor of Yobe State, Alhaji Geidam, traced the origin of Boko Haram to Seyyid Qutb and Qutbism in Egypt.[11] The politician traced the origin of Boko Haram from Egypt and the capital punishment meted out to Seyyid Qutb to a migration of Muslim brotherhood elements to Minna in Niger State, Yobe and Borno. This position merely obfuscates the history of the Boko Haram group. The militants that Governor Abba Ibrahim's government combated in Kananma Yobe in 2003/2004 are not the same as Boko Haram. Granted that Qutbism justified the violent overthrow of Muslim governments and largely influenced the establishment of the Al Qaeda network – which supported the Talibans in the war against the Soviet Union in Afghanistan – they are all separate groups. Aside from ideological fanatism and purity, and perhaps sharing of resources as jihadist movements often do, there is no evidence linking Boko Haram to Seyyid Qutb.

11

PRELUDE TO VIOLENCE

Boko Haram did not spontaneously go on the offensive in a campaign of bombings, maiming, abductions and killings. The organization between 2002 and 2009 was administered by Yusuf as a government subdivision in Nigeria. It was a government within a government.

In a 2006 press release signed by the Shura (Consultative Council), Boko Haram declared that Islam permits the sect to subsist under a secular government like Nigeria. The declaration stated that Boko Haram members could not join or support the government since their system structures and institutions contained unIslamic elements.

Yusuf was not allowed to preach in central mosques in an effort to restrict the propagation of his puritanical message. He was also denied television and radio appearances in Borno State.

However, despite the denial of airtime, Yusuf sold his preaching tapes which were very popular and in high demand. The income from tape sales was very high, so the sect had good cash inflows.

BOKO HARAM ADMINISTRATION

Ibn Tiammiya Masjid (mosque) was the headquarters of the religious sect. Sheikh Mohammed Yusuf and his hardline second-in-command, Abubakar Shekau, ran the organization from their mosque located at Anwar Doki, nicknamed Millionaires Quarters in Maiduguri.

The organization had three important organs including a cabinet which comprised the *langinas* (departments), the *Shura* (or Consultative Council) and the *Hisbah* (or Brigade of Guards and Militia). See Figure 1.3.

Cabinet: The cabinet comprised various service departments such as welfare, economic affairs, health, religious affairs, agriculture, etc. The *langinas* (departments) were headed by appointed officials to render services scheduled for the departments.

The Shura: This was the Consultative Assembly or parliament of Boko Haram. It made "laws" for the group. The laws were Sharia laws and not Nigeria's penal code or metropolitan laws. This organ was critical to the group as the Sharia code formed the foundation of its social control.

A 2006 release signed by the Shura declared that Islam permits the sect to subsist under a modern government like Nigeria. The declaration, however, cautioned that the members of Boko Haram could not join or support the Nigerian government as long as the governmental systems, structures and institutions contained elements that were contradictory to core Islamic principles and beliefs.[12]

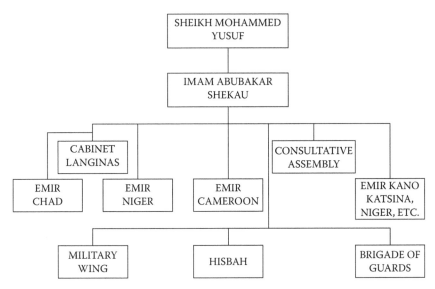

Figure 1.3 Boko Haram organizational chart 2009.

The Hisbah: This is the police force of Boko Haram. In the Muslim North, Hisbah agencies exist everywhere and their mandate is to enforce Sharia laws. The role of the Hisbah is to detect offenders, arrest them and charge them to the Sharia court system for adjudication and punishment if found guilty or culpable.

The Hisbah serve as an important organ for internal security and crime control. Since the BH communes were outside the purview of public security agencies (such as the Nigeria Police Force), the Hisbah provided law enforcement according to the Sharia code.

The Hisbah could arrest for drunkenness, indecent dressing, blasphemy and other conducts forbidden by the code. The Sharia code also abhorred stealing, corruption, white collar crimes, moral decadence, murder, assault, etc.

Aside from "laws," the Hisbah also enforced order in the communes. It ensured that boys and girls were not mixed under the same shade. Hisbah enforced the religious laws against blasphemy. Boko Haram beliefs, which included the consideration of banking, taxation and jurisprudence as infidel, were enforced by the Hisbah. The religious police ensured that "Western vices" did not overtake fundamentalist ethos.

13

Brigade of guards: The guardsmen had the role of protecting the spiritual leader Sheikh Mohammed Yusuf and his deputy, Imam Abubakar Shekau. This brigade constituted a close protection team for the spiritual leader, escorting him on several trips and providing security for venues where he chose to preach.

Military wing: This was an armed militia. Its role was the protection of the various communes where BH members lived and to protect BH against attacks by real or perceived enemies. The sect knew that it was unorthodox in many respects and the experience of the Yobe Talibans indicated that violence was in the offing in the not too distant future.

Muhammed Yusuf, as spiritual leader, was answerable only to Allah and might not have engaged in budgeting. This is pertinent as a BH budget analysis would have allowed a peep into the thinking of the leadership as it related to acquiring weapons for its military wing. Its expenditure priorities might have revealed the mindset of the leadership.

MILITANT ACTIVITIES

In April 2007, a group of Islamic militants later identified as Boko Haram members attacked a police station in the Pan-Shekara District of Kano. Armed with assault weapons, the militants killed 13 policemen and set the police station ablaze. This incident resulted in a call out of the military, which engaged the militants in a 24-hour gun battle supported by ground attack airplanes before the Boko Haram fighters could be defeated in what we may call the Battle of Pan-Shekara.[13]

Sheikh Mohammed Yusuf was a disciple of the Kano-based cleric, Sheikh Ja'afar Mahmud Adam. Yusuf used to visit Sheikh Adam in Kano to seek knowledge. However, when Sheikh Adam deplored Yusuf's extremism, the teacher and student relationship fell apart. Sheikh Adam often debated Yusuf on his extremist views, attempting to deradicalize his favorite student. Unfortunately, Yusuf was enamored with Salafi radicalism and was not willing to explore competing epistemologies.

The falling out with Mohammed Yusuf had fatal consequences for Sheikh Adam who was brutally murdered by Yusuf's loyalists inside the Dorayi Central Mosque in Kano on 13th April, 2007. Sheikh Ja'afar Adam was killed while he was leading the *subhi* (morning prayers).[14]

Prior to the assassination of Sheikh Adam by suspected Boko Haram hitmen, the two clerics were engaged in a caustic verbal diatribe. They exchanged hot religious arguments through the medium of audio cassettes sold to their loyalists in Kano and throughout the

14

Muslim North. Aside from the war of words, Boko Haram members on several occasions invaded Sheikh Adam's mosques to rudely interrupt his homilies.[15] Their quarrel was described succinctly: "While Yusuf opposed western education and contended that it bred corruption, Jafaru, who was trained in Saudi Arabia saw nothing wrong with western education."[16]

After the death of Sheikh Ja'afar Adam, the former mentor and later rival Mohammed Yusuf proselytized his brand of radical Islam across the entire Muslim North. He encouraged converts to leave their homes and "move east" to Maiduguri. With the immigration of fresh converts and adherents to the Boko Haram headquarters in Maiduguri, its capabilities grew in terms of committed followers. With an armed, trained, motivated militia commanded by Abubakar Shekau, Boko Haram was set to become a grave threat to Nigeria's secular government.

In 2008, Katsina Governor Alhaji Ibrahim Shema received an intelligence report that a large number of men and women from Dutsinma, Katsina State, who had been converted to Boko Haram ideology were leaving the state to migrate to Maiduguri. These migrants were later given training in weapons and tactics by foreigners from Chad and Somalia. The Boko Haram fighters were trained in guerilla tactics, the making of improvised explosive devices (IEDs) and marksmanship.[17]

TIMELINE OF BH INSURGENCY

1995	2002	2003	2004	2007	2008	2009	2010
Sahaba Group Founded by Mohammed Lawan	Lawan Resigns and Mohammed Yusuf heads Sahaba	Yusuf converted to Salafi Wahabism by Mohammed Alli	Yobe Talibans commence Jihad	April 13 2007 Sheikh Adam killed in Dorayi Mosque Kano by B.H	Gov Shema of Katsina State gets intell of BH recruitment	June 11th Custom Market roundabout massacres by "Operation Flush"	April 19th Shekau assumes leadership of BH
	Mohammed Alli founds Yobe Taliban	Yusuffiyas help elect Ali Modu Sheriff as Governor Borno State	Mohammed Alli killed	Pan-Shekara Police attack in Kano by B.H. 21 policemen killed	Borno Gov Ali Modu Sheriff establishes "Operation Flush"	July 26th Commencement of B.H Jihad	September 2010 Bauchi Prison Break
		Mohammed Alli goes on Hijra to Kanama Yobe				July 30th BH rebellion crushed Yusuf Killed	

Figure 1.4   Timeline of BH insurgency.

15

CONCLUSION

The radical Islamic sect, Boko Haram, grew from modest beginnings in 2002 when the mantle of leadership fell upon Muhammed Yusuf, a young charismatic cleric. Yusuf's destiny changed when he encountered Mohammed Alli, who converted him to Taliban-style fundamentalism. Alli put pressure on Yusuf to embark on a hijra to Yobe State, but Yusuf rejected the notion of hijra and jihad.

The growth of the Yusufiyya movement (better known as Boko Haram) into a major religious movement resulted in the deepening of its administration and development of coercive instruments such as a police force (Hisbah), Brigade of Guards for executive protection and a militia. The militia's known attack is that on the Pan-Shekara Kano Police Station in April 2007 where 13 policemen laid down their lives. The Nigerian military had to employ ground and air assets in order to neutralize the fundamentalists who had taken over the police facility (we shall examine attacks on law enforcement officers and facilities in Chapter 7). In another April 2007 terrorist attack, BH fighters killed Sheikh Ja'afar Adam while he was leading *Subhi* prayers at the Dorayi Mosque in Kano. The elimination of Sheikh Adam ensured that Sheikh Muhammed Yusuf's radical rhetoric was virtually unchallenged for some time in the North. The callous murder of Sheikh Adam also sent shivers down the spines of other clerics who might have spoken up against Yusuf.

With increasing wealth and influence, Yusuf was set to convert the entire Muslim North to his brand of radical Islam. Government security agents became aware of him and security reports were written here and there. Yusuf himself was arrested and harassed by the authorities several times without conviction.

Yusuf was banned from preaching in several mosques. He was denied television and radio appearances in Borno State. However, despite these feeble attempts by the Borno State government to curtail the activities of Boko Haram, the group's anti-corruption message resonated with poverty-ridden youths to whom the fundamentalist logic was refreshing and who were assured that in Boko Haram communes they would live under Sharia code and would not have to endure the horrors of secular life in Nigeria. Youths quit universities and schools to join the sect. Some workers quit their jobs to join Boko Haram. Many converts sold their belongings in order to contribute to the sect. Their goal was to fight the cause of Allah and save Islam from Western domination. The traditional and strict narrative had such a strong appeal to some Northern youths that they were ready to do "anything" for the movement. And many of them did.

16

NOTES

1. Shehu Sani. "Boko Haram: The Northern Nigeria (Hausaland)" **Vanguard** (July 1st, 2011): Page 16.
2. Ibid.
3. **Hijra** is a journey from the "bad world" to go and be closer to God. The Holy Prophet Mohammed undertook a *hijra* from Mecca to Medina.
4. Ahmad Salkida. "Boko Haram from the Beginning" **Sunday Sun** (May 18th, 2014): Pages 13–14. Mr. Salkida, a journalist with the **Daily Trust** newspaper, was a confidant of Sheikh Mohammed Yusuf, the leader of Boko Haram.
5. Sani (2011).
6. Ibid.
7. The Al Masifu sect is also known as the Maitatsine sect so named after its founder Alh. Mohammed Marwa Maitatsine, a Cameroonian-born fanatical Muslim cleric whose uprising in Kano, Nigeria, in 1980 paralleled that of Boko Haram. Seeking to purify the practice of Islam, Al Masifu had over 5,000 fighters. They attacked orthodox Muslims at the Kano Central Mosque on December 18th, 1980 killing many. This attack was a reaction to the expulsion order given to the sect by Kano State Governor Alhaji Abubakar Rimi who acted on their growing violent tendencies. In the ensuing violence, Al Masifu was defeated after the call out of the military and 4,177 deaths were recorded along with 8,712 casualties and massive property loss.
8. Sani (2011).
9. Ibid.
10. Raymond Gukas. "Talibans Strike Again in Borno" **Daily Champion** Vol. 17 No. 30 (September 22nd, 2004).
11. Sunday Aborisade. "Boko Haram Started In Egypt, Not Nigeria – Ex-Yobe Gov" **Sunday Punch** (August 9th, 2015): Page 8.
12. Shehu Sani. "Boko Haram: History, Ideas and Revolt (3)" **Vanguard** (July 4th, 2011).
13. Funsho Balogun. "Methods of a Killing Machine" **The News Magazine** (August 1st, 2011): Page 16.
14. Ibid: Pages 14–15.
15. Ibid.
16. Ibid.
17. Ibid.

2

Reign of Terror

The Boko Haram jihadi group has been described as an existential threat to the Nigerian nation (see Figure 2.1). At the onset of the armed conflict, the jihadis did not appear to pose a significant national security threat. However, due to poor management of the conflict, the jihadis won a number of battlefield victories and changed tactics from guerrilla warfare to conventional warfare and holding conquered territories. By 2014, the jihadis held territories larger than several Western European nations.

BH threat grew proportionally with the absence of serious governance in Nigeria. The tendency of Nigerian government officials is to ignore policy problems and pray to God for things to get better. It is a governance model based upon a lack of situational awareness, threat awareness and an inability to embark on structured thinking for problem solving.

In his inaugural speech on May 29th, 2015, the President of Nigeria, Muhammadu Buhari conducted the problem analysis as follows:

Boko Haram is the typical example of small fires causing large fires. An eccentric and unorthodox preacher with a tiny following was given post-humous fame and following by his extra-judicial murder at the hands of the Police. Since then through official bungling, negligence, complacency or collusion Boko Haram became a terrifying force, taking tens of thousands of lives and capturing several towns and villages covering large swathes of Nigerian Sovereign territory.[1]

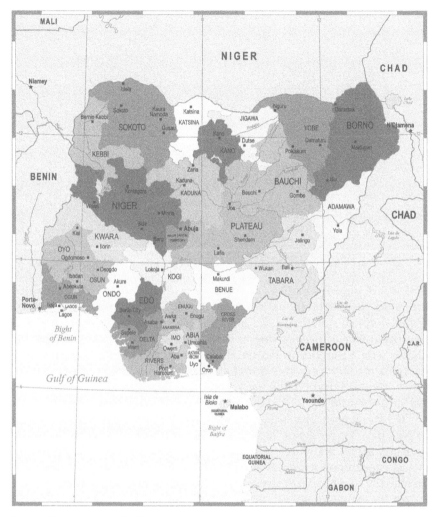

Figure 2.1   A map of Nigeria.

This chapter examines the transformation of BH from a fundamentalist Salafist sect to a terror machine which has claimed over 35,000 lives in Nigeria.

In July 2009, the leader of BH, Sheikh Mohammed Yusuf, changed the mission of his Islamist group from preaching and welfare to jihad. This change was provoked by the killing of 17 members of the sect by men of the Nigeria Police Anti-banditry Squad – Operation Flush in Maiduguri, Borno State, in June 2009.

THE JUNE 11TH MASSACRES

In 2008, the Borno State government established a joint police and military anti-robbery squad code-named "Operation Flush." Governor Ali Modu Sheriff directed that the commander of the anti-banditry response team report directly to him. At that time, given the high number of cross-border banditry cases in Borno State, the formation of Operation Flush as an elite and mobile anti-violent crime unit was good public policy.

Operation Flush exhibited a slight administrative anomaly. Usually, a joint police/military task force (JTF) of this nature would report to the Commander of the 21 Armored Brigade in Maiduguri. However, Borno Governor Ali Modu Sheriff took direct control of this task force. Initially, the task force was quite effective in meeting its mandate of combating violent armed banditry. However, like all non-properly supervised and monitored organizations, it experienced goal displacement and, due to its involvement in carrying out arbitrary arrests of citizens, extortion of cash from members of the public. The JTF involved itself in purely civil matters that were outside its purview.

On Thursday June 11th, 2009, near the customs market in Maiduguri, a detachment of Operation Flush intercepted a funeral procession of Boko Haram members. The law enforcement officers asked the large procession of mourners why the okada (motorcycle) riders among them were not wearing crash helmets, contrary to extant rules of the road.[2]

The Boko Haram members were on their way to the cemetery to bury four of their members who had tragically died in a car crash on the Biu–Maiduguri road. The mourners, who were paying their last respects to their departed colleagues, felt that the interception of their procession and threat to arrest the okada outriders was provocative and high-handed, so they stood their ground. In matters of this nature, the mourners should have parted with some cash to the JTF men (bribed them) and they would have been allowed to proceed. Unfortunately, one of the key tenets of Sunni Wahabism is its abhorrence of corrupt practices, and the BH men were not ready to compromise their religious practice on that fateful day.

The hot argument that ensued revealed the disregard of the lawmen for their situation. Sensing danger from the large number of mourners estimated at over 300, the Operation Flush men opened fire on the crowd, killing 17 BH members and three bystanders. The police and military authorities have not named the shooters on that occasion. The dead and wounded were promptly rushed to the University of Maiduguri Teaching Hospital.

Given the events that played out near the customs market in Maiduguri on June 11th, 2009, the JTF displayed poor judgment in crowd management, law enforcement, emotional intelligence and crisis resolution. The Operation Flush massacre of unarmed and defenseless civilians was the first shot in a war that has to date claimed over 35,000 lives, displaced over 2.5 million people and destroyed property worth several billion dollars. Since the Operation Flush men stopped that funeral procession and extra-judicially murdered 17 Boko Haram members without provocation, the North East of Nigeria can never be the same again. The JTF team acted as judge, jury and executioners.

Reaction of the Government

As is usual for Nigerian security agencies, no explanations were made to members of the public about the stressful street-level shooting incident that occurred on June 11th near the customs market roundabout in Maiduguri.

1. The decisions of the officers to discharge their firearms were not explained and the use of deadly force was not justified.
2. No officers were apparently debriefed or penalized or placed on administrative leave after the extra-judicial murders of about 20 citizens. The Boko Haram members were shot dead because they would not pay a bribe.
3. The Operation Flush men were not put in fear of their lives. They maintained that they would not pay a bribe.
4. Governor Sheriff who was the direct upline report of Operation Flush did not demand more details of the shooting.
5. Although law enforcement officers and men have to take the lives of bad guys in the course of their duty, such as the armed bandits, armed robbers and other violent actors common in Borno State at the time, it is not possible to mistake over 300 mourners in a funeral procession for a band of thieves and open fire on them. The action of Operation Flush was cold-blooded homicide and was not justified use of deadly force.

22

The Borno State government, following the lead of the government security agencies, also disregarded the incident of mass murder:

1. The government (under Governor Ali Modu Sheriff) did not issue a statement condemning the mass murders.
2. It did not issue a statement of condolence or sympathy.
3. The government neglected to conduct an inquiry into the mass murder.
4. There was no sympathy visit to the injured sect members at the University of Maiduguri Teaching Hospital.
5. There was no offer to defray the hospital bills of the injured persons.

Gov. Sheriff was said to have been advised by some officials within his government and members of the public to show some concern over the incident. The governor was warned that his total disregard of the tragic incident could be viewed by the sect as an intentional affront, but Gov. Sheriff acted as though nothing had happened.

To add insult to injury, the Operation Flush shooters were back at their usual road block spot on June 12th, 2009 – 24 hours after they had shot dead 20 Nigerian citizens and injured others who were still hospitalized.

Reaction by the Boko Haram Leader

In an interview in the *Daily Trust* newspaper, the leader of Boko Haram, Sheikh Mohammed Yusuf, alleged that the actions of the Borno State government showed that the murders were premeditated and perhaps ordered by the state government. He enumerated the following:

a. The Borno government did not condemn the killings
b. The Borno government did not inquire into the incident
c. The Borno government did not empathize with the sect over the killings.

The sect leader concluded that there was a government script being followed to eliminate his followers – *Yan Yusufiyyahs*.

After the newspaper interview, the usually tame and diplomatic Sheikh Mohammed Yusuf felt compelled to issue a call to arms. Yusuf delivered a widely circulated Friday sermon in Hausa language titled "Open Letter to President Umaru Musa Yar'Adua." In the sermon, he

23

described the security agencies and the Borno government as enemies of Islam. He boasted that BH was ready to confront all security agencies in Borno State as well as the government. Yusuf directed his followers to arm themselves in preparation of self-defense and eventful jihad in response to the murder of 17 BH members.

It is extremely shocking that the leader of a powerful religious sect like BH would issue such a threat, and his words be ignored by the federal, state and local governments and the security agencies. Obviously, Yusuf was crying out to be heard and perhaps offered an olive branch. However, in the usual way of governing in a non-accountable manner, no one took action. Governor Alli Modu Sheriff, his deputy, the police executives, the state security executives, the military commanders, the national security adviser, even the president of the country, Umar Musa Yar'Adua, and the vice president, Dr. Goodluck Jonathan, were all asleep at the controls. It is not customary for Nigerian leaders to prevent or head off crises. To them, that is a sign of weakness. Their attitude is "bring on the fight," then they wonder why there is so much loss of life, property and government credibility. The truth is, if you do not prevent or avert a crisis, then it will certainly confront you in time. The paradox of crisis is not in winning or losing; it is that it will result in loss, that is, a decrease in value.

RESOURCING FOR VIOLENCE

On Tuesday July 21st, 2009, nine members of BH were arrested by the police for possession of 74 empty bomb shells, a large quantity of gunpowder and other bomb-making materials. The men were arrested in Biu and on Friday July 24th, 2009, and paraded at the police headquarters in Maiduguri.

When questioned by journalists on why they had explosive materials in their possession, the leader of the nine BH members, Inusa Ibrahim Sabo, said the bombs were to protect them from Ali Modu Sheriff's Operation Flush. The men said they were directed by their leader Sheikh Mohammed Yusuf to arm themselves as they presumed that the Operation Flush massacre of June 11th, 2009 was intentional and that they were no longer safe.

On the same Friday July 24th, 2009 that the Biu nine were paraded at the police headquarters in Maiduguri, an explosion took place that night in the residence of a BH member known as Hassan Sani Badami from Biu. Badami, who had been trained in making improvised explosive devices, was building a device when it accidentally exploded in his face, killing him. A member of BH who was Badami's apprentice, his wife and child all sustained severe injuries and were taken to the headquarters of Operation Flush on Dikwa Road, Maiduguri, for interrogation. The proper procedure should have been to take the injured for medical attention. However, Operation Flush did not do this, thereby showing little regard for human life – especially that of BH members and their family, including small children.

It should be emphasized here that the line that separates law enforcement officers from terrorists is a thin one. The difference being that law enforcement is guided by rules and disciplined conduct, despite human emotions. Law enforcers cannot act outside their rules of engagement. If they do, then they become law breakers and not law enforcers. Perhaps those rules did not exist for Operation Flush. Perhaps the rules were simply jettisoned. Whatever the case, their acts – even in fighting terror – which were not exhibited in handling the victims of the Badami bombing accident of July 24th, 2009, were reprehensible and condemnable.

On Saturday July 25th, 2009, in reacting to Badami's death, Sheikh Mohammed Yusuf, the leader of Boko Haram, said that his act had earned him a place in paradise (heaven). This concept was very powerful as it was a coded call to arms in the holy war that was about to commence, but intelligence officials did not decipher it.

OUTBREAK OF HOSTILITIES

In an interview published by the *Sunday Trust* newspaper on July 26th, 2009, Sheikh Mohammed Yusuf reviewed the whole situation with the Borno State government, the Operation Flush murders and Badami's martyrdom and threatened that his sect would avenge the deaths.

a. **Dutsen Tashi, Bauchi:** Boko Haram broke the law at 6:00 AM on July 26th, 2009 when 30 BH youths invaded the Dutsen Tashi police station in Bauchi City. The young men were armed with locally made single-barrel shotguns, machetes, bows and arrows and daggers.

    The invaders were met by a hail of gunfire. The police, assisted by the military, routed the attackers, with five killed instantly. The police quickly overran the BH zonal headquarters in Jadaman

Mada on the outskirts of Bauchi, seizing military uniforms, boots, live ammunition, shotgun shells, improvised explosive devices and gunpowder. The BH compound was destroyed and all the occupants arrested.

b. **Potiskum, Yobe State:** BH jihadists attacked the central police station in Potiskum, Yobe State. The attack was repelled and the sectarians retreated to their headquarters in Mamudo Quarters. Security agents later surrounded their headquarters and after a fierce gun battle, three policemen and one firefighter were killed. BH suffered huge losses as 33 out of the 50 fighters holed up in the Mamudo compound were killed.

    The compound, which was situated near GCC Construction Company located on the Damaturu–Potiskum road, was immediately pulled down and destroyed.

c. **Wudil, Kano:** The BH attack on Kano State unfolded at Wudil police station. Again, the police swiftly repelled the attack and quickly proceeded to demolish the home and mosque of the sect leader in Wudil, Salihu – Al Amin and Sabon Gari.Explosive materials, bottles of petrol, Dane guns, local pistols, bows and arrows and charms were all recovered from the demolished homes, mosques and the attackers themselves.

d. **Maiduguri:** The hostilities by BH in Maiduguri were the largest. The fight got under way on the night of Sunday July 26th, 2009. That night, all GSM telephone lines were disabled apparently by the sect. No telecommunications network had service throughout the night. This was obviously a tactical maneuver to prevent communication among law enforcement agents.

    BH fighters selected and attacked several targets simultaneously. The State Police Headquarters (SHQ) was the epi-center of the gun battle. In a 3-hour long gun battle, about 50 BH jihadists were killed while the others retreated. Eight police personnel were killed, along with two soldiers and three prison wardens.

    The new Maiduguri prison was invaded by the jihadists and all inmates set free. This attack was meant to set free sect members who had previously been arrested by the police.

    The homes of police personnel were also attacked and set alight by the rampaging jihadists in the simultaneous attacks. Boko Haram fighters killed a police sergeant at the SHQ gate. They torched nine residences at the Police Mobile Force (MOPOL) training college. The jihadists murdered four policemen who were undergoing promotion training at the MOPOL college. The second-in-command of the MOPOL unit, SP Usman Farouk, was callously and mercilessly murdered by the BH fighters. An unnamed policeman whom the jihadists accosted at the residence of the commandant of the police training college was also killed.

The jihadists burnt down two police stations in Maiduguri – Laminsula and Gomaru. They caused extensive bloodshed, damage and mayhem on that night of July 26th, 2009.

In Damasak, Mobber Local Government Area of Borno State, the divisional police station was also attacked and one policeman killed.

Reactions to the Dutsen Tashi Attack

The Dutsen Tashi attack was a victory for law enforcement. The jihadists were routed by the combination of police and military defenders.

Then police affairs minister and a native of Bauchi State, Dr. Ibrahim Yakubu Lame stated that the police would investigate to ensure that all sectarians were arrested and their sponsors brought to justice.

Bauchi State governor Alhaji Isa Yuguda expressed satisfaction with the commitment and accuracy of security operatives in the operation. He gloated, "This calls for celebration as we have succeeded in pre-empting them."[3] Gov. Yuguda described the BH attacks as wanton militancy and declared them lunatics.

The Assistant Inspector-General of Police, Moses Anegbode, provided details of the violent clash (battle damage assessment) as follows:

a. 41 fatalities
b. 39 BH members killed
c. 1 police personnel killed
d. 176 sect members arrested
e. 200 weapons seized
f. 200 canisters seized
g. 2 bags of gunpowder seized
h. 7 bags of potassium seized
i. 1 bag of nitrate seized
j. 1 AK-47 rifle seized.

In his own reaction, BH leader Sheikh Mohammed Yusuf condemned the killing of dozens of his members in Bauchi. He said that BH members were ready to die to ensure the institution of a strict Islamic society.

Reaction the the Yobe Attack

Yobe State governor, Alh. Ibrahim Geidam condemned the sectarian attack, describing it as an embarrassment to Islam. He thanked law enforcement for containing the situation.

The Commissioner of Police of Yobe State, Mr. Mohammed Abba, gave the tactical report thus:

a. 33 extremists were killed
b. 6 rifles, 1 pistol, 1 Dane gun seized
c. 3 AK-47 rifles and 32 rounds of 7.62 mm live ammunition seized
d. Women and children held in captivity in the BH enclave released
e. Over 2,000 residents of Potiskum fled the city for personal safety.

Reaction to the Kano Attack

An arrested and injured BH fighter told newsmen at the State Police Headquarters (SHQ) on Bompai Road, Kano:

> Allah be praised. We are simply passing a period of tribulations and I know that even if I die now, I would be hugely rewarded by Allah. They cannot stop us. We must propagate the message of Allah. Only Sharia we believe and Western education is taboo.[4]

This statement was quite ominous and pregnant with meaning. It indicated why they were fighting and why they were ready to lay down their lives. It showed that it was a suicidal, loss–loss proposition. I lose and you lose. There is no winner.

It showed a fatalistic mindset that takes directives only from Allah or Sheikh Mohammed Yusuf. Since Yusuf had said it was okay to die fighting for the cause, then their martyrdom was an act of loyalty (*Bayat*) to Sheikh Mohammed Yusuf, and would result in a first-class ticket to heaven where the warriors for God would be rewarded bountifully. This author wishes that security and government officials did not casually start this conflict.

Reaction to the Maiduguri Attack

As the epi-center of the jihadi movement, the Maiduguri attack (which included the attack on a policeman in Damasak) was the fiercest and unsurprisingly the bloodiest.

President Umaru Musa Yar'Adua personally ordered the General Officer Commanding 3 Division of the Nigerian Army based in Jos, Major General Saleh Maina – to quell the insurrection. The president gave the order prior to his departure on a state visit to Brazil.

The army moved in with six armored tanks, troops, members of the Police Mobile Force (MOPOL) and regular policemen to Railway Quarters – the headquarters of Boko Haram. Once in position, the military made announcements ordering residents out of the BH enclave. Over 4,000 people took shelter in military barracks. Upon expiry of the deadline for safe exit from the BH enclave, the military commenced artillery bombardment of the mosques and homes in Railway Quarters.

After a four-day fight the sect was defeated by the military. Sheikh Yusuf was captured alive and unhurt by soldiers and taken to the Giwa military barracks in Maiduguri. While a captive in Giwa barracks on July 30th, 2009, Governor Ali Modu Sheriff went to see the leader of the insurgency, a man who had helped to bring him to political power and helped him to defeat Governor Mala Kachalla of the People's Democratic Party (PDP) – a man who was now his arch-enemy. Whether Gov. Sheriff went to confirm Yusuf's identity or to gloat is unclear, as the details of their meeting were not made public.

Sheikh Mohammed Yusuf was moved from army detention in Giwa Barracks to the SHQ Maiduguri, though it is not clear who gave this order. At the SHQ, he was video-taped and photographed hale and hearty sitting on the floor in handcuffs. However, it seems the indiscipline that has been the bane of professional policing in Nigeria since its independence in 1960 crept in. Some trigger-happy policemen shot dead the sect leader and gave the usual excuse that he had been trying to escape. It must be added here that extra-judicial murders are generally very rife in police custody in Nigeria. However, in a case of this nature which had involved the loss of police lives, it was sure fire that bringing Mohammed Yusuf to the SHQ was a death sentence.

The important questions that an independent panel of inquiry should ask are:

a. Who gave the order for Sheikh Mohammed Yusuf to be moved to the SHQ?
b. Who moved Sheikh Yusuf to the SHQ?
c. Why did General Saleh Maina who was carrying out a counter-insurgency operation on the orders of President Yar'Adua allow the extra-judicial killing of the sect leader?

    d. Did Gen. Maina receive clearance from above (e.g. Chief of Army Staff, Chief of Defense Staff) before allowing the removal of Sheikh Yusuf from Giwa barracks?

    e. What was the role of Borno State Commissioner of Police Mr. Christopher Dega in the cold-blooded murder of Sheikh Yusuf?

    f. Who ordered the killing of over 700 BH captives at the SHQ on July 30th, 2009?

These are questions that demand frank answers. The point here is that this preacher who had been forced to the point of defending himself was killed. However, the responsibility for the over 35,000 lives snuffed out by Boko Haram lies in the hands and conscience of those who gave the order to kill Yusuf on that fateful July day.

The pattern of arrogance, ignorance, impunity and idiocy that has characterized leadership in Nigeria's security sector played out here. It is a well-known axiom that you do not kill the head of an insurgency. You must keep the leader alive to call his men to order. After Yusuf's murder some people of feeble minds celebrated and jubilated. They did not know that that singular act would constitute a death sentence for tens of thousands of Nigerians and human misery for millions of internally displaced persons (IDPs).

General Saleh Maina and the gallant troops put down the insurrection. However, by condoning the murder of Yusuf, they lost the war. As at September 2018, over 35,000 people have been killed (and we are still counting), while over 2.5 million people have been displaced. The military has been humiliated in many battles, property worth several billions of dollars has been destroyed, and the conflict is still ongoing.

On that same July 30th, 2009, Alhaji Buji Foi, a prominent leader of Boko Haram and former Commissioner of Religious Affairs in the government of Gov. Ali Modu Sheriff was captured at his farm along the Biu–Damboa road. He was brought to the SHQ in Maiduguri where he was also summarily executed by police personnel.

Another pathetic extra-judicial murder on the same day was that of Alhaji Mohammed Fugu, a businessman and father-in-law to Sheikh Mohammed Yusuf. When he heard he was sought by the police, he went to the SHQ to report himself without his lawyers. He felt confident that he had done nothing wrong. He was also summarily executed. His compound was demolished by the government.

It was said that before Sheikh Mohammed Yusuf was shot dead, he asked Allah to receive his soul. The AK-47 rifle blast that killed him was

Figure 2.2   Abubakar Shekau.

merciless. The bullet exited the muzzle of the gun at a rate of 715 meters per second, striking the cleric on the head, opening up the cranial plate and splashing the gray matter on the floor.

It was a brutal end to Sheikh Mohammed Yusuf, but a new beginning for terror as never before seen in Nigeria. But on July 31st, 2009, no one knew what the future held. Boko Haram had been convincingly defeated and the threat of jihad had gone away with the death of the sect's leader. His second-in-command, Abubakar Shekau was said to have been killed in action – end of story (Figure 2.2).

CONCLUSION

This chapter has looked at the spark of the religious strife and the major battles that were fought in Dutsen Tashi, Kano, Potiskum and Maiduguri. In all the battles, the authorities were prepared for conflict and they prevailed. Eventually, on July 30th, the conflict which had commenced on June 11th came to a tragic end for the leader of the Boko Haram sect – Sheikh Mohammed Yusuf.

At the beginning of the chapter, we quoted Nigeria's President Muhammadu Buhari as saying that it was the extra-judicial murder of

Sheikh Mohammed Yusuf that sparked the Boko Haram conflict. Our analysis does not agree with that assertion. From the chronology of events and using causal connections, the June 11th massacres by Operation Flush in Maiduguri gave rise to the jihad. It was the *causus belli*. Sheikh Mohammed Yusuf personally declared the jihad in his "Open Letter to President Yar'Adua."

It was the conclusion reached by Yusuf after the June 11th massacre that rankled more because of the cavalier manner by which the state government treated the killing of 17 members of his sect that pushed him to declare jihad. Yusuf infact subscribed to a conspiracy theory that Operation Flush was set up by Gov. Ali Modu Sheriff not only to combat armed robbers and armed bandits, but also to exterminate members of the BH sect.

When Yusuf wrote to President Umar Musa Yar'Adua declaring jihad, nobody from the federal government reached out to him to assuage his feelings and convince him to embrace peace. The run up to the July 30th, 2009 military defeat of BH in Maiduguri showed that neither dual federalism nor cooperative federalism work in Nigeria. Federalism is about responsibility. Yet no level of government was responsible for ensuring peace after 17 citizens were callously murdered by government agents. The Nigerian Constitution (1999) guarantees freedom of worship, association and movement. Up until 6:00 AM of July 26th, 2009 when the Dutsen Tashi police station attack occurred, BH had not broken the law. They had been protesting, but no known law had been broken.

With the benefit of hindsight, if the unfortunate shooting incident of June 11th, 2009 had been handled with maturity, care and responsibility, perhaps Boko Haram would not have resorted to jihad. The murder of the 17 mourners was neither condemned, deplored nor investigated by any federal authority. In Nigeria's social contract, the federal and state governments have a duty and a responsibility to protect the human rights of citizens. When the Borno State government adopted an uncaring and cavalier attitude to the murder of Nigerians within its borders, cooperative federalism required that any of the following officers act in defense of those human rights:

a. President of the Federal Republic of Nigeria
b. Vice President
c. Secretary to the Government of the Federation
d. National Security Adviser
e. Director General, Department of State Services

f. Inspector General of Police
g. Attorney-General and Minister of Justice
h. Chairman of the National Human Rights Commission
i. Chief of Defence Staff
j. Minister of Police Affairs
k. Minister of the Interior
l. Minister of Defence
m. Chief of Army Staff
n. Chairmen of Relevant Senate Committees
o. Chairmen of Relevant House Committees.

All the officers enumerated above had the responsibility to investigate the killing of 17 citizens near the customs market in Maiduguri by armed soldiers and policemen. Yet no one did.

The June 11th, 2009 massacre exposed the soft under-belly of governance in Nigeria. Many agencies, bodies and officers consume a lot of public resources; however, there is little to show in terms of service to ordinary citizens. While these bodies would make a lot of noise if one eminent personality was hurt, the lives of 17 citizens seemingly meant nothing to them. It is a horrific narrative that needs to be changed if Nigeria is to become a modern democratic state.

NOTES

1. President Muhammadu Buhari's inaugural speech reproduced in **Saturday Tribune** (May 30th, 2015): Page 3.
2. In 2009, the Federal Road Safety Commission (FRSC) introduced a policy on the compulsory use of crash helmets by commercial and private motorcycle riders throughout Nigeria.
3. www.vanguardngr.com/2011/07/boko-haram-history-ideas-and-revolt-4/
4. www.vanguardngr.com/2011/07/boko-haram-history-ideas-and-revolt-4/

3

BH Reloaded

The military conquest of Boko Haram on July 30th, 2009 was final and decisive. The Al Jazeera television network based in Doha, Qatar, was later to air video footage of uniformed Nigeria police personnel executing hundreds of Boko Haram fighters who were made to lie down in a row at the Borno State Police Headquarters (SHQ) in Maiduguri. Some of the police officers identified in the video were later arrested and charged for culpable homicide for the extra-judicial killing of the BH fighters.

Life returned to normal in Maiduguri and the whole of the Muslim North. The calm and peace being experienced was actually the calm before the storm, but no one knew it at the time.

Although there was ample evidence of mass murders of BH members, there was no public outcry from any quarters on behalf of the sect members. They were simply forgotten and unmourned, at least not publicly. No government authority inquired into the matter. It appeared to be a case of good riddance to bad rubbish.

In a classified cable sent from the US Embassy Abuja in November 2009, which was made available on Wikileaks, the diplomats said:

> Borno political and religious leaders . . . asserted that the state and federal governments responded appropriately and, apart from the opposition party, overwhelmingly supported Yusuf's death without misgivings over the extrajudicial killing. Security remained a concern in Borno, with residents expressing concern about importation of arms and exchanges of religious messages across porous international borders.[1]

There were reports that Yusuf's deputy had survived, and audio tapes were believed to be in circulation in which Boko Haram threatened future attacks. However, many observers did not anticipate imminent bloodshed.

Security in Borno was downgraded. Borno government official Alhaji Boguma believed that the state deserved praise from the international community for ending the conflict in such a short time, and that the "wave of fundamentalism" had been "crushed."[2]

The cable that emanated from the United States Embassy in Abuja captured the mood of the times. However, it was mistaken. The fact that Abubakar Shekau was still alive meant that the conflict merely went underground – but only for a while. Shekau was not only the second-in-command of BH leader Sheikh Mohammed Yusuf, he was also the "Minister of War."

It was the charisma, diplomacy and leadership abilities of Mohammed Yusuf that kept the BH sect from towing the path of violence earlier. Acts of violence were directed against a few individuals; like the murder of Yusuf's teacher, Sheikh Adam. There is speculation that Adam was killed on the orders of Abubakar Shekau who was in control of the sect's military wing.

WHO IS ABUBAKAR SHEKAU?

After the mantle of leadership of BH fell on him in July 2009 with the extra-judicial murder of Sheikh Mohammed Yusuf, Shekau escaped to the Niger Republic where he was safe from the Nigerian authorities.

Abubakar Shekau was born in Shekau Village, Tarmuwal Local Govt. Area, Yobe State, between 1965 and 1975. There is no reliable birth record for him. He is of the Kanuri ethnic group. He speaks Arabic, Hausa, Fulani and Kanuri. He did not receive any formal Western education, and therefore does not speak or write English – unlike Sheikh Mohammed Yusuf.

As was customary for a poor Kanuri child in the Muslim North, Shekau relocated to Maiduguri in the late 1970s as an *almajiri* (street urchin) in search of Islamic knowledge and food. He enrolled with a local Islamic teacher (Malam) "without care from any parent" – a situation that toughened him.[3]

Shekau's one-time neighbor said: "He learnt in a very hard way, in abject poverty, living in same environment with his age mates who wore good clothes and rode in posh cars belonging to their parents, mostly government officials."[4]

The extremely tough circumstances of having to scratch out a daily living made Shekau grow up a hardened man. A neighbor said "the ugly experiences of his adolescent years formed the basis of Abubakar's anger against society.[5]

The future leader of the deadliest terrorist organization in the world (as of 2014), Abubakar Shekau found peace in the Islamic theology, especially the sayings of the Prophet (Hadith) which emphasize such virtues and values as equity, justice and love.

Abu Shekau later enrolled at the Mohammed Goni College of Legal and Islamic Studies (MOGOLS) at Mafoni, Maiduguri. The school, located in a densely populated neighborhood of the Borno State capital, ran afternoon classes which was convenient for the budding terrorist. Teachings at MOGOLS were given in either the Hausa or Kanuri language. Young Abubakar did not have the opportunity to learn English at MOGOLS. These circumstances would all combine to shape him.

A former schoolmate said of Shekau:

I knew him (Abubakar Shekau) at High Islam in MOGOLS in 1995. He was very slim, dark in complexion, always wearing a white but dirty gown (*jalabiya*). He had this hard look, often appearing wild and always aggressive even when talking. He used to carry around some Islamic text books that made students think he read a lot but someone in his class once said he only used the books to create the impression that he is a scholar.[6]

The former classmate further recalled:

He kept to himself and rarely associated with his mates. He regarded students who did not share his doctrine and understanding of Islam as "*Thabut*" meaning those who do not know Islam like unbelievers. He later bought a bicycle which he used in carrying his books.[7]

Sharing more historical facts on young Abu Shekau, the classmate also said:

He started selling some Islamic books and then changed his bicycle to an old Suzuki Jincheng motorcycle. I think he started influencing some students to accept his religious belief that time but I didn't get to see him again until when he started preaching at Angwar Doki, Millionaires Quarters, and some other places before 2009.[8]

Abubakar Shekau was nicknamed **Darul Akeem wa Zamunda Tawheed**, which was often shortened to **Darul Tawheed** (or monotheism expert) which means "the abode of monotheism." Shekau favored this nickname as it symbolized his absolute faith in Allah. His nickname has also been interpreted to mean "the oneness of Allah."

SECOND-IN-COMMAND

As the deputy head of Boko Haram, Shekau was quite unruly. He was more in the mold of Mohammed Alli – the cleric who radicalized Mohammed Yusuf. His belief system reached the jihadi level, while that of Yusuf did not. Yusuf and Alli parted ways in 2004 due to Yusuf's unwillingness to embark on *hijra* and eventual *jihad*. However, even though Shekau believed in jihad, he stayed on with Yusuf and played the role of head of the military wing and second-in-command (2 i/c).

BH leader Mohammed Yusuf was a charismatic, educated cleric who at one time had sought admission into the University of Maiduguri. Yusuf could speak English and drove a Mercedes Benz car during his lifetime. In contrast, Shekau was more radical, and more strategic in his thinking.

Shekau was ready for jihad, but Yusuf apparently kept him in check. However, his fiery preaching gave away his preference for revolutionary change over evolution. A Shehuri North resident remembers the first encounter he had with Shekau's preaching in late 2008:

> Shekau came for preaching that time at Shehuri. We learnt that Mohammed Yusuf who was the leader of the Yusufiyya Movement as they were called that time traveled to Kaduna and he (Shekau) stood in for him. . . The group appeared to be very popular among the youth that time and a friend invited me. Shekau started his preaching very well, he was talking about immorality in our society and corruption everywhere. He started abusing some Islamic clerics accusing them of conniving with those in government to cheat in the society.
>
> He said the day of reckoning was coming. Then he delved into so many things, threatening jihad and all sorts of things.[9]

The attendee at the Yusufiyya *tafsir* (lecture) continued his narration:

> Then I heard some of the lieutenants sitting beside him attempting to stop him from deviating from their teaching and he shouted at them. I was

38

later told by my friend who invited me that those trying to disagree with Shekau were Mohammed Yusuf's disciples and those resisting them were Shekau's lieutenants.[10]

Shekau had an interpretation of Islam that deviated from that of his spiritual leader, and he did not hide his true beliefs or tone down his rhetoric to align with that of Yusuf. While Yusuf presented a balanced, mature message in his *dawah* (preachings), Shekau was a die-hard jihadist and he surrounded himself with his disciples. Whenever he was opportune to preach in Yusuf's absence he would attempt to persuade his listeners to adopt his extremist religious beliefs and war-like disposition. While Yusuf was alive, Shekau portrayed himself as an Islamic scholar with deep knowledge of the religion. Aside from preaching extremist theology, Shekau did not openly rebel against Yusuf. He played the role of a second-in-command, representing the spiritual leader when he was so directed.

Shekau, an unrepentant protagonist of violence, is suspected of having ordered the assassination of Sheikh Ja'afar Mahmud Adam, the teacher of Mohammed Yusuf. After his radicalization in 2002, the relationship between Mohammed Yusuf and his former teacher fell apart. Sheikh Adam and Sheikh Yusuf held several debates where Adam challenged Yusuf's radical ideas. Adam, who was born on February 12th, 1960, was a Nigerian Salafist Islamic scholar. BH elements disrupted his lectures on several occasions. He was shot dead in his mosque in Dorayi Kano on April 13th, 2007. However, some people are of the view that Shekau was not responsible for Sheikh Adam's murder. They thought it was done by politicians who the cleric had threatened to expose during the 2007 general elections.[11]

A Nigerian journalist, Ismail Omipidan speculates that Shekau might have been a secret member of the Nigerian Taliban group which was an extremist group hiding under the umbrella of the moderate and popular BH. It is argued that Shekau's preaching and bellicose actions were indicators of his Nigerian Taliban leaning. Shekau is credited with over-ruling Yusuf as to the timing of the attack on the police and Borno State government. Yusuf desired a path away from confronting the government. However, the provocation of June 11th, 2009 rankled and the Borno government's cavalier attitude hurt even more. The hawks in BH were emboldened to the point of insubordination.

Mr. Omipidan writes:

The only time Shekau perhaps had the upper hand over the late Yusuf, and even went as far as over-ruling his decision, was when it was time to decide whether or not to go ahead with the onslaught on Maiduguri in 2009. And that singular action of Shekau changed the entire focus of the Boko Haram and it is responsible for the present posture of the group . . . Shekau was the real brain behind the timing of the launch of the insurrection in some parts of the North in 2009.[12]

It was said that Yusuf was urging his adherents to tarry a while over the planned jihad as Muslims were approaching the holy month of *Shaban* (the month before Ramadan). Yusuf had counseled against waging a war in the month of *Shaban*. Shekau objected. He argued that his troops had already been mobilized to strike, and that there should be no going back on the jihad. In effect, he over-ruled Yusuf, who appeared to doubt the efficacy and need for the jihad, despite the various provocations by the Borno State government and the Nigeria Police Force.

A SELF-PROCLAIMED LEADER

When the smoke cleared and the dust settled after the July 30th, 2009 conquest of BH in Maiduguri, Yusuf laid dead as did Alhaji Buji Foi and about 700 other BH members. The body of one man was not found; that of Abubakar Shekau alias Darul Tawheed. Although the police claimed that he was killed, they could not produce corpus evidence. Shekau escaped the military onslaught led by Maj. Gen. Saleh Maina with bullet wounds, as he later confirmed in a 25-minute video shot on April 19th, 2010 in Maiduguri.

Shekau said he was shot in the thigh during the four-day military offensive but was rescued by "fellow believers and protected by Allah."[13] In the video, Shekau vowed to retaliate over the killing of BH members in Maiduguri and other places.

The video dated April 2010 was the self-proclamation that Shekau needed to assume leadership of the BH sect. The leader Yusuf had been extra-judicially murdered. So, as the surviving second-in-command recognized and accepted by all as the heir to the throne, Shekau only needed to assume the role of the leader of BH. This he did.

In the same April 2010 video interview, Shekau was asked why he was clutching an AK-47 rifle, since guns were products of Western education which BH said was *haram* (forbidden). Shekau responded, "guns are not products of boko . . . we can also make guns. We even made and used guns."[14]

40

Asked about their source of arms and ammunitions in the video, Shekau replied:

> What we are saying is that it is not permissible to seek for boko (Western education) under the prevailing system and given the un-Islamic things introduced in boko.
>
> We are not fighting Western education itself. What we are opposed to are the various un-Islamic things slotted into it and the system upon which the study of Western education is rested. These are the reasons why we say it is not permissible to study it.[15]

THE RADICAL NARRATIVE

Abubakar Shekau epitomized Islamic radicalism and extremism. The environment in North East Nigeria – an area that is economically depressed, lacking major industries and a viable economic growth engine – was home to some of the poorest people in Nigeria. The area survived on subsistence farming. The growth business in the North East was government jobs, government appointments and the education industry which employed teachers, school administrators and menial workers such as messengers, cleaners, gardeners, etc. The local environment of deprivation and poverty provided fertile ground for an extremely radical narrative. With his extreme detest of Western civilization, Abubakar Shekau became the point man to deliver a twisted message from God.

His message was simple. He argued that the powers in Abuja and Borno State were corrupt and immoral. He said that a strict form of Islam would produce a better system of government. The government Shekau envisioned would implement strict Sharia code across Nigeria. His radical narrative carried with it a capability to carry out violence – a Kalashikov rifle and a license to plunder the ill-gotten riches on display by Nigeria's corrupt elite. To a discerning mind, Shekau's message was empty rhetorics and illogical. However, to a North Eastern youth who grew up begging on the streets or driving an okada (commercial motorcyle) or tricycle to survive the mean streets of Maiduguri, his message was a message from God. It was logical. It was infallible. It explained his down-trodden station in life and it provided justification for any bestiality that could be committed against other members of society. Since society and government were responsible for their lack of Western education, for their abject penury and woes in life, society had to pay. The logic of the

41

BH jihad was to build a just and egalitarian society where poverty would be abolished and Sharia code would be the law of the land.

This narrative helped Shekau recruit many fighters. Joining the war against the infidels and corrupt government was an avenue to financial reward on earth, and if one were to lose his life in battle, then it would be a ticket to *al jannah* (heaven).

In this narrative, the young impressionable minds saw their one-way ticket out of lack, penury, deprivation and desperation. Given the early victories of BH against the military which resulted in the loss of about 75% of Borno State to BH, the narrative became even more believable and seductive.

Aside from converting a large number of North East youths to Jihad, the BH extremist propaganda appeared to have radicalized youths in far Northwest Cameroon, Southern Niger and Chad. These countries share similar economic dislocations in areas proximate to Nigeria's North East. The governments in the countries are also as weak as their Nigerian counterpart, so the circumstances were similar and the message was provocative. It provoked an assessment by the youths of their circumstances in life. It provoked a yearning for a better life. And it apparently provoked acts of terror. Cameroon's Northwest region has been hard hit by BH. Nigeria's regional allies, Chad and Niger, have also been hard hit. They have experienced frequent suicide bombings, kidnappings and other forms of terrorist attacks. BH has Amirs (leaders) in those countries and has active terrorist organizations in play there. For example, the Nigerian border towns have a large number of jihadi fighters who often join in the battle. Recently, a Chadian court sentenced ten BH fighters to death. Nine of them were Chadians.[16]

THE MAN WITH NINE LIVES

The Nigerian authorities have made the argument on several occasions that Abubakar Shekau is dead. They claim that persons who pretend to be Shekau are impostors and doubles. The problem with the government's assertion is that it has not been able to provide corpus evidence that would prove that Abubakar Shekau is indeed dead.

Shekau was first thought to have died in July 2009 during the destruction of the BH Central Mosque in Angwar Doki, Maiduguri. He later surfaced and assumed leadership of BH in April 2010.

In September 2012, the military raided his home in Maiduguri when he sneaked in for the naming ceremony of his newborn son. He escaped with a gunshot wound to his leg. In that raid, the military arrested Shekau's wife and three children. Presumably, the newborn baby was also held as an insurgent. On October 7th, 2012, the military announced that Shekau was dead.

In another encounter in 2013, the military publicized the death of Shekau quite prominently with his photos splashed on the pages of the newspapers. In several news interviews, this author urged the government to provide forensic proof[17] that the man was in fact Abubakar Shekau. Later, Shekau again arose from the dead and made more video announcements and threats.

Although the military still insists that Shekau is dead, in October 2016, Nigerian government agents negotiated with Shekau for the release of 21 of the kidnapped Chibok school girls. The details of the negotiations have been kept secret. However, some sources maintain that 21 million US dollars was paid to the arch-terrorist in cash.[18]

Shekau has turned out to be the cat with nine lives. In August 2016, ISIS named a new leader for BH.[19] It was assumed by many experts, including this author, that Shekau was dead. A few days later, Shekau surfaced in a taped recording to say that he disagreed with the replacement decision. He maintained that he was still the leader of the terror group. His leadership was later acknowledged by the Nigerian government.

CONCLUSION

The Nigerian authorities missed an important opportunity to defang the proverbial BH snake when it failed to arrest or incapacitate Abubakar Shekau in the July 2009 encounter in Maiduguri. Trigger-happy policemen killed Mohammed Yusuf at the Borno SHQ, but allowed the really dangerous terrorist to escape with a bullet wound to his leg.

Shekau reportedly led the Maiduguri attacks that claimed about 300 lives in July 2009. Ironically, it was the leader of the sect, Sheikh Mohammed Yusuf, who was arrested, paraded and then murdered in cold blood.

The events of July 2009 indicate that there was very little intelligence information available to the Nigerian authorities about the BH group. There was a treasure trove of open source intelligence available from BH in the period between its radicalization in 2002 and July 2009; good intelligence on the group was available within its own words. A charismatic preacher, Yusuf was quite visible and voluble. He gave a lot of press interviews and his views were extensively published in the newspapers. What should have happened then was for the intelligence agencies to collect open source materials and conduct basic intelligence analysis. The lectures by Yusuf and Shekau were open *tafsirs* (lectures) and intelligence agents could have attended these to glean information about the threat. Deep cover agents could have and should have infiltrated the group in order to bring in information from the belly of the beast.

The ascendancy of Shekau and his continuing threat to Nigeria were simply a result of failure of intelligence. If intelligence officials had done a painstaking job in tracking the rhetoric, published materials, audio tapes and *tafsirs* (lectures) of the group they could have projected the trajectory to violence and then moved to nip the problem in the bud. Waiting for Yusuf, a reluctant warrior, to declare holy war was negligence of duty.

As said by President Muhammadu Buhari of Nigeria on his inauguration day (May 29th, 2015), "fires are easier to quench when they are small."[20]

NOTES

1. Wikileaks, www.wikileaks.org/plusd/cables/09ABUJA2014_a.html
2. Ibid.
3. Timothy Olanrewaju. "The Shekau We Know – By School Mates" ***Sunday Sun*** (May 18th, 2014): Page 10.
4. Ibid.
5. Ibid.
6. Ibid.
7. Ibid.
8. Ibid.
9. Ibid.
10. Ibid.
11. See "Revealed: How Gov. Shekarau Plotted the Assassination of Sheikh Ja'afaru" ***Sahara Reporters*** (April 12th, 2009). This report was very poorly argued and written with no evidentiary support. However, it is one of the conspiracy theories out there about the cleric's murder.
12. Ismail Omipidan. "Boko Haram: A Reporter's Perspective" ***Sunday Sun*** (May 18th, 2014): Page 16.
13. 25-minute video made by Abubakar Shekau on April 19th, 2010.
14. Ibid.
15. Ibid.
16. "Chad Sentences 10 Boko Haram Members to Death" ***BBC News*** (August 28th, 2015).

17. Kingsley Omonobi. "The Last Days of Shekau, Boko Haram Leader" ***Vanguard*** (August 25th, 2013).
18. Dr. Ona Ekhomu. Television Interview. "Death of Abubakar Shekau" ***Channels Television*** (August 26th, 2013).
19. "Nigeria: Boko Haram 'Releases 21 Chibok Girls'" ***Al Jazeera Television*** (October 13th, 2016).
20. "Boko Haram in Nigeria: Abu Musab Al-Barnawi Named as New Leader" ***BBC News*** (August 3rd, 2016).

4

Prelude to War

When the Nigerian Army troops led by Major General Saleh Maina of 3 Division, Jos, Plateau State defeated Boko Haram decisively on July 30th, 2009, it was assumed that the problem of Boko Haram had been permanently solved.

Unfortunately, that assumption was wrong. After going underground for a period of 14 months, giving the authorities the false impression that it had been vanquished, the sect re-emerged under new leadership – that of Abubakar Shekau. The new leader, Shekau, was very different to Mohammed Yusuf. Shekau was totally committed to jihad and violent conflict. He made no pretensions about diplomacy and moderation. He was bloodthirsty. He was an extremist. He was an implacable warrior for God.

The BH threat is continuing in West Africa. The authorities should learn an important lesson from the re-emergence of BH in 2010 that BH is a patient and purposeful enemy. It moves at its own pace. It executes its own agenda. It is a strategic enemy and knows how to use deception to its advantage. BH will take the time to perfect the art of war – be it marksmanship, bomb-making, IED delivery, ambush tactics, mass casualty events, etc. – before striking. It is common knowledge that while they were regrouping in the Niger Republic after their routing from Angwar Doki Quarters in Maiduguri, BH fighters received marksmanship training from Al-Shabbab fighters. This resulted in the first major threat that BH posed to Nigeria – the AK-47 threat. BH fighters infiltrated Maiduguri and other North East Nigeria cities. They would conceal the AK-47 rifles under their flowing gowns (*jalabiya*) and produce it at the right moment to carry out a summary execution – usually a headshot – before then driving away on their motorbikes.

Later, BH graduated its terror tactics to the IED threat. In the beginning, it suffered some reverses as some IEDs exploded on the bomb makers or bomb delivery personnel. However, that was a price of training which they were willing to pay. And as the saying goes, "practice makes perfect." Over time, BH bomb makers mastered the art of putting together IEDs. Now, suddenly, we are under grave IED threat.

A HISTORY OF VIOLENCE

This book has described Sheikh Mohammed Yusuf as a generally peace-loving and diplomatic leader of a Wahabi-Salafist sect. However, the seeds of BH violence were sown during his leadership and are a product of its organizational structure, its mission, its operational methods and its rhetoric.

In April 2007, armed Islamic militants attacked a police station in the Panshekara District of Kano. The fighters, armed with automatic weapons, killed 21 policemen and 21 bystanders. They also set the police station ablaze. It took the Nigerian Army 24 hours of counterattack supported by ground attack airplanes to defeat the militants.[1]

There were numerous speculations about the identity of the attackers. One school of thought was that the aggressors were a rump of the Yobe Taliban sect; another pointed the finger at the Yusufiyya sect.[2] The stated motive of the attack was that the Islamists were protesting against the police investigation of the Sheikh Ja'afar Mahmud Adam assassination which had occurred four days earlier. It is now believed in intelligence circles that Abubakar Shekau personally ordered the murder of Sheikh Adam. The assault on the Panshekara police station could logically be regarded as the handiwork of Abubakar Shekau as the Yusufiyya sect (Boko Haram) at that time was one of the few militant organizations that had a propensity to violence and had the capability (munitions of war, trained fighters and organization) to carry out such a large-scale attack. It should be recalled that, after their defeat in 2004, remnants of the Yobe Talibans rejoined the Yusufiyya sect and had now been fully integrated into the Islamist sect.

Among the membership of the BH sect, Abubakar Shekau had his own sub-group of ardent, ultra-militant loyalists who could have organized and executed the Panshekara attack, even without the knowledge of the group's spiritual leader, Sheikh Mohammed Yusuf.

Another causal factor of the Panshekara attack could be that the police investigation into the Sheikh Adam assassination irked Shekau who then ordered the torching of the police station and killing of the policemen. Unfortunately, a large-scale attack of this nature on public law enforcement was not thoroughly investigated and the findings made public. There is always a tendency to cover up facts from members of the public thereby leaving rumor mills and conspiracy theories as the only available sources of information. Aside from a vague description of Islamic militants, it would have been good to know the following:

a. Which group carried out the attack?
b. What was their grievance?
c. How did they obtain munitions of war?
d. Who was their spiritual leader?
e. Who were the field commanders?
f. How did they get logistics?
g. What was their end game?

These are important questions whose answers might have enabled law enforcement to predict the next attack and perhaps stop them. However, the indolent attitude of the Nigerian authorities to such matters, and lack of a rigorous analytical problem-solving culture led to a hasty closure of the issue which had in it the seeds of the next attack. Clearly, law enforcement cannot prevent some or all attacks. However, incidents that have occurred provide an opportunity for a post-mortem analysis that will enable us to learn how to prevent similar attacks in future; particularly when these incidents cost a large number of human lives, including those of law enforcement officers.

THE PURPOSE OF VIOLENCE

The jihad embarked upon by Sheikh Mohammed Yusuf was consistent with the rhetoric of his organization and its mission. When Yusuf was converted in 2002 to radical Islam, he adopted the goals of fundamentalism. The purpose of the BH jihad was to create an Islamic caliphate in Nigeria. The narrative was that since contemporary Nigeria society was corrupt, the duty of every true believer was to wage a relentless holy war until total victory was achieved and a caliphate created.

At the beginning, the purpose of BH violence was to fight for the implementation of Sharia law in the Muslim north and the eventual creation of a caliphate where holy men would rule in a just manner. The BH jihad had historical antecedents in post-independence Nigeria.

THE MAITATSINE JIHAD

Mohammed Yusuf and his followers had a role model in Mohammed Marwa Maitatsine, the Cameroon-born founder of the Maitatsine movement that claimed nearly 5,000 lives in Kano in 1980. The Maitatsine sect, which could be considered a forerunner of the BH group, was based upon fundamentalist Islam and jihad.

Mohammed Marwa Maitatsine led the Al Masifu sect with about 5,000 members. The Al Masifu denounced ostentatious living, including owning houses and wearing fancy Muslim fashions. They also rejected facing Mecca while praying. The Al Masifu sect was intent on "purifying" the "practice" of Islam by replacing traditional orthodoxy with its fundamentalist doctrine.

Nigerian security agencies promptly arrested Maitatsine and some of his lieutenants in 1978 and deported Maitatsine to his native Cameroon. Exploiting the porous borders, Maitatsine returned to Nigeria in late 1978. During the next two years, the Al Masifu sect grew in membership and exhibited large-scale violent behaviors in Kano. The sect members frequently intimidated citizens who lived close to their enclave in Kano. In 1980, a policeman was murdered by members of the sect.

Angered by the excesses of the Al Masifu sect, the governor of Kano State, Alhaji Mohammed Abubakar Rimi, sent a letter to Maitatsine demanding he and his followers leave Kano city immediately. This expulsion order was ignored by Maitatsine.

On December 18th, 1980, the Al Masifu sect members attacked other Muslims praying at the Kano Grand Mosque. Police intervention to maintain law and order was rebuffed by the sectarians. The governor then requested the federal government's assistance. The military was called out to quel the rebellion.

The Maitatsine jihad was a bloody confrontation. Orthodox Muslims joined the security agencies in the fight against the sect. Muslims identified sect members and lynched them. The sect members were armed with bows and arrows and firearms seized from security agents. The fighting raged on until January 3rd, 1981, when the Al Masifu sect was defeated.

The fighting took a huge toll in human lives – over 4,177 people were killed. This included the sect's leader, Mohammed Marwa Maitatsine himself, Al Masifu sect members, policemen and a reporter with the *Daily Times* newspaper. The number of people injured in the conflict was 8,712. The violence also resulted in huge loss of property.[3]

Our argument is that BH merely followed the jihadi script of Maitasine. The Al Masifu sect was focused on its concept of fundamentalist religious purity. It adopted the rigid position that those who do not convert to its brand of Islam were unbelievers and deserved to die. That is what informed the attack on other Muslim faithfuls on December 18th, 1980 at the Kano Grand Mosque.

The Al-Masifu sect was indignant that Kano residents did not readily see that it (Al Masifu) was practicing the true faith. Efforts to proselytize the larger population on its fundamentalist doctrine did not yield much result. Between 1978 and 1980 the sect gained many followers, but its membership of 5,000 was very small compared to the population of Orthodox Muslims in the city. This fact did not sit well with the fundamentalists. They felt that it was now time to take matters into their own hands and force citizens to take notice and adopt the fundamentalist doctrine; the bottom line was that citizens must either convert or lose their lives. However, the government did not agree with the sect members so military force was used to overwhelm the jihadists and restore peace to Kano.

The violent conflict between the Al-Masifu sect and the Nigerian authorities appears to have inspired other Islamic fundamentalists to violence in Northern Nigeria. This Al-Masifu violence continued until about 1985 with deadly clashes in Bauchi, Bulumkutum (Maiduguri), Yola (Adamawa State), etc.

THE TRIAL OF DAMAGUN

On January 16th, 2007, 50-year-old Alhaji Mohammed Bello Damagun, a Muslim cleric and director of Media Trust Ltd, was arraigned in a Federal High Court in Abuja on charges of money laundering for a terrorist organization. The charge sheet stated that Alhaji Damagun had transferred the sum of US$300,000 from the Al Qaeda network in the Sudan to a London bank named Habibson for the purpose of carrying out terrorist acts. The charge sheet further revealed that the funds were transferred in late 2002 when Damagun was a member of the Yobe Taliban. It is worth

51

recalling that the leader of the Yobe Taliban, Mohammed Alli, converted Mohammed Yusuf to his radical and fundamentalist ideology. In 2003, when Alli determined that BH was not ready to confront the Nigerian authorities he left in frustration on a *hijra* to Yobe State. In Kanama Yobe, the group became known as the the "Nigerian Taliban" or the "Yobe Taliban."

In the indictment of Damagun in January 2007, it was also alleged that he had facilitated 17 people to undergo terrorism training at the Mauritanian Qurah Islamic Camp.

Alhaji Damagun was also accused of funding Sheik Mohammed Yusuf and Boko Haram. He was alleged to have given large sums of cash and donated a bus and loudspeakers to Mohammed Yusuf for the evangelizing of radicalism and extremism. These acts were alleged to have been committed in September and October of 2006. The federal indictment identified Mohammed Yusuf as an operative of the Nigerian Taliban.

The Damagun trial was presided over by Hon. Justice Binta Murtala Nyako. Justice Nyako granted Damagun bail after she was persuaded by the defense counsel that Damagun was not a flight risk. It is shocking and incomprehensible that the judge allowed bail in an important terrorist finance and support case of this magnitude. A remand decision would have served the cause of justice. Since bail was granted there has been no further trial of the case, there was no discharge or acquittal of the case and it is reasonably assumed that Damagun has evaded justice despite the gravity of the offences committed and the charges laid. The Damagun case appears to be an example of impunity.

Prior to the extra-judicial murder of BH leader Mohammed Yusuf on July 30th, 2009, he gave many important interviews to the *Daily Trust* newspaper. He used the news medium to explain his views in his running battles with the Borno State government. After the June 11th, 2009 customs market roundabout massacres (when 17 members of the sect were killed by "Operation Flush" in a funeral procession), Yusuf alleged that the June 11th murders were premeditated and probably ordered by the Borno State governor, Ali Modu Sheriff. He alleged that there was obviously a script that was being followed to eliminate *Yan Yusufiyya*.

The *Daily Trust* newspaper alone got the scoop of an interview with Mohammed Yusuf which was published coincidentally on Saturday July 25th, 2009, the eve of the Dutsen Tashi Bauchi attack (which was the start of hostilities by BH). In the interview, Yusuf threatened that BH would avenge the deaths of the 17 killed in the funeral entourage, and the martyrdom of Badami who was mortally injured by a bomb he was building in Biu and later died. On the same July 25th, 2009, Mohammed Yusuf said Badami's martyrdom earned him a place in *Al Jannah* (heaven). Unfortunately, this thinly veiled call to arms was missed by the intelligence agencies and the security agencies. The next day, BH fighters struck. We have been at war ever since.

There appear to be broken links between BH management under Mohammed Yusuf and the *Daily Trust* newspaper, which was partly owned and directed by Alhaji Mohammed Bello Damagun who was accused by the federal government of money laundering and terrorism financing for the Al Qaeda network. Damagun was also accused of providing logistical support to BH and was identified as a member of the Yobe Taliban (or Nigerian Taliban). To analyze the broken lines in a link analysis, we will assume that the link that exists between BH and the newspaper could actually be a solid line. The solid line indicates that there is a direct relationship, and not an indirect one (see Figure 4.1). The question now is, was the *Daily Trust* newspaper obtaining excellent scoops from Boko Haram or was it propagating Sheikh Mohammed Yusuf's message? Perhaps it could be said here to media organizations in Africa that they should subscribe to journalistic best practices of objectivity and fact checking in order to avoid being labeled as providing material support to a terrorist organization – even if unwittingly. While Mohammed Yusuf, as the leader of a terrorist organization, was eager to be heard and increase his notoriety value, the media should have only reported facts and not granted him the publicity he sought. Part of the strategy of terrorists is to speak to a large audience – the world – and be heard. If a terrorist quietly killed themselves in their home, only their immediate family would know and bury them in shame. However, if they tried to kill a VIP or a large number of people, then they would be on the evening news and on the pages of newspapers. Gaining wide publicity for their exploits is central to the reckoning and actions of terrorists.

It is often difficult to tell when the media is being used to send coded messages to other terrorists. In Abubakar Shekau's videos, he is often shown to be twisting, scratching and making unrecognizable hand movements. Some Nigerian security experts maintain that Shekau is sending coded messages with his hand and body signals to his field commanders. This analysis has not been proven, but is plausible. For example, when Mohammed Yusuf said that Badami had secured a

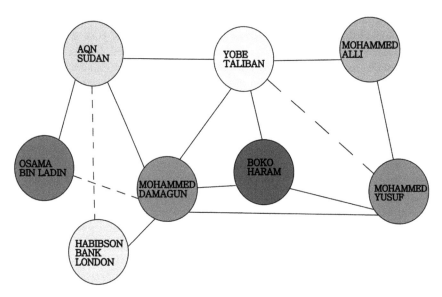

Figure 4.1 Link analysis between Damagun and jihadi groups.
Source: Author.

place for himself in heaven with his act of martyrdom, it is argued by some intelligence analysts that he was giving orders for the violence to begin. At 6:00 AM on Sunday July 26th, 2009, BH fighters attacked Dutsen Tashi Police Station in Bauchi.

KATSINA INTELLIGENCE REPORTS

In 2008, the Governor of Katsina State, Alh. Ibrahim Shema, received an intelligence report that a large number of men and women were departing from Dutsin Ma town in Katsina State and heading towards Maiduguri in Borno State.[4] The purpose of the out-migration of Katsina indigenes was to join the Boko Haram group or the *Yan Yusufiyyas*.

The security report revealed that the men were receiving training in weapons handling. Foreigners from Chad and Somalia were said to be teaching them marksmanship.[5] Aside from musketry, the men were also taught basic guerrilla warfare tactics and the making of improvised explosive devices (IEDs).[6]

This big handwriting on the wall was again apparently missed by the Nigerian intelligence officials. While the Yusufiyya movement recruited large numbers of followers and fighters, then trained them in the art of modern guerrilla warfare, the federal, state and local governments were oblivious to the threat of armed insurrection, or worse a holy war. There is no record of action taken by Governor Ibrahim Shema to dissuade Katsina citizens who were migrating from Dutsin Ma and other towns in Katsina State from going to join the jihadists. It is not clear what the governor's thought process about this threat was. However, he appeared to have the characteristic "government can handle anything" mentality:

1. There was no press conference called by the governor to appeal to the citizens to stop the migration.
2. There was no debate of the security situation in the State House of Assembly.
3. There was no evidence that Governor Shema passed this intelligence report to the federal authorities. President Umar Musa Yar'Adua, an indigene of Katsina State, was not briefed on the security situation in his home state. This might have prompted him to take some action. After all, it is still illegal in Nigeria to train a large number of people in musketry, guerrilla tactics and bomb making.

The rise of Boko Haram as an armed terror group in Nigeria occurred in plain slight. In the organization of the group, Abubakar Shekau was the head of the military wing. Shekau, an unrepentant jihadist, prepared for war long before hostilities broke out. He had a well-trained, resourced and motivated army ready to go to war against the Nigerian State and people. One did not need to gaze into a crystal ball to know that all that was left was the spark to violence. Meanwhile, the men would engage in skirmishes to hone their fighting skills. When not practicing the art of warfare, they were listening to *tafsirs* (lectures) on jihad and learning how corrupt and amoral the Nigerian government and society were. The indoctrination was thorough and deep. The men had pledged *bayat* (loyalty) to their leader, Mohammed Yusuf, and were ready to lay down their lives for him in order to go to heaven. That was their scripting.

YOU BE THE ANALYST

A large number of young men and women migrate to the largest state in the country. They settle down in communes and compounds, to avoid dealing with other members of society. You receive information that weapons handling training is being provided by foreign fighters to this large number of people. You also learn that they are being taught bomb-making skills and guerrilla tactics. **What will you report to your executive is going on?**

The answer is that the executive does not need a crystal ball or "the eyes of the gods" (the local diviner) to tell him that war is afoot. Belligerence does not occur in one day. Prior to conflict, there is a prelude which involves planning, resourcing, financing, training and eventual deployment.

The elected officials who encountered the prelude to war one way or another did not decipher the clues that were abundant. They erroneously thought that nothing could happen. Yet the Maitatsine uprising of the 1980s should have provided sufficient lessons about the nature of religious conflict. Once the militants have the capability, the motivation and the intent, this completes a threat matrix and makes them deadly.

When BH transformed from an organization that preached Islam and served widows, orphans and *almajiris* into a jihadi group, the authorities did not pay the necessary attention. The Panshekera Police Station attack was missed along with the assassination of Sheikh Ja'afar Adam, and the resignation of Alhaji Buji Foi from the Borno State Cabinet when Gov. Ali Modu Sheriff reneged on his promise to implement full Sharia code in Borno State. These were precursor events.

Undoubtedly, the Nigerian military is quite fearsome. However, it is unwise to wait until a crisis spirals out of control and then call out the military. The political elite must concentrate on risk mapping (see Chapter 15 of this book) in order to identify risks far enough ahead of time and take actions to mitigate them before they become threats. The Nigerian authorities handled this rather delicate situation with kid gloves and it metamorphosed into a full-blown insurgency.

The political situation in the country was rather unsettled. The general election of 2007 produced President Umar Musa Yar'Adua and Vice President Goodluck Jonathan. However, the Niger Delta militancy and the agitations of the Movement for the Actualization of the

Sovereign State of Biafra (MASSOB), which were based in the southern part of the country, were some of the key security threats of the day. Nigerian leaders were distracted and did not notice the major national security challenge that was incubating in the North. Nigeria had seen many deadly religious riots including the Miss World riots of November 2002, which killed over 250 people, and the Danish Cartoon riots of February 2006, which left over 100 dead. This might have fooled intelligence analysts into thinking that the Panshekera Police Station attack of 2007 was an isolated incident. Dark and ominous jihadi clouds were forming but the government security agents did not recognize them. As early as 2004, a top police executive, Sir Mike Okiro, raised an alarm about Islamic terrorists in Nigeria. His assertion was hushed by Nigerian politicians. The US authorities in the same year alerted that Nigeria had a new threat – the Yobe Taliban (or Nigerian Taliban). This was after the December 2003 to January 2004 armed confrontation by the Nigerian military, which ended in the defeat of the terrorists.

MIGRATION TO THE EAST

A key indicator of impending conflict with the authorities was the huge internal migration of Northern Muslim youths to Angwar Doki in Maiduguri and other BH communes in the North East. It was common knowledge that young Northern Muslims were quitting their jobs and "going east" to join Boko Haram, yet no alarm bells sounded to the political elite. The truth is that anytime one man acquires the resourcing and capability that Mohammed Yusuf commanded in 2008, the potential for abuse is great. Power is nothing until it is used.

DEMOCRATIC INSTITUTIONS

Nigeria held general elections in April 2007 and swore in new political leaders on May 29th. However, their legitimacy was in question as electoral fraud was widespread. Election results did not appear to be based upon votes cast, but on votes "allocated" to candidates by electoral officers. These electoral malpractices – including perverted election petition judgments – eroded the legitimacy of democratic institutions. This legitimacy deficit tended to undermine the authority of the political elite who had a propensity to be self-serving in their programs, and weak in their decision making. This weak democratic structure had a tendency

57

to alienate citizens from the leaders, making it justifiable for people to engage in acts of violence without compunction.

POLITICAL STABILITY

In 2008, the government of Nigeria was stable. The presidential election petition was not a threat to the presidency of Umar Musa Yar'Adua. Despite the superficial political stability, the political risk profile of Nigeria was high as several separatist movements were in operation including MASSOB, Niger Delta militants, the Oodua People's Congress (OPC) and the Northern Muslim jihadists who were not a well-known threat at the time. In 2008, BH was a thriving religious fundamentalist group with an agenda of violence, yet the intelligence agencies did not recognize them as the grave threat that they were. The focus of Nigerian security and intelligence agencies has always been the security of governance. In this model, the emphasis is on protection of the political class, rather than on protection of the nation. This model emphasizes "eye service" to the executive rather than effectiveness in public safety and security. The measure of performance is to build an impregnable wall of protection around the VIP while security risks, threats and trends that affect the citizens are left unattended. So long as the political elite are safe, the nation is safe. The citizens appear to be expendable. The Boko Haram conflict has shown that providing effective public security can better ensure political stability.

HUMAN RIGHTS

Upon assumption of the presidency in 2007, President Umar Musa Yar'Adua stated that the rule of law and respect for human rights were cardinal planks of his administration.[7] He kept his promise on both issues. However, many other political leaders in the system were committed to violating the human rights of others. The murder of 17 Boko Haram members in a funeral procession on June 11th, 2009 was a grave human rights violation. Yet, at the time it happened, the facts were not well grasped. The murders were handled with levity and the perpetrators went unpunished. The BH leader saw this human rights violation as an effort to systematically "exterminate" *Yan Yusufiyya*, hence he declared war on the government. Yusuf had stated in an interview that if the government of

Ali Modu Sheriff had reached out to him to sympathize over the loss of lives, he would have told his followers that there was no need for jihad as the government had apologized to the group. However, no such apology was offered which made the loss hurt even more.

JUSTICE SYSTEMS

The justice system tended to provide justice to the rich and privileged. The police, the prosecutors, the courts and corrections favored the rich and powerful and did not hold much promise for the underprivileged. This made people resort to self-help remedies and violence, since they could not rely on the justice system to protect, preserve and promote their rights. The narrative of BH – that corruption and immorality had supplanted justice in Nigeria – was evident for "all" to see and agree with. The corruption and perfidy of state actors was the strongest argument of BH leaders for a jihad. Unfortunately, a justice system that was broken and dysfunctional did not produce a logic that would enable intelligence analysts to predict the rise and resort to extremism and fundamentalism by the BH sect. A corrupt and perverted justice system is self-seeking and therefore does not have the ability to serve the larger society. Since it is disconnected from society – except perhaps to persecute and punish perceived errant members – it cannot act as a societal regulatory mechanism as it should.

CIVIL–MILITARY RELATIONS

In 2008, the military was an instrument of coercion and enforcement of state power. The police agency in Nigeria from 2007 and 2009 was headed by Sir Mike Okiro, one of the best inspectors general of police (IGPs). Prior to his tenure as an IGP, the force had been decimated by 16 years of military rule and was on the verge of rebirth under Okiro's two predecessors; namely, Mr. Musiliu AK Smith and Mr. Tafa Balogun. The Panshekera Police Station attacks of April 2007 needed military might to quell. The Niger Delta militancy had gone beyond police control and was now an entirely military matter. In 2008, the police agency was able to grapple with the OPC and MASSOB crises.

In an environment of adversarial civil military relations brought on by frequent call out of the military to quell violence, it was easy to miss the onset of an insurgency by the jihadis.

CORRUPTION

This cankerworm seemed to have eaten deep into the fabric of Nigerian society. Corruption was quite widespread and tended to reduce the respect of citizens for social institutions and public officials. The corruption argument informed the name of Boko Haram which means that since *Yan Boko* (the educated elite) were corrupt, then *Boko* is *haram* (Western education is sinful). Corruption provided the strongest *raison d'etre* for the jihadists.

INSURGENCY/TERRORISM

Boko Haram formulated its radical ideology, recruited followers, recruited fighters, and hired trainers for weapons handling, bomb making and guerrilla tactics. It also raised funds and even gained political prominence in the government of Borno Governor Ali Modu Sheriff, whom it helped to elect in 2003. Boko Haram built its own communes and avoided contact with other members of the general public. What did the Nigerian authorities think they were doing when they were not praying or studying the Holy Quran? They were preparing for armed conflict, which eventually came in July 2009.

President Umaru Musa Yar'Adua had to order General Saleh Maina to put down the rebellion by force, which the military did. However, the other mistakes are now history. Again, Nigeria's intelligence and security chiefs were oblivious to the fact that a full-blown insurgency and terrorism had erupted on their watch. While they were asleep at the controls, BH insurgency/terrorism had become fully developed. A threat that might have been prevented is still claiming lives in to this day.

CONCLUSION

The BH insurgency/terrorism did not suddenly arise on the Nigerian scene. It was in the making from 2002 to 2009, at which point it eventually blew open into a full-scale war at Dutsen Tashi Police Station in Bauchi State in July 2009. However, the Nigerian authorities had not understood the threat which the jihadis represented.

BH terrorists had a role model in the Al-Masufi sect led by Mohammed Marwa Maitatsine, which caused thousands of deaths in Kano in 1980 and continued until 1985. It also had the Yobe Taliban as another example of armed struggle against the Nigerian authorities. When BH fighters attacked Panshekera Police Station in April 2007, they fought against the military. Two years later, the real armed conflict began.

The road to insurgency was a long one for BH and many of its actions were overt. However, due to intellectual laxity and incompetence, relevant security and intelligence agencies in Nigeria were not able to analyze the problem and present it to a responsible executive who would understand the gravity of the threat and direct appropriate action. Unfortunately, only after BH commenced its reign of terror did Nigerians realize that we were facing a dangerous future where suicide bombings would be common currency.

NOTES

1. "Extremists Kill 21 Policemen in Kano" *The Guardian* (April 17th, 2007).
2. Funsho Balogun. "Methods of a Killing Machine" *The News Magazine* (August 1st, 2011): Page 14.
3. Shehu Sani. "Boko Haram. The Northern Nigeria (Hausaland)" *The Vanguard* (June 30th, 2011): Page 16.
4. Funsho Balogun. "Methods of a Killing Machine" *The News Magazine* (August 1st, 2011): Page 15.
5. Ibid.
6. Ibid.
7. George Agba. "Yar'Adua Warns Human Rights Violators" *Leadership* (November 8th, 2008).

5

Funding of BH

A question that has often been asked about the Boko Haram insurgency in Nigeria, but not given a satisfactory answer, is: who is footing the bill? The terror group was not known to have large financial resources, so policy analysts often wondered how they funded the purchase of assault weapons, improvised explosive devices (IEDs), bullets, anti-aircraft (AA) guns, general purpose machine guns (GPMGs) and other munitions of war that they deploy in tactical operations. At one point, Boko Haram fighters rode around in convoys of new Toyota Hilux pickups. The question is: how did they acquire their fleet of 4×4 vehicles? It was once reported that 700 cars were seized from the terror group.[1] How did they purchase that large fleet of motor vehicles? Aside from the cost of weapons and logistics, the terrorists also pay salaries to their fighters.

Furthermore, the insurgents pay large sums of money to suicide bombers prior to delivering their ordinance to target. Boko Haram also incurs expenses in the production and dissemination of its propaganda and recruitment videos. The insurgency is acutely aware of its propaganda messaging and the ability of creative video images to sway young minds to its cause. We will also contend that ISIS borrowed this recruitment tactic from the Boko Haram playbook as BH has been using video propagation of jihad since Abubakar Shekau took over the mantle of leadership in April 2010.

THE POLICY PROBLEM

The Boko Haram insurgency in Nigeria has utilized expensive military hardware in its conflict against the Nigerian military, and indeed the Multinational Joint Task Force (MNJTF) patrolling the Lake Chad Basin area. The policy problem is that analysts need to identify important sources of funding of this terror group so that they can be shut off. Various political actors have been accused of funding the jihadi group – but these accusations have not been substantiated with weighty evidence. For example, it has been alleged that governors of Northern states used to pay protection monies to BH so that their states would not be attacked.[2] It is common knowledge that the former governor of Borno State, Senator Ali Modu Sheriff in 2003, enlisted the help of Boko Haram to win the gubernatorial contest. Aside from the political office offered to BH members,[3] the governor was also said to have paid monthly subventions to the group. These payments stopped when the relationship between BH and the Borno State government soured.

The goal of this chapter is to present evidence of sources of funding of the ongoing BH insurgency. BH funding has come from a variety of activities including kidnapping, slave trading, political financing (sponsorship), foreign charities, foreign terrorist groups such as the Al Qaeda network, bank robberies, cattle rustling, extortion and racketeering, taxation, drug trafficking, etc.

The evidence presented here is tenuous as the parties concerned often deny their involvement due to the nature of the criminal acts that the recipients engage in.[4] Borno Governor Ali Modu Sheriff, who forged an alliance with Boko Haram to win election to high political office in 2003, has not disclosed how much he paid to BH for their service. The funds were paid through the governor's discretionary security vote which he is not obliged to disclose and which is not audited.

Funding provides capability for the terror organization. With adequate funding, insurgents can carry out their threats as they can buy sophisticated weapons, procure top-of-the-line logistics, pay good salaries to fighters and mercenaries and engage in activities that enable them to challenge the legitimate government and threaten the peace and good governance of the state.

Without funding, insurgents can be compared with toothless bulldogs – they may bark but they cannot bite. The terrorist may have evil intentions, but without the funds to execute terror plots it is tantamount to an overrated schoolyard bully.

The Boko Haram group is the biggest threat that the Nigerian government has confronted since the country's independence in 1960. Even though Nigeria endured civil war from 1967 to 1970,[5] the BH insurgency has tested the soul of the nation in a profound manner.

Carefully analyzing the funding sources of the current conflict will enable the government to learn how insurgents fund their operations which threaten the government and the citizens.

THE STRUCTURE OF TERRORIST FINANCING

In their excellent report, the Financial Action Task Force (FATF) and the Inter-Governmental (GIABA) devised a structure of terrorist financing.[6] They theorized that terrorist financing has three structural elements – raising funds, funds movement and instrument/mechanism.

Raising Funds

Terror groups in West Africa generate income through legitimate and criminal means. Funds are raised through donations/alms giving/compulsory levies, trade proceeds, organized crime such as kidnapping for ransom, extortion, armed robberies and smuggling. The study found evidence that there was exploitation of the zakat, one of the pillars of Islam which mandates Muslims to give 2.5% of their annual income to charity. "Children, the physically challenged, the elderly and the poor are used to begging for alms. Donations received are used to support terrorist activities."[7] The problem is that it is extremely difficult to differentiate between begging that funds terrorism and begging that is for the survival of the beggar – "because of widespread poverty, unemployment and underemployment."[8]

Funds Movement

This relates to the ways, techniques or mediums used by terrorists to move their funds. These include smuggling of cash and small arms and light weapons across the nation's borders. The terrorists "exploit porous national borders and weak border surveillance"[9] to move their funds in and out of Nigeria. Another method is bank/wire transfers; charities, NGOs and politically exposed persons tend to use this means for fund movement. Terrorists were said to use proxy accounts to transfer funds to their members. The FATF/GIABA study concluded that "most often these funds are withdrawn using the automated teller machines (ATMs)."[10] The third method of funds movement is the misuse of the non-profit organization (NPO) sector. In this method, compromised NGOs and charities use the cover of humanitarian work to move funds to terrorists.

Instrument/Mechanism

The third element of the FATF/GIABIA study of terrorist financing is the instrument/mechanism. The report states that the main instrument used is cash – which reflects the cash-based nature of the West Africa sub-region's economy.

The cash instrumentality makes it extremely hard for the authorities to track BH funds through the banking system. However, this could prove to be a vulnerability for BH as utilizing a cash mechanism requires couriers or a system of moving the cash from the point of collection to the terror group and from the terrorists to the point of use (e.g. payment of salaries, purchase of munitions of war, payment to informants, purchase of logistics, etc).

The Nigerian economy runs on a cash infrastructure. In recent years, the Central Bank of Nigeria has put policy measures in place to try and change the strong orientation toward cash usage. The apex bank has instituted a cashless policy which penalizes large cash deposits or withdrawals. This policy is proving to be effective for ordinary Nigerians. However, BH does not normally make bank deposits and seldom makes withdrawals. When BH extorts money from citizens or when it receives ransom payment, it usually does so in cash. It does not accept cheques or wire transfers for these and other transactions. The cash is arranged in "Ghana must go" (jute) bags and brought along to make the ransom or extortion payments.

Ransom payments in foreign currencies have also been made in cash. Some intelligence agents who have taken part in these negotiations and ransom payments have confided in the author that it is all raw cash – no matter what the amount of money involved.

The Buhari government reportedly paid about US$13 million for the release of 21 Chibok girls in May 2016.[11] The government supposedly negotiated down an initial demand of US$80 million and paid roughly one quarter of the sum demanded as ransom. It must be emphasized that the federal government has never confirmed these ransom payments.

TYPOLOGIES OF TERRORISM FINANCING

The FATF/GIABA Report on Terrorism Financing in West Africa also enumerated four broad categories of typologies of terrorism income generation. They included:[12]

a. Terrorism financing through trade and other lucrative activities.
b. Terrorism financing through NGOs, charity organizations and levies.
c. Terrorism financing through smuggling of arms, assets and currencies by cash couriers.
d. Terrorism financing through drug trafficking.

Typology 1: Trade

Arrested BH fighters have revealed to their captors that BH raises money by buying goods and commodities and shipping them to places where they are sold for profit.[13] Intelligence operatives interviewed by the author disclose that the fish trade in Baga, Borno State, is a major income earner for the sect. They sometimes seize fish from traders for direct sale, or compel fish merchants to pay protection fees to them. In return, the traders would be allowed to carry on their business without harassment.[14]

BH also receives funding from businessmen who own telecommunication service companies in Northern Nigeria. In 2011, a businessman confessed his membership of BH and that he shared his business profits with BH. He also confessed to supplying pre-registered SIM cards to BH fighters.[15]

Typology 2: NGOs

Arrest records in 2012 have shown that voluntary and mandatory donations were collected from non-governmental organizations (NGOs) to fund Boko Haram activities.[16] The donations were received from members and sympathizers of the sect. It was also discovered by intelligence agents and investigators that BH was using *almajiris* (street vagrant children), the physically challenged and the elderly to solicit alms from the public which were then back-channeled to the insurgents. The beggars were usually positioned in strategic places.[17]

Typology 3: Smuggling

This involves the illegal importation of arms, women, cash and other assets across Nigeria's porous borders. In a recent arrest, the security forces were informed that arms smuggled into Nigeria were sold in the black market and proceeds donated to BH.[18] It was also revealed that female couriers were preferred as they are not often searched due to Muslim sensibilities. The couriers ferry arms and cash into and out of Nigeria.[19]

Typology 4: Drug Trafficking

The FATF/GIABA study did not provide any evidence of drug trafficking by BH. The study provided evidence of terrorism financing by other groups in the sub-region.

The FATF/GIABA study did not categorize the funding of BH by politicians and it failed to categorize income generation through ransom kidnap. The study cited kidnap as a tactic used by AQIM, even though BH had been engaged in ransom kidnap since Shekau had become leader of the sect.

A discussion of "Curbing the Funding of Global Terrorism: The Role of the Financial Sector" listed the following emerging platforms for terrorism financing[20] that relate to BH:

a. Human trafficking.
b. Illegal trade in commodities (cigarettes, shoes, general goods).
c. Sale of counterfeit pharmaceutical drugs and medicines.
d. Illegal trade in human body parts and organs.

Malcolm Nance identified the following methods of terrorist financing, most of which are used by BH to funds its activities:[21]

a. Cultural or ethnic support organizations
b. Legal investments
c. Protection rackets
d. Legal businesses
e. State support
f. Charitable organizations
g. Collection of tributes
h. Kidnapping for ransom
i. Smuggling

j.   Illegal banking activities
k. Fraud
l.   Drug trafficking
m. Illegal taxation
n. Government subsidy fraud (not used by BH)
o. Private donations
p. Document forgery (not used by BH)
q. Counterfeiting (not used by BH).

No two insurgent or terrorist organizations are exactly the same. The difference also manifests in how they are funded. Let us now look at financing sources that are peculiar to BH.

GOVERNMENT SUBVENTIONS

It is alleged that BH receives significant government subvention primarily from the Borno State government.[22] During Governor Ali Modu Sheriff's administration (2003–2011) BH allegedly received steady subvention from the state government. Kano State government under Governor Ibrahim Shekarau was said to have paid monthly subventions of N10 million (about US$28,000 at the exchange rate of US$1.00 = N360.00 in September 2019) to guarantee peace in the state.[23] Although this allegation is widely believed to be true, Governor Shekarau denied it during interrogation by intelligence officials. He disavowed his statement that the reason Boko Haram was attacking Kano under his successor – Governor Rabiu Musa Kwankwaso – was because Kwankwaso refused to "provide necessary support for some of the structures he established while in office."[24] These "structures" are believed to be pay offs, since there was no other visible structure that the governor could be referring to. Boko Haram had itself lent credence to the funding by politicians when it announced that it was on the payroll of some Northern governors.[25]

The BH sect identified the former Bauchi State Governor, Alhaji Isa Yuguda, as one of its major financiers. In January 2012, the insurgents claimed that in addition to the financial support, the Bauchi governor "was also an admirer of the military prowess of the group."[26] The Bauchi governor denied the assertion.

The Boko Haram jihadists were clear that the payments from state governments were aimed at keeping the group from attacking the affected states. Governor Kwankwaso (Ibrahim Shekarau's successor in

Kano State) claimed legalistically that Shekarau did not indicate in his handover notes the financial agreement he had with Boko Haram.

Clearly, subvention to BH was not a line item in the state annual budget estimates. Such payments came out of the security vote which is a discretionary fund (slush fund) controlled by the state governor and is not subject to audit. This creates a difficulty for researchers since security votes are disbursed in secret and the recipients or amounts disbursed are not made public.

It is indisputable that in 2003, Borno Governor Ali Modu Sherrif went into alliance with BH in order to gain the group's support for his election bid. After his victory, he created a religious affairs ministry and appointed Alhaji Buji Foi as the first commissioner (chief executive) for that ministry. Governor Sheriff was said to have placed BH on subvention in order to compensate them for helping him win high political office. It should be restated that at this time BH had not commenced jihad.

Virginia Comolli[27] stated that in the early days a number of local politicians would have hired some BH members as their political enforcers, basically local thugs used to intimidate political opponents.

The subventions from state governments remain opaque to investigators as the funds were mostly security votes which are not subject to audit or line-item rendition in the state budget.

It is believed that the following Northern states paid subvention to BH when it began its jihadi phase. They are Yobe, Adamawa, Gombe, Bauchi, Jigawa, Kano and Taraba. The subventions apparently bought "protection" from attacks for the paying states. Understandably, the governors would deny making such payments in order not to appear to be funding the insurgency. The reality was that if they did not pay up, then they could be viciously attacked by the insurgents.

Aside from subventions, some state governments provided government facilities for use by the terrorists. For example, Borno Governor's Lodge was used by BH kingpins. A top shot of BH was arrested by the Nigeria Police Force in the Borno State governor's lodge in Abuja.[28]

The suspect, Kabir Sokoto, was the mastermind of the Christmas Day 2011 bombing of St. Theresa's Catholic Church, Madalla, Niger State near Abuja. The vehicle-borne improvised explosive device (VBIED) attack killed over 40 people. Kabir Sokoto, who was arrested in the company of a serving military officer was later tried and convicted.

Then governor of Adamawa State, Vice Admiral (Rtd.) Murtala Nyako accused the federal government of sponsoring the BH sect[29] to destabilize the North East region. This claim was never substantiated.

The governor was later impeached and removed from office by the State House of Assembly.[30]

Elizabeth Donnelly of the Africa Program with the London-based Chatham House wrote: "Politicians and traditional leaders in Nigeria often accuse their opponents of supporting Boko Haram financially but there is no hard evidence from any side that this is true."[31]

PROFIT KIDNAP

The Boko Haram jihadi group receives a very significant portion of its income from ransom kidnap. The terrorists kidnap Nigerians and foreigners and demand ransom payments for their release. The major kidnap incidents included the seizure of 276 school girls from the Government Girls' Secondary School, Chibok, Borno State, as they were preparing for their examination on April 14th, 2014; the abduction of 110 girls from the Government Girls Technical and Science College, Dapchi, Yobe State, on February 18th, 2018; the kidnap of three members of an oil exploration team in Borno State in 2017; the June 21st, 2017 kidnap of ten policewomen after an attack on a military/police convoy along the Damboa–Maiduguri highway, near Chibok.

Chibok Girls

Boko Haram gained worldwide notoriety with the kidnap of 276 school girls from Chibok in the southern part of Borno State on April 14th, 2014. In a mass kidnap event which has characterized the group's operations, they seized female students from their dormitories as they studied for their school certificate examinations. The school compound was minimally guarded and the terrorists pretended to be Nigerian soldiers sent to evacuate the girls for their own safety. The girls were placed in waiting lorries and driven away into the nearby Sambisa forest – the hideout of the insurgents. About 50 girls managed to escape their captors and gave the narration of the mass abduction. The Nigerian government in May 2016 paid an unconfirmed ransom of US$13 million which resulted in the release of 21 of the girls. The federal government later negotiated with the Islamists and secured the release of 82 more school girls, presumably after payment of a ransom. The second mass release also involved the release of some insurgent commanders in government custody.

71

Prior to the presidency of Muhammadu Buhari, his predecessor had held several botched negotiations with BH for the release of the Chibok girls. The terrorists negotiated ransom and ceasefire deals with President Goodluck Jonathan, but none of the girls were released (see Chapter 13).

Dapchi Girls

On February 19th, 2018, Boko Haram fighters executed another mass kidnap event when they seized 110 school girls from the Government Girls Science and Technical College, Dapchi, a small town located 100 km north of Damaturu, the Yobe State capital.

As was the case in the Chibok abductions, several lorries were brought to the girls' school by people dressed in military uniforms who pledged to take them to safety. The girls were seized and taken to an unknown destination.

Granting audience to the visiting US Secretary of State, Mr. Rex Tillerson, on March 12th, 2018, President Muhammadu Buhari stated that Nigeria's government would prefer to negotiate the release of the remaining 106 Chibok school girls and 110 Dapchi school girls. He said that in order to ensure safe release of the girls, the government was taking the military option off the table.[32] President Buhari disclosed that his government was working in collaboration with international organizations and negotiators to secure the release of the girls. The Nigerian president said: "We are trying to be careful. It is better to get our daughters back alive."[33]

As was the case in the release of the first and second tranches of the Chibok girls, a ransom was paid and BH commanders were released from captivity. As past is prologue to the future, the International Committee of the Red Cross (ICRC) and the Swiss government, along with the intelligence service and hostage negotiators, struck a deal with the insurgents/terrorists. Abducted girls numbering 104 were released by Boko Haram in March 2018. It is suspected that that this was another multi-million dollar pay day for the remorseless terrorists. However, this could not be confirmed from any of the groups involved.

Prior to the dramatic release of the Dapchi girls by their captors, this author advised the government on a live television interview program on March 13th, 2018 to exhaust all available investigative leads prior to negotiating with terrorists.[34] The author urged the security agencies to engage in a focused hot pursuit of the missing girls. Investigative strategies suggested included the establishment of a dedicated tips hotline, announcement of a substantial reward for information leading to the rescue of the girls, and forensic debriefing of the girls who were fortunate enough to escape captivity.[35]

It is obvious that the motive of the BH insurgents in the Dapchi mass kidnap event was to earn ransom income. This is another strategy in their playbook. Aside from poking a finger in the eyes of the Nigerian government, the huge income potential of mass kidnap of vulnerable populations like innocent school girls makes it rather irresistible. The implication of this is that we should expect to experience more mass abductions of this nature unless meaningful actions are taken to ensure better school security in North East Nigeria.

Kidnap of Foreigners

In April 2013, the Islamist sect received US\$3.15 million in ransom payment brokered by French and Cameroonian negotiators for the release of a French family of seven people kidnapped in Northern Cameroon.[36] In addition to getting the ransom payment, BH secured the release of some of its members who were in custody in Cameroon.

French citizen, Tungay Mouin Fournier, his wife, brother and four young children were seized on February 19th, 2013 while on holiday near the Waza National Park in Cameroon – 10 km from the Nigerian border. They were believed to have been held in Sambisa forest during captivity. Mr. Fournier was employed by the French utility firm CDF Suez.

Boko Haram leader Abubakar Shekau, who personally handled the negotiations, insisted on double the ransom received. However, he later asked for some detained members of the sect to be thrown in as part of the deal.[37]

On May 3rd, 2013, BH terrorists kidnapped elder statesman and former Minister of Petroleum, Alhaji Shettima Ali Monguno from the Mafoni Mosque in Maiduguri after *Jumaat* prayers.[38] Initial contact with the family of the victim focused on demands for release of arrested Boko Haram members. It was, however, believed that a multi-million naira ransom was paid for his release. Four years later, in May 2017, troops of 31 Artillery Brigade Nigerian Army took down a terrorist cell in Mokwa, Niger State, arresting Mustapha Mohammed (aka Adam Bitri) and other BH fighters.[39] Preliminary investigations revealed that Mustapha was among the band of BH terrorists who snatched the 92-year-old elder statesman off the Maiduguri street, hustled him into a waiting car and fired a lot of shots to scare off bystanders before taking him into captivity.

Another kidnap incident was the seizure of the General Manager of the Borno State Water Board, Alhaji Baba Gujbawa. He was seized in April 2013.[40] He was later set free by BH after a ransom was paid.

Virginia Comolli argues that Al Qaeda in the Islamic Magreb (AQIM) trained Boko Haram in kidnapping for ransom. She wrote that there have been several reports indicating that disputes within Boko Haram had taken place over how ransom money would be split. We're talking about fairly large sums of money that would have allowed the funding of several operations.[41]

Jacob Zenn of West Point's Combating Terrorism Center contends that kidnapping has been a lucrative source of cash for Boko Haram. He said that BH is widely suspected of carrying out dozens of other abductions for ransom in northern Nigeria. He adds: "Virtually all of the kidnap victims were mid level officials, or their relatives, who were not wealthy enough to have security details, but could afford modest ransoms of about US$10,000.00."[42]

According to then US Assistant Secretary of State for African Affairs, "Our suspicions are that they are surviving on very lucrative criminal activities that involve kidnappings."[43]

An investigation conducted by the *Daily Trust* newspaper[44] in 2014 found that Boko Haram conducted targeted abductions in Maiduguri, Bama, Konduga, Damboa, Gwoza, Marte and Malam Fatori towns and cities. Male and female abductees from wealthy families regained freedom after their families paid ransoms. The reporters wrote: "The wife of a prominent politician and a businessman from Damboa was abducted and released the next day. The father of a serving commissioner in Borno State was also kidnapped and released."[45]

A 41-year-old female gold trader had a hard time in captivity as she was brutally and repeatedly raped for 17 days. Her abductors stole her stock of gold when they invaded her home to seize her in the Muna General Area of Maiduguri in 2013. She was held in Bulabulin Ngarannam. She was raped by 18-year-old jihadists. Her words:

> They learnt that I trade in gold. As such, while in their enclave, the boys would come over every morning look at me with disdain and said that I accumulated a lot of money but was not willing to give sadaqa (alms). They would then forcefully have sex with me.[46]

In April 2013, the Nigerian military battling Boko Haram code-named Joint Task Force – Operation Restore Order (JTF-ORO) informed members of the public that BH had resorted to kidnapping and ransom demand to finance their terror operations.[47] Military spokesman Col. Sagir Musa said that the terrorists resolved to concentrate more on kidnapping than armed robbery. The military's intelligence information was that BH preferred kidnapping because it was "more lucrative, less dangerous and requires short time to plan and execute."[48]

The military warned the public that "a special kidnapping squad had been earmarked and tasked by Boko Haram to kidnap persons who could have wealthy relatives, politicians, businessmen, businesswomen, traditional rulers, senior civil servants and foreigners."[49] The military advised citizens to be vigilant about the trend, be wary and security conscious.

In a ransom kidnap incident in June 2014, Boko Haram seized 30 nomads near Chibok in southern Borno State and demanded cattle for the release of the female abductees.[50]

ARMED ROBBERIES

Boko Haram has committed a large number of bank robberies, highway robberies and home invasions as a way of financing its terror operations. In 2011, armed Boko Haram fighters targeted Ibo traders in Maiduguri dispossessing them of cash and goods at gunpoint. A building materials merchant named MC Tom suffered a fatal heart attack in April 2011, when he was twice robbed of large sums of money by BH.[51]

In 2011, furniture showrooms owned by Ibo traders in Gwange Area of Maiduguri were violently robbed by Boko Haram. Some of the store robberies had tragic consequences as three Ibo traders were killed in one Gwange robbery incident.[52]

At Mairi, Sabon Layin and Umarari areas of Maiduguri, pharmacies owned by Ibo indigenes were violently robbed by the terrorists. At Mairi and Umarari, pharmacy owners were shot dead in cold blood.[53]

In July 2011, Boko Haram switched from robbing merchants to robbing banks. They robbed a Finbank branch on Bama Road, Maiduguri. A six-man BH tactical team assaulted the bank on motorbikes. They detonated 12 IEDs during the heist and killed a security guard who attempted to close the bank gate. They snatched three cash-loaded bags and exited the bank.[54] In a throwback to the Robin Hood mentality of robbing the rich to give to the poor, the terrorists threw up crisp currency notes as they left, shooting into the air. Members of the public who took cover from the shooting and bombing came out to hustle for some of the "free" cash.

75

In another armed takeover bank robbery[55] which took place on the same day, the terrorists laid siege to Gwange Police Station which is located beside a bank. Five police personnel lost their lives in the encounter. They then proceeded to rob the bank unchallenged.

Commenting on the change of targets from merchants to banks, then spokesman of the sect, Abu Ziad "admitted that the sect had carried out two bank robberies because banks support causes that contravene Islamic injunctions."[56]

David Doukhan of the International Institute of Counter Terrorism stated that although bank robbery does not sound ethical for a fundamentalist religious sect: "the robbery is justified by Koranic interpretation that bank robbery is permitted, since the money from the bank is considered spoils of war."[57] Doukhan estimates BH's bank robbery spoils at about US$6 million.[58]

TAXATION

Another source of financing for Boko Haram from 2012 to 2015 was taxation of citizens in large parts of Borno State, Yobe State and Adamawa State. These were areas under Boko Haram occupation at the time. The federal, state and local governments were supplanted by the terrorists who took full control and became the *de facto* governments. The terrorists renamed the territories they held as part of the Caliphate and renamed cities such as Mubi to Modinatu Islam. The citizens under Boko Haram rule were tortured, forced into marriages, publicly flogged and some executed. Above all, they paid whatever tax was apportioned by the terrorists.

In a Voice of America News interview in May 2013, Clement Nwankwo of the Policy and Legal Advocacy Center in Abuja confirmed the taxation of citizens by Boko Haram: "Some even say they (Boko Haram) are in control of various local governments in the northeast and are collecting taxes and running the show in those places."[59]

In a paper[60] this author presented at the ASIS International Annual Seminar and Exhibits in 2015, he concluded (after studying the map of the North East region of Nigeria when about 75% of the entire region was under the control of Boko Haram) that there was a paradigmatic shift among terrorist organizations. He said they now seek to govern territories. Controlling the lives of citizens including taxation was presented as a goal of the new paradigm of terrorism. The ISIS takeover of much of Iraq and parts of Syria at that time (2014) was referenced.

The real estate controlled by BH included areas that are notorious for trafficking in petrol and diesel, textiles, fish, cigarettes, counterfeit drugs and human beings. According to Sasha Jesperson, a London-based researcher with the Royal United Services Institute for Defence and Security Studies, "They are not conducting the trafficking themselves, but it's likely that they are taxing the trade when it passes through the areas they have control over."[61]

HUMAN TRAFFICKING AND SLAVERY

The BH sect is also suspected of being involved in human trafficking. Shekau had boasted of selling women into slavery. It is speculated that some of the Chibok girls were sold outside Nigeria to become sex slaves. Sasha Jasperson concurred: "If they have women and girls who have been kidnapped they will (potentially) sell them to human traffickers."[62]

DRUG TRAFFICKING

The United Nations Office on Drugs and Crime (UNODC) has determined that Boko Haram benefits from the drug trafficking trade that pervades the Sahel region. Speaking at an International Conference in Doha, Qatar, in April 2015, the UNODC Executive Director, Yuri Fedotov, said that Boko Haram was levying taxes on the illicit trafficking of drugs and natural resources.

INTERNET SCAMS

The ECOWAS regional anti-money laundering agency, the Inter-Governmental Action Group Against Money Laundering in West Africa (GIABA) has said that internet scams have been another source of funding for BH.[63] The agency documented how BH contacts Westerners proposing romantic relationships. Victims are later blackmailed if nude photos have successfully been obtained from them.

CONCLUSION

At the height of its power, BH rode around in long convoys of Hilux vehicles like the ISIS convoys in Syria and Iraq. Clearly those days are over now for the Islamist insurgency. However, the terrorists continue to attack targets in Nigeria, Cameroon, Chad and Niger. This chapter has examined the ways and means by which BH acquired its wealth. The methods identified included financing by politicians, subventions by some Northern state governments, kidnapping for ransom, armed robberies, charities, taxation, trafficking and internet scams.

The terror group relied mainly on cash to do business. It said it did not believe in the banking system, so it largely avoided bank transfers or the regular financial system. The cash trade is a vulnerability due to the fact that cash couriers must transport the asset from origin to destination.

Unfortunately, the vulnerabilities of Nigeria to terrorism financing are high. These include porous borders, poor governance, corruption among public officials and lucrative criminal enterprises which could be exploited due to weak criminal justice institutions.

NOTES

1. "Boko Haram: What Does Nyako Really Know?" *The Punch* (March 27th, 2017).
2. "SSS Quizzes Shekarau Over Alleged Boko Haram Funding" *The Punch* (February 1st, 2012): Page 14.
3. The Governor of Borno State, Senator Ali Modu Sheriff appointed top member of the Boko Haram group, Alhaji Buji Foi, as the Commissioner for Religious Affairs.
4. "Secret Intelligence Report Links Ex-Governor Sheriff, Chad President to Boko Haram Sponsorship" *Premium Times* (September 12th, 2014).
5. Over one million persons died of severe malnutrition during the Nigerian civil war which recorded about 100,000 military casualties.
6. Financial Action Task Force (FATF) and Inter-Governmental Action Group Against Money Laundering (GIABA). **FATF Report on Terrorist Financing in West Africa**. FATF/GIABA (2013).
7. Ibid: Page 32.
8. Ibid.
9. Ibid.
10. Ibid: Page 33.
11. Gbenga Bada. "Boko Haram: FG Reportedly Paid \$13m for Release of Chibok Girls" *Pulse-Ng* (November 12th, 2016).
12. FATF/GIABA (2013): Page 18.
13. Ibid: Page 19.
14. Author's interview notes with an Assistant Director of the Department of State Services. Interview conducted in September 2013 in Lagos.

15. Ibid.
16. Ibid: Page 21.
17. Ibid.
18. Ibid: Page 24.
19. Ibid.
20. Dr. David Wodi Tukura. "Curbing the Funding of Global Terrorism: The Role of the Financial Sector" Discussion Paper Presented at International Seminars on Managing Asymmetric Security Challenges in the 21st Century. Organized by the Nigerian Army Resources Center. Abuja, Nigeria.
21. Malcolm W. Nance. **Terrorist Recognition Handbook: A Practitioner's Manual for Predicting and Identifying Terrorist Activities (2nd Edition)**. Boca Raton, Florida: CRC Press (2008).
22. Alh. Sanda Umar Kondugha reportedly made confessional statements to the Department of State Services in Abuja that Senator Ali Ndume, former Borno State governor Senator Ali Modu Sheriff and Nigeria's former ambassador, Ambassador Saidu Pinda were financial backers of Boko Haram.
23. "SSS Quiz Ex-Gov Shekarau" *Vanguard* (January 21st, 2012).
24. Ibid.
25. Emmanuel Aziken, Abdulsalam Muhammad, Victoria Ojeme and Ndahi Marama. "We're on Northern Govs' Payroll – Boko Haram" *Vanguard* (January 24th, 2012).
26. Ibid.
27. Virginia Comolli. **Boko Haram: Nigeria's Islamist Insurgency**. London: Hurst & Co. Publishers (2015).
28. "Boko Haramist Arrested in Governor's Lodge" *The Village Square* (January 16th, 2012).
29. Sani Tukur. "Governor Nyako Accuses Jonathan Administration of Genocide Against Northern Nigeria" *Premium Times* (April 19th, 2014).
30. "Governor Murtala Nyako of Adamawa State Impeached" *Sahara Reporters* (July 13th, 2014).
31. Heather Murdock. "Analysts: Nigeria's Boko Haram Funding Vast, Varied" *The New York Times* (March 20th, 2014).
32. Terhemba Daku. "Nigeria Will Rather Negotiate Abducted Girls Release than Military Option" *The Guardian* (March 13th, 2018): Page 3.
33. Ibid.
34. Television interview. Your World Today Program. TOPIC: FG Negotiation with Abductors of Chibok and Dapchi Girls *Channels Television* (March 13th, 2018).
35. "Ekhomu Calls for Special Task Force to Rescue Dapchi Girls" *Daily Sun* (February 27th, 2018): Page 10.
36. "Boko Haram Gets $3.15 Million to Free French Hostages" *The Nation* (April 27th, 2013): Page 58.
37. Ibid.

38. "Boko Haram Kidnaps Borno Elder Statesman Shettima Ali Monguno" *Sahara Reporters* (May 3rd, 2013).
39. Michael Olugbode. "JTF: Boko Haram Resorts to Kidnapping to Raise Funds" *This Day* (April 29th, 2013): Page 11.
40. "Troops Arrest Boko Haram Terrorists Who Kidnapped Former Petroleum Minister Shettima Ali Monguno in 2013" *Daily Correspondents* (May 26th, 2017).
41. Comolli (2015): Page 67.
42. Peter Weber. "Who's Financing Boko Haram?" *The Week Magazine Online*. New York, NY (May 12th, 2014).
43. Phil Stewart and Lesley Wroughton. "How Boko Haram Is Beating US Efforts to Choke Its Financing" *Reuters*. Washington, DC (July 1st, 2014).
44. Hamza Idris and Ibrahim Sawab. "Life in Boko Haram Camps, by Female Ex-Captives" *Daily Trust* (May 26th, 2014): Page 3.
45. Ibid.
46. Ibid.
47. Olugbode (2013): Page 13.
48. Ibid.
49. Ibid.
50. Tunde Sulaiman. "Boko Haram Demands Cattle for 30 New Abductees" *New Telegraph* (June 11th, 2014): Page 1.
51. Funsho Balogun. "Inside Boko Haram: Methods and Tactics of a Killing Machine" *The News Magazine* (August 1st, 2011): Page 16.
52. Ibid.
53. Ibid.
54. Ibid.
55. Ibid.
56. Ibid.
57. Peter Weber (2014).
58. Ibid.
59. Ibid.
60. Dr. Ona Ekhomu. **Approaches to Countering Terrorist Threats in Africa**. Paper Presented at the ASIS Seminar and Exhibits. Anaheim, CA (September 2015).
61. Michel Arseneault. "Nigerian Intelligence Chief Calls for Untangling of Boko Haram Funding" *Africa RFI*. Paris, France (May 21st, 2015).
62. Ibid.
63. FATF/GIABA (2013).

Part Two

Choice of Targets

6

Targeting Military and Corrections

INTRODUCTION

The Boko Haram insurgency in Nigeria has been marked by the large number of souls lost to the intentional acts of violence. The killing field for the insurgents is quite large. It includes all Christians in Nigeria (about 100 million people), all Shiite-Muslims (about 5 million people), all Sunni Muslims who are not of the same narrowly focused Wahabi-Salafi persuasion (about 95 million). At the height of their power in 2009, the group's membership was estimated at 50,000 persons. Although Sheikh Mohammed Yusuf's charisma attracted casual bystanders and politicians seeking miracles from Allah, the community of committed adherents remained small – perhaps due to the extremist views espoused.

Following the events of July 2009 which resulted in the extra-judicial killing of the top leadership of the sect, the new leader who resumed the campaign of violence was less discriminating and seeking vengeance. He set his sights on the group's number one enemy – the Nigeria Police Force. The sect also targeted the Nigerian military[1] as this was the force that subdued them at Angwar Doki – Millionaires Quarters, Maiduguri – and pulled down their spiritual headquarters, the Ibn Tiamiyya Masjid.

THE DEADLIEST TERROR GROUP IN THE WORLD

In November 2015, the Global Terrorism Index named Boko Haram as the world's deadliest terrorist organization for the year 2014. Boko Haram overtook ISIS as the world's deadliest terror group. Boko Haram accounted for 6,644 deaths in 2014, which was an increase of 317% from 2013. In contrast, ISIS was responsible for 6,073 deaths in 2014.[2]

Up until September 2019, BH was still producing deaths at a steady rate. Although the group is no longer holding Nigerian territory, its new strategy is to launch lone wolf, wolf pack and frontal attacks that produce a constant flow of fatalities in the North East.

The terror group evolved from carrying out targeted murders using AK-47 rifles hidden under the *jalabiya* gown to bombings – vehicle-borne IEDs (VBIEDs), person-borne IEDs (PBIEDs) (i.e. suicide vests), home-borne IEDs (HBIEDs) or the booby-trapping of homes with bombs. The sect utilized roadside bombs as well as unattended packages.

This chapter focuses on the targeting of military and corrections institutions/personnel by the Boko Haram insurgents. The security agencies have long been declared the enemies of Boko Haram. Following the customs roundabout incident of June 11th, 2009, BH founder and spiritual leader Yusuf pinpointed the police and Borno State government as the group's key enemies.

TARGETING PRISONS

Boko Haram appeared to be quite brilliant in its choice of targets. Its first major attack in 2010 targeted Bauchi Prison on September 7th where it set free 759 inmates, including 150 BH fighters. The BH detainees freed from Bauchi Prison were awaiting trial for the July 26th, 2009 attack on Dutsen Tashi Police Station, Bauchi. The prison break, which involved the use of AK-47 gunfire, resulted in the deaths of one soldier, one policeman, two prison wardens and one civilian. Six people were also injured in the attack.

The choice of Bauchi Prison[3] appeared to be strategic. In their first attack after their routing in July 2009, the terrorists successfully freed 150 members in one fell swoop. The detainees were now at liberty to rejoin the jihad (holy war) against the Nigerian state and people.

The Comptroller General of the Nigerian Prisons Service, Mr. Olusola Adigun Ogundipe, described the attack as unfortunate. The prisons boss said it was a "surprise package by the attackers who overpowered the few armed squad of the Prisons Service and forcefully gained entrance into the main prison yard."[4]

Fifty perpetrators took part in the violent prison break. The attackers smashed the locks on the prison cell doors while conducting a cell–by-cell search and set fire to part of the prison.[5] They struck during *ishai* (evening) prayers in the holy month of Ramadan. During the initial breach, they laid down a heavy line of fire. A joint security patrol that responded to the sound of heavy gunfire was overpowered by the attackers.

The gun battle sent nearby residents fleeing for cover. The Emir of Bauchi Alh. Rilwan Suleiman Adamu was said to have gone into hiding.[6] Speaking on the violent prison break, the Emir said "By the grace of Allah this is the last we will see of the Boko Haram. We will work with the government as well as other security agencies to ensure that this does not happen again."[7] What the revered traditional ruler did not know at the time was that BH insurgents were just commencing the implementation of a strategy to break-out their fighters from prison. Bauchi was only the second in a long line of prison breaks which began during the July 2009 disturbance, as shown in Table 6.1.

Table 6.1 Prison Breaks by BH 2009–2014

S/N	Facility Name	Date of Attack	No. of Prisoners Freed
1.	Maiduguri	July 27, 2009	482
2.	Bauchi	Sept 7, 2010	759
3.	Yola	April 22, 2011	14
4.	Koton-Karfe, Kogi State	Feb 2012	119
5.	Damaturu, Yobe	June 2012	41
6.	Malha, Adamawa	Dec 2012	35
7.	Maiduguri Farm Center	Jan 2013	79
8.	Gwoza, Borno	March 2013	118
9.	Bama, Borno	May 2013	105
10.	Mubi, Adamawa	Oct 2014	366

Source: Compiled by the author.

Outlining government strategies to forestall future prison breaks, the Comptroller General of the Prisons Service, Mr. Ogundipe said:

> There are a few vulnerable prisons in the country including Maiduguri, Gombe and Azare. We have increased the presence of armed security operatives there in order to ensure that there is no repeat of what happened here at those places.[8]

The Bauchi State Commissioner of Police, Mr. Danlami Yar'Adua, confirmed that 36 inmates voluntarily surrendered to the prison authorities in order to serve out their sentences.[9]

Analysis of the Bauchi Prison Break

This major security breach deserves a post-mortem as it would presage the pattern of attacks that we observed for the next five years of the BH insurgency. The risk of an attack on the prison was quite high. In a video released in April 2010, the new leader of the Islamist sect vowed retaliation for the 700 Boko Haram members killed in Maiduguri.[10] Using a risk management approach, the authorities should have predicted which targets might be attacked by BH and then strengthened them. Let us look at elements of the attack using a threat matrix. The matrix comprises three factors: intentions, motivations and capabilities.

Intentions

In April 2010, Shekau announced on a video that he intended to retaliate against the deaths of BH members.[11] This was a declaration that violent action was imminent. There was apprehension close to the first anniversary of the routing of BH that they might strike then, but nothing happened. However, the intention to commit acts of violence had clearly been declared.

Motivations

Bauchi Prison appeared to be a logical target as a large number of jihadists was held there. These were detainees from the Dutsen Tashi attacks of July 26th, 2009. Breaking them out would give Shekau a motivated army, providing a clear motivation for carrying out the attack. A second motivation

86

was vengeance. In July 2009, the sect was vanquished by the military in Maiduguri. Many sect members were extra-judicially murdered at the Borno State Police Headquarters (SHQ) in Maiduguri. Vengeance was an obvious and declared motive.

Deepening the loyalty of sect members was another motive. By forcefully setting free incarcerated members, Shekau was showing his fighters that he cared.

There was also the just cause motivation. The narrative was that since Salafi jihad was a just cause, Allah allowed the detained members to regain their freedom.

Capabilities

The September 7th, 2010, prison break involved 50 attackers, armed with automatic weapons and incendiary devices. The deployment of the aggressors was professional. While a group of attackers breached the facility and shot dead two prison wardens, another group of attackers remained outside the facility and engaged the passing joint military/police patrol in a shoot-out resulting in the deaths of the soldier and another policeman.

The weaponry used in the assault was remarkable. GPMGs and AK-47 rifles were used which was an indication that automatic weapons were being proliferated into the hands of the Islamists.

The capabilities displayed in the Bauchi prison break included the following:

a. **Weaponry:** Machine guns (GPMGs), AK-47 rifles[12] and incendiary bombs with which they set fire to the prison.
b. **Logistics:** The attackers came in a convoy of sundry vehicles. These became useful in evacuating their brothers who they had come to rescue from detention.
c. **Manpower:** Fifty attackers. The two or three wardens and lone armed policeman at the prison were no match for this large number of attackers – all armed.
d. **Training:** Musketry training was evident. The panic which ensued during the assault on the prison showed that the weapons were used with great dexterity. This further confirms intelligence reports that after the routing of BH in Maiduguri in July 2009, they relocated to the Niger Republic and other places such as Algeria and Somalia for better training in conducting violent campaigns.

87

e. **Leadership:** Tactical deployment that fended off any attempt by military patrol to disrupt the prison break evidenced good field leadership of the insurgents.

f. **Intelligence:** Knowledge of the capability of the guardians.

The threat matrix only gives us a snapshot of the aggression. However, there were loopholes and weaknesses (existing conditions) which the threats (BH) exploited to cause the loss event. What were these vulnerabilities?

Vulnerabilities

The Bauchi prison break was made possible by vulnerabilities that existed there. These vulnerabilities included:

a. Poor security awareness on the part of the correctional facility management

b. Poor prison security program

c. Over-crowding in the facility

d. Lack of accountability of prison officials.

a) Security Awareness

The Bauchi prison managers maintained a low-security posture. The facility was poorly defended as evidenced by a lone armed policeman on site – in a facility holding 150 terrorists. The wardens did not display security awareness. They lowered their guard because the holy month of Ramadan was coming to an end in a few hours, as verbalized by both the Emir of Bauchi and the Governor of Bauchi State. The attackers were said to have infiltrated the prison by pretending to join in the *ishai* prayers.

b) Prison Security Program

The Comptroller General of the Nigerian Prisons Service acknowledged that there were vulnerabilities in the prison. The Bauchi prison did not have the full complement of layered security appropriate for a high-security prison facility. Aside from fencing and locks on the cells, the facility was porous. Let us consider the four Ds of a security program:

Deterrence: The perimeter fencing might have provided some deterrence to law-abiding citizens. However, a determined attacker (like an Islamist) was not easily deterred.

Detection: The second line of protection is detection. Aside from the human beings (wardens and police personnel), there was no electronic detection capability at the facility – no magnetometer detectors, no CCTV equipment, no intrusion alarm systems, no fire alarm systems.

Delay: The third layer of protection is delay. The security architecture and engineering of the facility appeared to be so flawed that the structural barriers did not provide adequate elongation of time to enable response to the security breach. It was easy for the terrorists to smash the locks in the cells and set the inmates free.

Denial: The last layer of protection is deny/defend. The guardians were no match for the force arrayed against them (an army of 50 men) and the weaponry of the aggressors. The facility simply did not have a strong security program.

c) Over-crowding

The prison was over-crowded, holding about 50% more inmates than its capacity. CG Ogundipe stated that the facility was designed for 500 inmates. However, on the day of the security breach it held 759 inmates.[13] The over-crowding of inmates and non-segregation of BH inmates from the general population created a toxic environment. In fact, it might have created further radicalization within the prison. However, there is no evidence available to substantiate this. Furthermore, most of the inmates freed never came back to prison.

d) Poor Accountability

An important weakness in the Nigerian correction system which the Bauchi incident of 2010 revealed was poor accountability on the part of government executives. Four government officials commented on the incident; namely, the Bauchi State Commissioner of Police, the Comptroller General of the Nigerian Prisons Service, the Governor of Bauchi State and the Minister of Interior. None of the officers – three federal and one state – took responsibility for the unfortunate incident or gave assurances of how such a breach would be prevented in future.

The police: The Commissioner of Police said his agency would investigate the prison break. He did not take responsibility for the serious security breach. A security incident that resulted in the death of several persons, freedom of 759 prison inmates (including 150 battle-hardened jihadi fighters) and threatened the Emir of Bauchi receives a threat rating of critical. Yet the chief law enforcement officer of Bauchi State did not acknowledge the inability of his agency to prevent or respond effectively to the security breach.

The Prisons Service: The Comptroller General of the Nigerian Prisons Service admitted that his service was *surprised* by the capability of the terrorists. He admitted that the security safeguards were inadequate for the facility protection. However, he did not take ownership of the security failure. He defended the few armed wardens and declared the incident as "unfortunate." He did not fire the Comptroller of Prisons in Bauchi State nor did he opt to resign for poor leadership of the corrections institution. This is a feature of political leadership in Nigeria – no executive takes responsibility for a failing and resigns. The CG did, however, recognize that vulnerabilities existed in other correctional facilities in the North East. Ironically, these facilities were all later successfully attacked by Boko Haram.

The state governor: Governor Isa Yuguda of Bauchi State lamented[14] that BH exploited the element of surprise by striking during the month of Ramadan when all true Muslims were expected to be fasting and not engaging in anything that will lead to the shedding of blood.[15] He warned rather unconvincingly: "Let me warn all Boko Haram members to steer clear of Bauchi and relocate outside the country or be prepared to face their waterloo."[16] The governor did not need to take responsibility for the prison break, and he did not. However, his words of warning sounded hollow and uninspiring.

Minister of Interior: Captain Emmanuel Iheanacho, whose ministry oversees the Prisons Service, stated that the federal government was committed to the security of Nigerians – words that were not matched with action when it came to the Bauchi prison break. There was no explanation of the security breach that had occurred, nor was any disciplinary action taken. In fact, given the gravity of what had occurred the minister should have resigned his appointment, yet he did not.

This entire lack of accountability has proven to be a vulnerability as most public officials do not see the need to put in their best in order to avert security breaches. The pattern that has emerged since the Boko Haram insurgency is to blame them (Boko Haram) for being evil people. However, such an observation is neither enlightening nor constructive. The question is: how are we going to protect our assets against these malevolent actors?

Other Prison Attacks by Boko Haram

The Bauchi prison break of September 2010 was one of several which the insurgents would carry out. Yola Prison (Adamawa State) was hit in April 2011 and 14 inmates were set free. A total of 119 inmates were broken out of prison in Koton Karfe Federal Prison in Kogi State in February 2012. Kumshe Prison in Borno State was hit in 2012 with 20 inmates set free. Damaturu Prison was hit in June 2012 with 41 inmates released. In December 2012, 35 inmates were broken out of Malha Prison in Adamawa State. In all the prison breaks, the stated reason by BH was to release their members from captivity.

MILITARY BASE ATTACKS

The Nigerian military can rightly be considered the principal enemy of BH. The destruction of Ibn Tiamiyyu Masjid in 2009 was carried out by the military. It was also the military that defeated BH in the Battle of Maiduguri in July 2009. Furthermore, the military also captured Sheikh Mohammed Yusuf, but mysteriously handed him over to the police authorities which resulted in his extra-judicial murder.

When BH resumed its campaign of terror in 2010, the key indicators of the incipient insurgency were missed. The government thought that the killings in Maiduguri were random acts of criminal violence. Neither *modus operandi*, ballistic match nor good old detective work enabled the police detectives to discover that the attacks were indicative of a grave security threat.

It took the bombing of the Police Force Headquarters building on June 16th, 2011 and the UN headquarters on August 26th, 2011 before the government realized that it was being faced by a determined enemy. Before the bombing of the UN headquarters in Abuja, many criminal explosions had been perpetrated by BH, yet the federal government appeared not to comprehend the threat. The government responded with police action and dialogue. Unfortunately, BH was actually becoming stronger, more audacious and increasing its capability.

The Mogadishu Barracks Bombing

The intentional targeting of military barracks, bases, posts, patrols and checkpoints by Boko Haram began on December 31st, 2010 when the mammy market at AHQ Garrison Asokoro Abuja was hit by two pre-planted IEDs, killing 30 people.[17]

A chemical analysis of the bomb particles revealed the presence of the following constituents: Nitrate ions (NO), Sodium ions (Na), Ammonium ions (NH4) and Potassium ions (K). The chemical components proved that this was an ammonium nitrate fuel oil (ANFO) bomb.[18]

Bomb detectives concluded that the two IEDs were fabricated from locally sourced materials without any ordnance incorporated. The detectives also opined that there were two IEDs – secondary and primary devices. The secondary device contained more explosive materials than the primary.[19]

The secondary device detonated 30 minutes after bomb detectives exited the crime scene. Apparently, it was intended as a double-tap bomb where the secondary device was designed to kill emergency responders. However, the bomb detectives had their IED jammers with them at the scene. Either the jammers prevented the secondary detonation or there was a device malfunction.

The Bombing of the 1 Division Headquarters

An audacious VBIED attack occurred on February 7th, 2012 at the head-quarters of the 1 Mechanized Division of the Nigerian Army, Kawo, Kaduna. The aggressor, dressed in military fatigues, attempted to bluff his way into the military facility. His intention was to ram the front of the building as the top army brass held their weekly meeting. However, an alert sentry smelt a rat and tried to stop the perpetrator. The suicide terrorist refused to stop and was fired upon by the sentry. His bomb payload detonated causing blast damage to the military facility. The suicide bomber was the only fatality.[20]

The attack was a close shave with death for the General Officer Commanding (GOC) 1 Division, Major General Garba Wahab, who was chairing the divisional meeting when the attack occurred. It was speculated that the attack targeted the military as punishment for several successful counterterrorist operations in Kaduna against BH. Aside from blast damage to the façade of the building, the bombing jarred a lot of nerves and resulted in tighter security by the military in Kaduna. Coincidentally, 15 minutes after the attack on 1 Division HQ, there was a bomb blast outside the gate of the Nigerian Air Force base in Kaduna. The blast occurred outside the gate and did not harm anyone or any property in the military facility.

The Bombing of St. Andrew's Church, Jaji

This place of worship located inside an elite military facility was hit with two VBIED attacks on Sunday November 25th, 2012. The Armed Forces Command and Staff College (AFCSC) in Jaji, Kaduna State, is a huge military complex dedicated to the training of middle-level military officers. The complex also houses the Nigerian Army School of Infantry (NASI).

The complex houses offices, schools, churches, mosques, homes, guest houses and has vast real estate for field training exercises. The complex is manned by armed sentry around the clock.

Two suicide bombers attacked the St. Andrew's Military Protestant Church. One terrorist rammed the church building and penetrated inside with his explosive payload detonating instantly. The second bomb detonated outside building. The attack was similar to the double-tap bombing of the Mogadishu Cantonment mammy market in Abuja.

The weapon was a fertilizer bomb in an explosive train packed into a mini van (bus) and a Toyota Camry. The bus rammed the church building at 12:05 PM after the second service. As the exiting crowd gathered to watch the fireball, the secondary weapon in the Toyota Camry was deployed at 12:15 PM, resulting in high casualties.[21]

The military authorities denied access to journalists and first responders including the National Emergency Management Agency (NEMA), the Kaduna State Emergency Management Agency (KSEMA) and the Nigerian Red Cross.[22] The military evacuated the dead and injured to the military hospital in Kaduna and other area hospitals. The death toll was estimated at over 50. A one-star general of the Nigerian Air Force, Air Commodore Alechenu Ekagbo, was listed among the official casualty figures of 11 dead and 30 injuries provided by the military.

The military was highly embarrassed by this deadly assault, resulting in a knee-jerk crackdown. The suicide bombers had evaded detection by the military checkpoints mounted at the entry and exit points of the cantonment by driving in through the unprotected bush. The rear of the military complex backs onto a wooded area. It was speculated that the bombers drove in through the Maraban–Jos axis.[23]

In the St. Andrew's attack, the terrorists flew below the radar to deliver a double-tap strike causing a large number of deaths and hurting pride and careers. The commandant of the AFCSC, Air Vice Marshal Ibrahim Kure, and the commandant of the Nigerian Army Corps of Infantry, Major General Mohammed Isa, were both replaced five days later.[24] Military provost and intelligence officials were arrested, detained and given general court martial as a result of the brazen attack.

Assaults on Borno Military Facilities

Borno State, the epi-center of the Boko Haram insurgency is home to several military facilities. From an operational vantage point, the facilities have aided the fight against the insurgency, yet their physical location in Borno State has made them vulnerable to attacks. Between 2013 and 2015 at the height of its power, BH overran several military facilities in Borno State.

The NAF Base Assault

On December 2nd, 2013, hundreds of Boko Haram fighters laid siege to the Nigerian Air Force (NAF) base in Maiduguri. In a coordinated assault, about 500 militants besieged the Air Force base and Army base, setting fire to buildings and other assets.[25]

Maimalari Barracks

The insurgents attacked the 21 Armored Brigade of the Nigerian Army (Maimalari Barracks) in Maiduguri on March 14th, 2014. They targeted the military detention facility where hardened BH terrorists were detained.[26]

Military intelligence of the impending attack provided a tactical edge to government special forces who were prepared for the insurgents. Three hundred and fifty people were killed in the clash. Most of the fatalities were insurgents who had invaded the facility, along with some of the hardened terrorists in detention.[27]

Despite being successfully repelled by the military with heavy casualties inflicted on the insurgents, the Maimalari Barracks attack was worrisome for the following reasons:[28]

a. The insurgents were able to advance to their objective – the detention facility – with ease.
b. The Shilka tank, a multipurpose self-propelled anti-aircraft artillery weapon positioned to secure the barracks, failed to fire.
c. The insurgents stormed the military base with some armored personnel carriers from Pori, near a tomato farm close to the barracks. That meant that the military facility did not have a secure perimeter.
d. The insurgents torched the MRS (a traditional medical facility within the barracks) and the detention facility.
e. Four children of a soldier were killed during the attack on Maimalari Barracks.
f. Air assets were deployed in the counter-attack against the insurgents. About ten Air Force jets were deployed in the operation.

The invasion of Maimalari Barracks was successfully repelled by the military with heavy casualties for the invaders. However, the lessons offered by the assault were numerous. The capabilities that the insurgents displayed were worrisome. The large number of fighters, their weapons, the armored personnel carrier (APC) and other logistics employed in the assault indicated a high level of resourcing by the enemy. The military's Shilka tank malfunction was unfortunate as that technical hitch almost turned the combat in favor of the invaders. The special forces had to engage the enemy in a direct firefight after the Shilka tank failed. The original plan for repelling invasions was to fire the "big guns" at the invaders as they reached a designated kill zone. The military was well served by advance intelligence of the impending attack, yet the battle raged for hours and air assets had to be called in to subdue the enemy.

Other barracks attacks, such as Giwa Barracks (March 2014), 202 Tank Batallion barracks in Bama (September 2014), Baga (January 2015) and Monguno Brigade Headquarters (January 2015), followed the same pattern. Bama,[29] Monguno[30] and Baga[31] were totally overrun and the terrorists took physical control of the large military facilities, along with the weapons and other assets.

The fall of the Multinational Joint Task Force facility in Baga was particularly tragic as over 2,000 citizens were killed. The insurgents rode into town on motorbikes and other vehicles while throwing explosives. They torched buildings and engaged the military in a major firefight. The soldiers battled the attackers for several hours but were forced to withdraw when no reinforcements came. With the withdrawal of the troops came the humanitarian tragedy as residents fled into the bush or headed for Lake Chad. Many residents drowned in the lake while the insurgents shot others dead. Citizens said that the troops appeared to run out of ammunition.[32]

Amnesty International described the January 3rd, 2015 attack on Baga town as the deadliest in the history of the Boko Haram insurgency.[33] In an editorial captioned "Baga Massacre: Diminishing Value of Nigerian Lives," *The Punch* newspaper[34] lamented that the world's attention was focused on seven people who were killed in a Jewish chicken stall attack by Al-Qaeda linked extremists in Paris, but the world did not notice 2,000 residents of Baga murdered by Boko Haram terrorists. The editorial stated:

> Two traumatic terror attacks thousands of kilometers apart, in Nigeria and France last week caught the attention of the world in unequal proportions . . . The difference is in leadership. About a week after the heinous crime by Boko Haram, President Goodluck Jonathan is yet to officially make a statement on the atrocity.[35]

Attacks on Military Facilities in Yobe State

Damaturu, the capital of Yobe State, came under attack in October 2013 from BH Islamists. They attacked an army barracks 20 km from Damaturu, overpowered the soldiers and seized an armored vehicle. The terrorists looted the armory and then set the barracks alight, detonating IEDs at the facility.[36]

On January 17th, 2017, Buni Yadi in Yobe State came under insurgent attacks. The BH insurgents attacked the 27 Task Force Military Brigade, killing a captain and four soldiers.[37]

A military base in Sassawa town in Tarmuwa LGA of Yobe State was also attacked by Boko Harm terrorists on February 6th, 2017. The insurgents mounted a dawn attack and ambushed soldiers deployed there. They later set the military base ablaze.[38]

Military Facility Attacks in Adamawa State

On Wednesday October 29th, 2014, the second-largest city in Adamawa State, Mubi, fell to BH insurgents. They engaged troops in a deadly shoot-out and eventually overwhelmed the military with superior fire power. Soldiers and residents fled in different directions – mostly southward towards Yola, the state capital. The brevity of the battle (only 2 hours) resulted in a lot of residents being trapped in the city.[39]

Vintim, the hometown of then Chief of Defense Staff, Air Chief Marshal Alex S. Badeh, was also overrun by the insurgents who set his country home ablaze. The sacking of Vintim occurred 24 hours after the fall of Mubi. The military troops stationed in Vintim and villagers were evacuated ahead of the capture of the town by the insurgents who proceeded to loot and burn the town.[40]

Adamawa State Governor, Mr. Bala James Ngilari, made several pleas to the federal government for reinforcements in order to prevent the fall of the whole state.[41] He later dispatched over 100 buses to attempt to pick up citizens from the outskirts of Mubi and transport them to Yola.

Other Attacks on the Military

Aside from these attacks on military barracks and bases, there were also attacks on military posts, checkpoints, and ambushes of the military. For example, troops on the 113 Battalion in Kareto, Borno State, were attacked in April 2016. After a 3-hour gunfight, the soldiers defeated the insurgents, killing scores of them. The military announced that some soldiers were wounded.[42]

Sabon Gari Kimba town in Damboa LGA of Borno State was hit by insurgents on April 16th, 2017. The militants invaded the military barracks in the town and engaged the soldiers in a gun duel that lasted several hours. The invaders, armed with rocket-propelled grenades (RPGs), anti-aircraft guns (AAs) and two armored personnel carriers (APCs), outgunned the military. Upon winning the battle, the terrorists looted weapons, vehicles, fuel and food before setting the military base on fire.[43] Eight soldiers including an officer were killed in action. Several other service members were also injured in this encounter.[44]

In another military base attack in Gudbori village, Borno State, in April 2017, four soldiers were killed and five injured.[45]

A suicide bombing attack on a military post in Gwoza, Borno State, near a secondary school, killed three soldiers and injured three others.[46] The attacker drove a bomb-laden vehicle into the military post with detonation occurring on impact.[47]

A female suicide bomber clad in a *hijab* and a soldier were killed when the quarterguard of the 301 Artillery Regiment of the Nigerian Army was attacked in Gombe. The bombing occurred on June 8th, 2014 when the young female approached the entrance of the military facility. The soldier went to intercept the girl who pretended to be a visitor. The female terrorist exploded her suicide vest, killing herself, the soldier and injuring other soldiers.[48]

A military post in Bulabulin Ngaram, Damboa LGA, Borno State, was attacked by BH fighters on June 24th, 2014. Sixteen soldiers were killed in the shoot-out. One soldier who managed to escape from the scene of the armed clash informed journalists in Maiduguri:[49]

> We were totally subdued by the insurgents. Some of my colleagues were abducted while many others escaped with bullet wounds. Dozens of Boko Haram insurgents stormed our checkpoint at Bulabulin on Tuesday night.
>
> The terrorists came in a convoy of over 30 vehicles mounted with Anti-Aircraft guns (AA). I was at the checkpoint when the terrorists came. We tried our best but they had the advantage over us. They had AA and we had AK-47 rifles that were not fully loaded. When we realized that they had taken over the place, some of us escaped to Maiduguri and other places but many could not make it.[50]

A female suicide bomber on June 4th, 2015 detonated explosive devices strapped on her body near a military checkpoint in Maiduguri. The attack occurred at Shagari Estate along Baga Road. A civilian JTF named Isah was killed in the blast.[51]

Military convoys also came under attack from BH ambushes in the theatre of war. Six soldiers were killed and 12 injured on December 10th, 2017 in the ambush of a convoy near Damboa (96 km from Maiduguri). The troops were on patrol between Nyeneri and Falawani villages when the attack occurred. The terrorists came in large numbers and attacked the convoy using IEDs and gun trucks. The jihadis looted the weapons of the convoy and escaped.[52]

Two soldiers of the 81 Task Force Battalion, 22 Brigade of Operation Lafiya Dole died in an ambush by Boko Haram terrorists on the Dukje–Mada road in Gulumba village in Borno State.[53] Their vehicle was destroyed by a roadside IED. Four other soldiers sustained injuries in this August 2017 attack. However, the soldiers fought back after the IED attack killing the attackers and recovering weapons.

In another roadside bomb attack, BH killed four soldiers along Kukawa and Alagano road, Borno State, in June 2017. Three soldiers were injured in the bomb attack. The troops, members of the 133 Special Forces Battalion, captured two children who were spying for the insurgents.[54]

CONCLUSION

The Nigerian military has been targeted by the BH insurgents. Since 2015, the war on terror has turned in favor of the Nigerian authorities. The military has recaptured all real estate seized by the terrorists and there is no jihadi flag flying over Nigerian territory.

As in all battles, progress came at a great cost. Troops paid the supreme price in many battles and ambushes. In one horrific case, an airforce fighter pilot was shot down and then beheaded on tape by Boko Haram.[55] Wing Commander Chinda Hedima (aged 39), who was described as a "true Nigerian hero," parachuted to safety when his jet was crippled by enemy fire during a combat mission. His life was terminated by mindless terrorists in a video as they chanted "*Allah Akbar*" ("God is great").

NOTES

1. Olaleye Aluko "Army Has Suffered Tragic Human Loss to Boko Haram – Buratai" *The Punch* (December 11th, 2017): Page 13.
2. Katie Pisa and Tom Hume. "Boko Haram Overtakes ISIS as World's Deadliest Terror Group, Report Says" *CNN*. Atlanta, GA (November 19th, 2015).
3. Susan Edeh. "How Boko Haram Killed 5, Set 759 Prison Inmates Free" *Vanguard* (September 8th, 2010).
4. Ibid.
5. David Smith. "More than 700 Inmates Escape During Attack in Nigerian Prison" *The Guardian*. International Edition. London (September 8th, 2010).
6. Ibid.
7. Susan Edeh (2010).

8. Ibid.
9. David Smith (2010).
10. 25-minute video made by Abubakar Shekau on April 19th, 2010.
11. Ibid.
12. Adam Nossiter. "Prison Raid in Nigeria Releases Hundreds" *New York Times* (September 8th, 2010).
13. Edeh (2010).
14. Ibid.
15. Ibid.
16. Ibid.
17. "Many Dead in Nigeria Market Blast" *Al Jazeera Television* (December 31st, 2010).
18. Nigeria Police Force. Case Studies of IED Incidents in Nigeria. Paper Presented at the 2012 CCW Groups of Experts Meeting on IED. UNOGCH.
19. Ibid.
20. Tony Akowe and Kolade Adeyemi. "Boko Haram Bombs Rock Military Base in Kaduna" *The Nation* (February 8th, 2012): Page 1.
21. Soni Daniel et al. "Many Killed as Suicide Bombers Hit Military Church in Jaji" *Vanguard* (November 26th, 2012).
22. Ibid.
23. Ibid.
24. Kingsley Omonobi and Luka Bamiayat. "Jaji Bombings: Military Removes Two Generals" *Sunday Vanguard* (December 2nd, 2012): Pages 1, 5.
25. Ndahi Marama. "Scores Killed as Boko Haram Attacks Air Force Base in Maiduguri" *Vanguard* (December 2nd, 2013).
26. "350 Killed in Boko Haram, Army Clash" *The Punch* (March 15th, 2014).
27. Ibid.
28. Ibid.
29. Lanre Ola. "Scores Killed as Boko Haram Insurgents Overrun Nigerian Town: Sources" *Reuters International* (September 2nd, 2014).
30. "Boko Haram Captures Monguno Town in Maiduguri – Security Sources" *Vanguard* (January 25th, 2015).
31. Anne Look and Abdulkareem Haruna. "Boko Haram Overruns Nigeria Military Base" *Voice of America*. Washington, DC (January 5th, 2015).
32. Ibid.
33. Adelani Adepegba and Eric Dumo. "2000 Likely Killed in Nigeria's Deadliest B'Haram Attack – AI" *The Punch* (January 10th, 2015): Page 35.
34. Editorial. "Baga Massacre: Diminishing Value of Nigerian Lives" *The Punch* (January 16th, 2015): Page 28.
35. Ibid.
36. "B'Haram: Death Toll in Yobe Attack Hits 127" *The Punch* (October 20th, 2013): Page 13.

37. Kabiru Hamisu Matazu et al. "Boko Haram's Renewed Attacks Spread Fear in North-East" ***Daily Trust*** (April 30th, 2017).
38. Ibid.
39. Segun Adebowale. "Boko Haram Overruns Mubi, Adamawa's Second Largest Town" ***The Eagle Online*** (October 30th, 2014).
40. Daniel. "Vintim, Badeh's Home Town, Taken Over by Insurgents" ***Information Nigeria Radio*** (October 31st, 2014).
41. Segun Adebowale (2014).
42. Daniel (2014).
43. Timothy Olanrewaju and Juliana Taiwo – Obalonye. "Boko Haram Fighters Invade Military Base" ***Daily Sun*** (April 19th, 2016): Page 6.
44. Kabiru Hamisu Matazu et al. (2017).
45. Ibid.
46. Abdulsalami Ahovi et al. "Three Feared Killed, Others Injured in Borno Suicide Bombing" ***The Guardian*** (June 23rd, 2014): Page 5.
47. Ibid.
48. Yusuf Alli et al. "Woman Suicide Bomber Hits Military Barracks" ***The Nation*** (June 9th, 2014): Page 1.
49. Kayode Idowu. "B'Haram Kills 16 Soldiers in Borno" ***The Punch*** (June 26th, 2014): Page 13.
50. Ibid.
51. Kayode Idowu. "Suicide Bombers Hit Maiduguri, Yola Again" ***The Punch*** (June 5th, 2015): Page 12.
52. Ademola Babalola. "Six Soldiers Killed in Boko Haram Ambushes" ***This Day*** (December 12th, 2017): Page 46.
53. Blessing Olaifa. "Two Soldiers Killed in Boko Haram Ambush" ***The Nation*** (August 8th, 2017). Page 43.
54. Olaleye Aluko. "B'Haram Kills Four Soldiers, Army Arrests Child Terrorists" ***The Punch*** (July 1st, 2017): Page 12.
55. Yusuf Alli. "Boko Haram: Military Vows to Avenge Beheaded Pilot" ***The Nation*** (October 5th, 2014): Page 3.

7

Targeting Law Enforcement

The Global Terrorism Index (GTI) report for 2017 ranked Nigeria as the third most terrorized nation in the world for that year, even though Boko Haram killings fell by 80%.[1] Nigeria's third-place ranking placed it ahead of Iraq and Afghanistan, but behind Syria, Pakistan, India, Turkey and Libya.[2]

The intentional targeting of law enforcement officers – police, immigration, customs security officials – contributed to this poor ranking. In Chapter 6 we examined the targeting of the military. The conventional wisdom is that terrorists and criminals usually avoid targeting law enforcement in order to avoid swift and excessive reprisals and crackdown. Unfortunately, the Boko Haram terrorists have taken the fight to law enforcement in Nigeria.

WHY PICK ON LAW ENFORCEMENT?

A study of violence by the jihadi group from the onset of the conflict phase in 2009 reveals the following six reasons why BH attacks law enforcement.

1. Capability

Boko Haram tends to pick on law enforcement targets because the jihadists feel they can prevail. Their assessment of police capabilities (personnel and facilities) has led them to the conclusion that they would win in combat. Police personnel and facilities are spread throughout the

774 local governments of the country. Most police facilities are poorly constructed, poorly equipped and poorly defended. The police agency in Nigeria has suffered severe neglect under successive military regimes from 1966 to 1999. The agency has also suffered neglect under civilian administrations since the return to democratic rule in 1999. Given these multiple vulnerabilities, the terrorists have apparently concluded that police facilities and personnel are fair game.

2. Neutralization

This is a card that is often played by BH to gain tactical operational advantage. During most bank robberies, Boko Haram fighters would attack the nearby police station – detonate IEDs and kill many policemen – before proceeding to rob the bank. The aim is to neutralize or eradicate any opposition to their evil designs.

3. Revenge

The jihadis nurse a deep-seated animus toward the police agency. After the leadership of BH parted ways with then Gov. Ali Modu Sheriff of Borno State, the Nigeria Police Force in Borno State began exhibiting high-handedness in their dealings with sect members. This culminated in the shooting incident at the customs market roundabout in Maiduguri by the men of Operation Flush. BH has long sought to avenge the deaths of those 17 sect members at the hands of police personnel.

The greatest anger against the police agency was the extra-judicial murder of Sheikh Mohammed Yusuf on July 30th, 2009. The police also murdered Alhaji Buji Foi, a top executive of Boko Haram, along with about 700 other sect members. Some were shot dead in cold blood in full view of video cameras. Abubakar Shekau is bent on getting his pound of flesh over these murders.

The perceived ills against Boko Haram committed by the police agency had to be avenged. So, to attack the police and any law enforcement agent appeared to be a duty for BH extremists.

4. Thirst for Blood

BH terrorists intentionally pick on police personnel to satisfy their thirst for human blood. BH jihadists love killing people. However, killing police personnel holds a greater thrill for them, adding to their job satisfaction.

5. Vulnerabilities

Police facilities such as police stations, police posts, area command offices, etc. are very vulnerable structures which often do not receive adequate physical security protection measures. The police stations and housings are not built with terrorist attacks in mind. Police executives continue to count on the fact that Nigerian citizens are docile and law-abiding. However, terrorists have shown that there are multiple weaknesses that can be exploited in attacking police facilities.

Aside from facility vulnerabilities, the outdated weaponry of police personnel is a vulnerability in the circumstance as well as the fact that the men and women do not receive continuous musketry and combat simulation training to help them address the threat.

6. Strategic Risk Assessment

Boko Haram has continued to pick on law enforcement because they (law enforcement) have not conducted a strategic risk assessment that would have helped them to identify the intentions, motivations and capabilities of the adversary enabling them to conduct and deploy effective security countermeasures. Due largely to poor strategic leadership, the threat posed to the law enforcers by the jihadis was not properly assessed. In fact, it was missed. It was just a question of time before the terrorists discovered the archilles heel of the police agency.

The factors enumerated above and others embolden the jihadis to attack police headquarters, police barracks, police stations, police posts and police checkpoints with impunity. The jihadis shoot dead police personnel on checkpoint duty and seize their weapons. The terrorists raid police stations and cart away arms and ammunition. The campaign of wanton violence has resulted in a high number of police fatalities.

THE FHQ BOMB

The most brazen and audacious attack of the BH insurgents against law enforcement was the June 16th, 2011 bombing of the Nigeria Police Force Headquarters (FHQ) in Abuja. This critical infrastructure facility houses the entire conical apex of the police agency in Nigeria. The weapon, a vehicle-borne improvised explosive device (VBIED) was intended to topple the magnificent high-rise building.

With the intervention of the traffic policeman, Assistant Superintendent Dantim, the bomb-laden vehicle was redirected into the outdoor parking lot and then parked at a distance of about 100 meters from the building's shell, creating a stand off distance that saved the building from significant structural damage. Additionally, the bomber's vehicle was sandwiched among several other vehicles which helped absorb the blast energy. However, the other vehicles contributed to the thermal event as there was a huge fireball which created very scary optics in this first suicide bombing event in Nigeria.

This event was an SVBIED (suicide-vehicle-borne improvised explosive device) attack which claimed seven lives. However, the police agency maintains that there were only two fatalities.[3]

Surveillance cameras mounted on the FHQ building showed the relocation of the suspect vehicle from the front of the FHQ to the parking lot. The video footage also captured the exact moment of detonation signaled by a bright flash of yellow light and smoke – the thermal event.

The bomb blast not only destroyed over 70 vehicles in the parking lot and smashed out glazing from the windows, but also destroyed furniture inside offices within the seven-storey building. The blast pressure knocked down TV sets, refrigerators and office file cabinets.[4]

The fact that the attack occurred only 48 hours after the police chief, Inspector General of Police (IGP) Hafiz Ringim, declared in Maiduguri, Borno State, that "Boko Haram's days are numbered"[5] fueled speculation that it was an attempt to murder Ringim himself. However, such speculation was not supported by the fact that more time would have been needed to build such a massive weapon, conduct surveillance of the FHQ building, create a fake police ID card for Mohammed Manga (the suicide bomber), and even pose for martyrdom shots with the iconic AK-47 rifle.

BH spokesman Abu Zaid praised the martyrdom of Mohammed Manga, a successful businessman aged 35 who was married with five children, and said that the bombing had targeted IGP Hafiz Ringim. He said that Manga had driven overnight from Maiduguri to Abuja to attack the police chief. He had an accomplice who exited the car prior to entry into the FHQ. Manga reportedly left N4 million in cash to his five children in his will.[6]

Analysis of the FHQ Bombing

The bomb attack was made possible by the failure of access control procedures at the FHQ.[7] Using a fake police ID card, Mohammed Manga was able to tail-gate the IGP's convoy into the compound.

The police personnel on access control duty did not exhibit adequate security awareness. Given the various attacks carried out by the BH sect it was conceivable that the FHQ could be targeted. However, there was no proper threat assessment to understand how a determined aggressor could attack the police facility.

ASP Dantim, who was responsible for enforcing parking in the IGP's parking lot, did his duty but paid with his life as the suicide bomber detonated the bomb, killing both of them. The aggressive enforcement action by Dantim saved the FHQ from destruction. Dantim's sacrifice also shows that one man can make a difference.

THE BORNO STATE SHQ ATTEMPTED ATTACK

On October 4th, 2011, Boko Haram terrorists targeted the Nigeria Police Force Borno State Command Headquarters (SHQ) in Maiduguri. A VBIED attack was averted by an eagle-eyed policeman who disabled the vehicle and a treasure trove of IEDs was recovered.

THE YOBE STATE POLICE ATTACK

Boko Haram terrorists attacked several police targets on November 4th, 2011. Five police facilities were attacked in addition to the federal government building in Damaturu, 11 churches and two banks. The terrorists used VBIEDs, IEDs, RPGs, incendiary devices (i.e. fuel bombs, Molotov cocktails) and small arms fire.[8]

The police targets attacked included:

a. NPF State Headquarters
b. NPF Anti-Terrorism Squad (ATS) HQ
c. NPF Division A
d. NPF Division B
e. NPF Division C.

In the attack, the terrorists destroyed the SHQ and burnt down the police commissioner's office. The entrance of the SHQ had several bullet holes and sustained an RPG strike.

The police ATS facility was hit with a VBIED attack. The explosive shock wave destroyed the front of the building and left a wide blast

107

crater measuring 3.62 × 3.6 m. Shrapnel from the attack struck the light pole and flag pole in front of the building. A civilian car parked in the vicinity of the blast seat was heavily impacted.

THE ATTACKS ON POLICE IN KANO

Boko Haram insurgents brought war to Kano City on January 20th, 2012.[9] The BH attacks targeted Nigeria Police Force facilities; two offices of the Nigerian Immigration Service and the headquarters of the Department of State Services in Kano. A suicide bomber rammed the Zone 7 Police Headquarters with a massive VBIED and caused significant property damage and loss of lives. Other terrorists attacked other police targets using IEDs and automatic gunfire.

Over 140 bodies were accounted for at the Murtala Muhammad Hospital mortuary as a result of the attacks. Witnesses reported counting over 100 bodies around the police zonal headquarters building.

Subsequent to this horrific attack which witnesses say claimed over 500 lives, this author called on the Federal Government of Nigeria to declare outright war on the Boko Haram terrorists in 2012. He wrote: "In this unconventional warfare, Boko Haram has no front-lines but the goals are clearly to kill Nigerians."[10]

THE SARS ABUJA ATTACK

On November 26th, 2012, 40 Boko Haram fighters attacked the headquarters of the Special Anti-Robbery Squad (SARS) in Abuja and freed 30 inmates, some of whom were members of the Boko Haram sect.[11] Two policemen were killed in the attack on the elite police agency dedicated to combating violent crimes. The pre-dawn attack resulted in a fierce gun battle between the police personnel and the intruders. The terrorists achieved their mission of setting their colleagues free.

THE ATTACK ON CP TARABA

The Commissioner of Police (CP) in Taraba State, Mr. Mamman Saleh, narrowly escaped death when his convoy was hit by a suicide bomb attack on April 30th, 2012 in Jalingo, the capital of Taraba State.[12] The attack which this author christened an "Okada-borne improved explosive device" (OBIED) occurred at 8:45 AM as the convoy of the commissioner of police was close to his office. Eleven people were killed instantly in the terrorist attack. The bomb-laden motorcycle rammed the CP's convoy destroying his car and killing his aide and ten others.

THE POLICE DIVISIONS IN GOMBE STATE

In September 2015, the Police Area Commander of Bajoga Area Command, Gombe State, disclosed that in one year BH terrorists destroyed four out of five police divisions under the command, killing several police personnel. Mr. Abimbola Sokoya said that the insurgents torched most of the police facilities after the attacks.[13]

THE GWOZA ATTACKS

Twenty-seven policemen were seized and taken away by Boko Haram in Gwoza, Borno State, in an August 2014 attack.[14] The missing police personnel were never rescued or found and are presumed dead. The terrorists are reputed for cutting the throats of captured policemen.

Initially, 35 policemen were declared missing on August 20th, 2014. However, eight of them managed to escape the terrorist onslaught on this city where the Police Mobile Force Academy is located. The terrorists took control of Gwoza after the attack.[15]

THE DAMATURU ATTACK II

The city of Damaturu came under insurgent attack again on December 1st, 2014. The terrorists made their way to Government House, Damaturu, before they were repelled by the military. The casualty figures stood at 33 policemen, 6 soldiers and 20 insurgents killed.[16] The police agency lost the largest number of service personnel in the Battle of Damaturu.

TEN POLICEWOMEN ABDUCTED

A military/police convoy came under attack in June 2017 along the Damboa–Maiduguri road and ten policewomen were abducted.[17] In a video posted on Sahara Reporters, BH leader Abubakar Shekau said: "I want to tell you that we are responsible for the work. We thank Allah.

We got victory from our creator. That work that happened along the Damboa–Maiduguri Road. It was Allah who did it. Not us."[18]

The ten policewomen were released unharmed in February 2018[19] after negotiations between the Federal Government of Nigeria and the extremist sect. It is widely believed that the federal government paid ransom to the insurgents.

THE ONSLAUGHT ON POLICE PERSONNEL

Boko Haram has carried out a deadly onslaught against police personnel in the North. However, the frequency of attacks in Borno State has been the highest.

Let us enumerate some attacks captured in the author's terror diary:

1. January 3rd, 2011 – Policemen killed in Maiduguri
2. February 20th, 2011 – Policemen killed in Maiduguri
3. February 23th, 2011 – Another police fatality at the hands of the terrorists
4. February 28th, 2011 – Police Commander's home attacked – two policemen killed
5. March 2nd, 2011 – Two policemen shot dead in Maiduguri
6. April 20th, 2011 – Policeman killed in BH bomb attack
7. May 17th, 2011 – Policeman killed in Maiduguri – headshot
8. August 25th, 2011 – Attack on police station in Gombe, Adamawa State
9. January 9th, 2012 – Secret police operative shot dead in Biu, Borno State
10. January 10th, 2012 – Five policemen killed in a beer garden attack in Damaturu, Yobe State
11. February 3rd, 2012 – Four persons killed in an attack by BH on a police station in Kogi State
12. April 25th, 2012 – Borno State Police Headquarters attacked by BH – seven killed, several injured.

CONCLUSION

Boko Haram's animus for the police agency has been manifested in the terrorists' choice of targets. They have tended to attack police personnel and facilities in an endless orgy of violence. Coincidentally, Dutsen Tashi

Police Station in Bauchi State was the first target of the Yusufiyya sect when they chose the path of violence.

It is hoped that police facilities in North East Nigeria would be designed and engineered to withstand extant threats of bombings and sundry security breaches. Perimeter security enhancements and strict access control including weapons searches must be implemented to keep police personnel and facilities safe. Designers of police stations should build reinforced strongrooms as armories. The current high incidence of seizure of arms from police facilities by Boko Haram must be curtailed by effective physical security safeguards.

Police facilities should have hotlines to nearby military facilities which could be contacted in the event of a terrorist breach. Using a well-designed security arrangement, police personnel and facilities in the North East can survive incessant Boko Haram attacks.

NOTES

1. Segun Olaniyi. "Nigeria Remains Third Most Terrorized Nation, Says Report" *The Guardian* (November 16th, 2017): Pages 1, 8.
2. Ibid: Page 8.
3. Jide Ajani and Kingsley Omonubi. "Force HQ Bomb Blast. How Ringim, 7 Storey Building Were Saved" *Vanguard* (June 19th, 2011).
4. Ibid.
5. Joe Brock. "Nigerian Islamist Sect Claims Bomb Attack: Paper" *Reuters Agency* (June 17th, 2011). https://www.reuters.com/article/ozatp-nigeria-bomb-idAFJO E75G0BF20110617
6. Ahmad Salkida. "The Story of Nigeria's First Suicide Bomber" *Sahara Reporter Online*. New York, NY (June 26th, 2011).
7. Chux Ohai. "Odita, Ekhomu Condemn Bomb Attack on Force Headquarters" *Saturday Punch* (June 16th, 2011): Page 4.
8. Major Abdulrasaq Kazeem and Tajudeen Adeshina Adigun. "Case Studies of IED Incidents in Nigeria" Paper presented at Session of the Group of Experts, UN Convention of Certain Conventional Weapons (CCW) held in Geneva, Switzerland (April 23rd – 24th, 2012). www.unog.ch/80256EDD006B8954/ (httpAssets)/F327DCED62227034C12579FE/$file/Nigeria_IEDs+2012.pdf
9. Mike Oboh. "Islamist Insurgents Kill Over 178 in Nigeria's Kano" *Reuters Agency* (January 22nd, 2012). https://www.reuters.com/article/us-nigeria-violence/ islamist-insurgents-kill-over-178-in-nigerias-kano-idUSTRE80L0A020120122
10. Sesan Olufowobi. "Expert Urges FG to Declare War on Boko Haram" *The Punch* (January 23rd, 2012): Page 6.

11. Kingsley Omonobi. "Gunmen Attack SARS Headquarters in Abuja" *Vanguard* (November 27th, 2012): Page 1.
12. Madu Onuorah et al. "Horror as Police Chief's Aide, 10 Others Die in Taraba Blast" *The Guardian* (May 1st, 2012): Page 1.
13. Vincent Ohonbamu. "Boko Haram Hits Four Police Stations in Gombe" *The Nation* (September 14th, 2015): Page 50.
14. "Boko Haram: 27 Missing Policemen Yet to Be Declared Dead, Say IG" *The Nation* (June 17th, 2015).
15. Ibid.
16. Onyedi Ojiabor et al. "33 Policemen, Soldiers, 20 Insurgents Die in Yobe Battle" *The Nation* (December 3rd, 2014): Pages 4, 57.
17. John Alechenu. "We Abducted 10 Policewomen, Attacked Military – Shekau" *The Punch* (June 28th, 2017): Page 17.
18. "How UNIMAID Lecturers, 10 Policewomen Were Released by Boko Haram" *The Vanguard* (February 10th, 2018).
19. "Boko Haram Frees 10 Abducted Policewomen and UNIMAID Lecturers" *Sahara Reporters*. New York (February 10th, 2018). www.saharareporters. com/2018/02/10/boko-haram-frees-10-abducted-police-women-and-unimaid-lecturers

8

Targeting Schools and Students

INTRODUCTION

Boko Haram insurgents have targeted schools – killing, maiming, burning, kidnapping, raping school children. Their most widely cited school atrocity is the April 14th, 2014 mass kidnap of 276 girls from the Government Girls Secondary School in Chibok, Borno State. However, the mass cremation of students in Buni Yadi and the mass throat slittings at the Federal Polytechnic Mubi were more gruesome school attacks. The horrific deaths and the systematic extermination of students placed these, the Government Secondary School, Mamudo massacre and a few others on the totem pole of BH atrocities against schools (as shown in Figure 8.1).

Aside from the loss of lives and loss of freedom, palpable fear is felt by many students in many Northern states. The school terror footprint extends to the states of Benue,[1] Taraba, Plateau, Nasarawa, Jigawa, Kaduna and the Federal Capital Territory. In these states, no actual school attacks have been carried out. However, fear of attack is palpable and the authorities have occasionally ordered school closures in response.

The greatest consequence of BH's targeting of schools is the chilling effect it has on education in the region. The North East is educationally disadvantaged with low school enrollments and a large population of out of school children which is estimated by the United Nations at three million.[2]

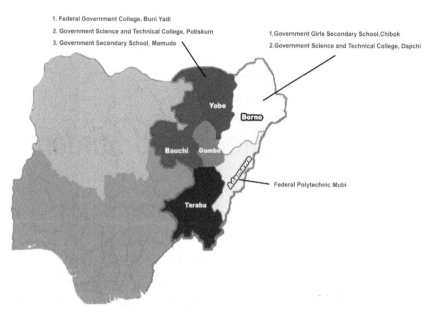

Figure 8.1   Boko Haram school targets.

The prolonged insurgency has resulted in frequent and prolonged school closures as well as decisions by parents to withdraw their children and wards from schools due to safety concerns. The targeting of schools by BH is directly "mortgaging" the future of Nigerians and ensuring that the ills which the extremists claim to be fighting will be entrenched in society.

Some of these are poverty, frequent school strikes, prostitution, immorality, etc. Boko Haram, because it is not a knowledge-driven insurgency, is ignorant of the fact that by targeting schools, it is committing the sins of the *Yan Boko* by creating these same social vices that it claims to be fighting.

WHY TARGET SCHOOLS?

BH insurgents have attacked a myriad of targets from churches to mosques, refugee camps, hotels and bars ("beer gardens"), telecommunication installations, district head palaces, government buildings, private residences, etc. However, the terrorists have deliberately concentrated attacks on schools, burning 254 by 2014 (see Table 8.1).[3]

Some reasons for the targeting of schools include:

1. **Book is Haram**: "*Book*" or "*Boko*" is the Hausa word for Western education and Western civilization (see Chapter 1). *Haram* means forbidden or sinful. So, if Western education is sinful, then the thing to do from the standpoint of Boko Haramisim is to root it out. Therefore, schools and students are legitimate targets of the extremists. At the initial stages of the conflict, Shekau pledged that school children would not be targeted.[4] However, in 2012, he changed the narrative justifying attacks on primary and secondary schools. He falsely claimed that government security forces were arresting Muslim children in *almajiri* schools.[5]
2. **Targets of opportunity:** Schools are spread throughout the conflict zone. Primary schools, secondary schools and tertiary institutions dot the landscape. An insurgent trying to achieve an imaginary quota of attack for a day, week, month or quarter will find a convenient target in the ubiquitous schools. The large number of schools provides more targets for the terrorists, hence the frequency of attacks on schools which creates a higher statistic than any other target group.
3. **Vulnerabilities of schools:** Schools in the region were built in a time when peace, law and order existed. There is no perimeter fencing, no alarm systems, no CCTV cameras, no locks on the doors except in the staff office and principal's office, no safe haven, no sheltering in place from the active shooter threat. After the suicide bombing attack on the Federal College of Education,

Table 8.1 Impact of BH on NE Schools/Children

State	Number of Schools Destroyed	Number of Out of School Children
Adamawa	73	
Borno	171	113,635
Yobe	56	73,894
Total	**300**	

Source: National Emergency Management Agency

Kano, in September 2014, which claimed 17 lives, this author called for the following security countermeasures for schools:[6]

a. Deployment of armed security personnel on school campuses
b. CCTV surveillance systems
c. Security lockdown hardware
d. Intrusion detection systems
e. Air raid sirens that could be manually triggered in the event of an insurgent attack
f. Suicide bomber detection training for the student population
g. Emergency drills
h. Employment of security professionals as chief security officers.

This author argued that since Kano State had been hit repeatedly by BH insurgents, schools needed to become proactive in their security to prevent the recurring mass murder of students.

4. **Revenge:** Boko Haram's spiritual leader, Abubakar Shekau, announced in 2012 that the sect would target schools as a reprisal against the federal government's arrests of Muslim children from *almajiri* schools.[7] However, there is no truth to the allegation that the security forces were arresting children from the Muslim schools. Unfortunately, Shekau has his own reality which he often makes up to suit himself. Once he determined schools to be a legitimate target, he issued the *fatwa* which his troops have been carrying out.

5. **Shekau's illiteracy:** Shekau did not receive formal Western education unlike his predecessor, Sheikh Mohammed Yusuf, who applied for admission into the University of Maiduguri but was not accepted. Shekau, on the other hand, grew up as a street urchin (see Chapter 3 of this book). He was a typical *almajiri*. His lack of formal education appears to inform his total disregard for Western values. It hints at envy of Western civilization and the artifacts it can produce. His response to this has been to try and tear down Western education. Clearly, the insurgency led by Shekau has retarded formal education in the North East region, but it has not and cannot stop it. Education is the ladder for the ascent of Nigeria to a greater future. One mentally deranged terrorist and his band of killers, rapists, kidnappers and thieves must not succeed in tearing it down.

6. **Wickedness:** The insurgents appear to love inflicting pain and suffering on people. Targeting a vulnerable population like school

116

children in bestial ways shows that BH insurgents lack human empathy and have little regard for human life. Their actions of destroying young lives in the most gruesome fashions are quite appalling and indicate deep psychopathy. Boko Haram slit the throats of dozens of students in Mubi and cremated 59 students in Buni Yadi. BH is so far off the mark of decency that the Al Qaeda network has denounced them as "unIslamic" and disavowed them.[8] Conversely, ISIS, the world's most horrific jihad group, fully endorses the outlandish actions of BH insurgents. In August 2015, ISIS leader, Sheikh Abubakar El Baghdadi, appointed Abu Musab Al-Barnawi as the leader of Boko Haram.[9]

7. **Terrorism financing:** Boko Haram has done well financially by demanding ransom payments from the federal government after the mass kidnap of school girls. The Chibok and Dapchi mass kidnap of girls were huge income earning (profit kidnap) ventures for the insurgents. Chapter 5 of this book dissects profit kidnap as a strategy of terrorism financing.

8. **Young brides:** BH insurgents come from the lowest strata of Northern society. Suddenly, with the acquisition of AK-47 rifles they have gained a lot of power and prestige. Secondary school girls have generally attained puberty and it is acceptable in the Muslim culture to marry girls as young as 10 or 11. BH fighters go to schools, conduct mass kidnaps and then marry these girls off. Those who refuse to convert to Islam are raped, brutalized, used as sex slaves and some killed.[10] So, targeting schools is a way of getting a flow of young brides for BH fighters. This is something that would normally have been beyond their reach – so it is a fringe benefit of the insurgency. Shekau considers abducted school girls as the spoils of war.

Let us now look at some major school attacks by Boko Haram.

BUNI YADI MASSACRE

In an act of unconscionable bestiality – BH fighters laid a 4-hour siege to the Federal Government College, Buni Yadi, Yobe State, on Tuesday February 25th, 2014. The terrorists, armed with AK-47 rifles, hunting knives and jerry cans of petrol, first set the administration block of the school on fire and then proceeded to the hostels where the children were already asleep. The terrorists shut the gates of the school and then set the hostels on fire. They shot students who tried to escape the crematorium, others were caught and their throats slit.[11]

The insurgents struck at 2:00 AM and operated unchallenged[12] until they left at dawn. Forty buildings were burnt down in all. Many students were burnt to death in their hostels. In all, 59 students met their untimely deaths at Buni Yadi.[13]

A survivor, who was lucky to be alive, said that the insurgents selected some female students from the girls' hostel and took them away. The 14-year-old junior secondary school student named Ibrahim Musa Lampo was shot in the leg as he escaped the inferno in his dormitory, captured and taken to the female hostel where he was placed in custody.[14]

The insurgents burnt hostels, classrooms on the school campus.[15] The school had just resumed from mid-term break when the terrorists struck. Several bodies were burnt beyond recognition and had to be given a mass burial.[16]

Isa Buba, a staff member of the school, said that the terrorists came through Biu Road from the Gujba Forests in 27 Hilux pick up vehicles and motorcycles laden with IEDs.[17]

The security guards were shot dead at the gate before the fighters proceeded to the staff quarters where they killed three teachers. Before leaving the town of Buni Yadi, the terrorists torched the local government secretariat building and the high court.[18] Buni Yadi is the headquarters of Gujba Local Government Council. It is 54 km south of Damaturu, the Yobe State capital.

The Buni Yadi attack was the fourth school attack in Yobe State in one year. It followed two terror attacks on the College of Agriculture in Gujba and Mamudo Secondary School, which claimed 42 lives. It should be pointed out here that the state of emergency declared by the federal government in the North East was in effect when Buni Yadi occurred – yet it could not stop the massacre.

Two weeks before the Buni Yadi attack, BH leader Abubakar Shekau released a video in which he threatened to kill some political leaders and innocent school children.

In an editorial on the Buni Yadi massacre, *This Day* newspaper concluded:

> Boko Haram is already succeeding in its agenda to stop education in a section of the country by means of terror. If we allow them, it is from the same young men and women who cannot go to school that they will recruit

members tomorrow. And since the sanctity of life means nothing to the blood-thirsty terrorists to the point of killing unarmed students, no effort should be spared in tracking and bringing an end to their madness.[19]

BAYERO UNIVERSITY KANO (BUK)

This university was attacked on April 24th, 2012. The terrorists invaded the old campus killing two professors and 13 others. The insurgents attacked an indoor sports hall and an open space used by the Christian community in the school for their Sunday service.[20]

About 15 gunmen carried out the attacks on the Christians who were already conducting Sunday Service. Prof. Jerome Ayodele and Prof. Leo Ogbonyomi were among the victims of the gun and IED attacks which lasted about 30 minutes before the assailants got away.[21]

Twenty-four hours after this attack, the police found a time bomb on the first floor of the sociology department[22] on the new campus.

Analyzing the BUK attack, this author concluded that campus security officials were negligent "as the attack was foreseeable and preventable."[23] He said that the attacks highlighted the need to appoint knowledgeable and passionate persons to sensitive security positions."[24]

FEDERAL POLYTECHNIC MUBI (FPM)

The horrendous terrorist attack that took place at this school on the night of October 1st, 2012 was simply unbelievable. Over 40 people, mostly students of the FPM were systematically shot dead or had their throats slit by scores of Boko Haram fighters.[25]

The terrorists besieged a block of hostels, called out names on a hit list and proceeded to eliminate their targets. The irony was that Mubi was under a dusk to dawn curfew on the night of October 1st when the gory mass murders occurred.

Soldiers and police immediately commenced a search for the terrorists.[26] However, they were apparently trying to solve the wrong problem. The authorities had modeled the problem as a normal criminal incident. President Jonathan, appalled by the mass casualties and the gruesome manner of the killings, ordered a "probe" of the incident.

Complicating the situation further was a denial by an unknown member of the sect.[27] The denial was not credible as the *modus operandi* of the mass murders including the following elements:

119

a. **No. of attackers:** There was a large number of attackers. BH usually operates that way.
b. **Weapons:** The terrorists used AK-47 rifles and hunting knives to slit throats. These are methods used by the sect.
c. **Procedure of attack:** The assailants called out students by name killing only Christians and sparing the Muslims.
d. **Operation during hours of curfew:** Only daredevil terrorists like BH could brave the curfew that was enforced by the military and proceed to commit mass murder.
e. **Signature of the aggressors:** "If it walks like a duck and quacks like a duck, then it must be a duck." In October 2012, only BH could commit such a brazen act of mass murder. An intelligence analyst presented with this evidence would be able to connect the dots and confidently conclude that to the exclusion of all other perpetrators, that this was a BH job.

A lecturer in Mubi who witnessed the massacre said that he and his family feared that the terrorists would come for them. He said that the Wuro Pategi side of town was populated by Christians and southerners who moved there because of the high number of Boko Haram religiously inspired killings occurring in Mubi. The lecturer described hearing screams, and dead silence close to his home.[28] The extermination of the Christians and southerners was ongoing in the Wuro Pategi neighborhood of Mubi, he concluded.

Unfortunately, the perpetrators of the Mubi massacre have never been detected or brought to book.

UNIVERSITY OF MAIDUGURI

This university is located in Maiduguri city, the epi-center of the BH insurgency. The campus is located on the outskirts of Maiduguri along the Maiduguri–Kondugha–Bama road, adjacent to the main entrance of the Sambisa Forest at Kawuri village. Sambisa Forest is the sanctuary of the terrorists. The university has been bombed and threatened with bombings[29] and nearby villages have been attacked with IEDs and automatic weapons.[30]

On March 14th, 2014, BH fighters attacked Malari village near the university. The terrorists shot dead six residents before setting several houses and a primary school ablaze with IEDs and petrol bombs.

The terror suspects advanced toward the university but they were repelled by soldiers from the Dalori military post. The exchange of automatic gunfire lasted over 3 hours causing considerable panic on campus.[31] Three students were killed in the terror attack. After the March 14th incident, due to the fear of serious bodily harm or death in an insurgent attack, many students left for other schools. Prospective students rejected admissions to the university.[32] It was reported in 2014 that enrollment figures between 2010 and 2014 had declined sharply.[33] In June 2014, the outgoing vice chancellor of the university, Prof. Mala Daura, said that the prevailing insecurity in Borno State had affected the university as some staff members had been attacked and killed by the insurgents or were felled by stray bullets. "This is why some of our staff have left the University."[34]

On January 16th, 2017, suicide bombers struck at the University of Maiduguri. A Professor of Veterinary Medicine, Prof. Aliyu Mani, and two students of the institution were killed in the suicide terrorism attacks along with the bombers.

In another terror attack, two female suicide bombers detonated their suicide vests (person-borne improvised explosive devices – PBIEDs) at the edge of the university in April 2017. The suicide bombers were targeting a mosque in the Jiddari Polo district. Four people were injured while the two bombers died from their weapons. The attack was carried out outside the perimeter fence of the university.

The university was again attacked using explosives on May 13th, 2017 by a wolf pack of insurgents that included two male and one female bomber. A security guard who intercepted the bombers died from blast pressure when the men detonated their suicide vests. The guard was questioning the men about their mission at the institution of higher learning when suddenly they detonated their PBIEDs. The female bomber hid beside a church on campus and later blew herself up causing property damage to the church but not injuring anyone else.

The university also came under twin explosives attacks on May 18th, 2017. An IED was detonated at about 10:50 PM while the second IED went off at about 12:50 AM.[35] The faculty of the Department of Veterinary Medicine and the BOT female hostel were the apparent targets.

Within the first six months of 2017 (January 16th to June 25th), the university community experienced six suicide bombing attacks. The attack of January 16th, 2017, which targeted early morning Muslim worshippers, involved four suicide bombers and killed five people including Professor Aliyu Mani of the Department of Veterinary Medicine.

The sustained onslaught on the school made it imperative to deploy effective security countermeasures. The size of the campus is roughly 40 km², so perimeter fencing would be quite expensive in territorial reinforcement. The university's neighboring communities such as Zannari, Gwozari, London Ciki, Mairi and Dalori all farm on the university's land, further compounding the issue of perimeter fencing. Due to its extensive real estate, the porous nature of the university was a vulnerability that the insurgents exploited to attack the university.

The successful campaign of the Nigerian military against Boko Haram at their nearby Sambisa Forest hideout has caused the displacement of some BH fighters into communities neighboring the university. This appears to be responsible for the rise in attacks as the timing of the offensive against the university in early 2017 coincided with when the Nigerian military first kicked the insurgents out of their Sambisa base – December 2016.

Another factor that has exacerbated insurgent attacks is the reduction in troop strength in Borno State because of the impressive military victory against the insurgents. With troop reductions came a sharp decline in the number of patrols thereby creating a security vacuum which was exploited by the insurgents. Troop reductions appear to have emboldened the terrorists.

It has been estimated that the university needs N2.6 billion to build the perimeter fence.[36] Unfortunately, the school does not have such financial resources available for the project. In June 2017, Borno State Governor Kashim Shettima donated N50 million to the university towards the fence project.[37]

In May 2017, the university hired 50 local hunters to conduct patrols and intercept suicide bombers. The military has also intensified patrols at the university.[38] This has resulted in the interception and neutralization of several suicide bombers.[39] Agents from the Department of State Services and undercover police detectives have been deployed to the university. However, given the large size of the campus, the number of government security assets deployed is considered inadequate.[40]

GOVERNMENT SCIENCE SECONDARY SCHOOL, POTISKUM

The attack on this school stands out as one of the most horrific terrorist attacks by BH. It is comparable in body count (52 dead) and savagery with the Buni Yadi school massacre (59 dead).

On November 10th, 2014, a suicide bomber disguised as a student mingled with around 2,000 students – some of them as young as 11 years old – who were waiting for the principal's address during the morning assembly.

The Government Science Secondary School is located in Potiskum, the second-largest city in Yobe State. Potiskum, located 100 km west of Damaturu, is the commercial capital of Yobe State.

The bomber, dressed in school uniform, had a bomb-laden back-pack which he detonated in the midst of the boys. Fifty-two boys died instantly, while 79 others were injured. It was a horrific bombing incident that targeted innocent young boys.[41]

Eyewitnesses described the horror of body parts all over the compound – it was carnage. This incident occurred one week after BH refused a ceasefire which was unilaterally declared by the federal government in an attempt to hold peace talks with the insurgents.

The loophole exploited in this bombing was the backpack that was allowed into the assembly area. The high death toll resulted from the explosive payload which the bomber could carry in his backpack. This threat could have been minimized if the school authorities had been proactive by banning backpacks from assembly halls. The attack was foreseeable based upon the fact that the Nigerian military had discovered a bomb factory where explosives were being sewn into rucksacks in Kano.[42]

OTHER SCHOOL ATTACKS

The attack on the Government Secondary School in Mamudo, Yobe, was the forerunner of the Buni Yadi cremation. BH gunmen killed 42 school children in this attack which began at 5:30 AM on July 6th, 2013. The insurgents mercilessly slaughtered the students, some of whom were half asleep. The assailants shot the children and then doused their hostel with petrol before setting it alight. Some of the kids were burnt beyond recognition. A teacher said most school children fled into the bush.[43]

In May 2015, another Boko Haram fighter carried out an active shooter attack at the College of Administrative and Business Studies, Potiskum. The terrorist stormed the College at 8:00 AM and opened fire on students and teachers. When he ran out of ammunition – after a prolonged shooting – he detonated the IED he was carrying and was killed instantly. Fourteen people were injured in this active shooter attack.[44]

A bomb explosion, preceded by sporadic gunfire left over 20 people dead in an attack on the Federal College of Education, Kano, on September 17th, 2014. Police personnel from nearby tactical operations responded to the sound of gunfire killing two assailants (see Table 8.2).[45]

In another school attack, a suicide bomber killed eight people at the School of Hygiene Technology, Kano, on June 23rd, 2014. The suicide bombing attack occurred inside the school premises located along BUK Road around 3:00 PM.[46] The school was conducting a screening exercise for new students when the suicide terrorist joined the queue and subsequently detonated an IED, killing seven others.[47]

A 14-year-old female suicide bomber attacked the Kano State Polytechnic on July, 30th, 2014, killing three students. The bomber

Table 8.2 Selected School Attacks by BH

Date	No. Attackers	Time	Institution	State	Deaths	Seizures
25/2/14	50	1:30 AM	FGC Buni Yadi	Yobe	43	16
			College of Agric. Gujiba	Yobe	40	0
19/6/13	4	12 NOON	Innovative Sec. Sch. Miu	Borno	6	0
6/7/12		5:35 AM	GSS Mamudo	Yobe	30	0
17/6/14	12		Ansarudeen PVT School Miu	Borno	9	0
1/10/12			Fed. Poly Mubi	Adamawa	40	0
12/12/12	10	2:00 AM	GGSS, Bama	Borno	5	0
13/2/14	200		Govt Sc. Snr. Sec. Sch. + Ashigar Sch of Business Kandogha	Borno	67	20
14/4/2014	100	12:00 AM	GSS Chibok	Borno		276

Notes:
1. April 10th, 2013, Shekau claimed ordering attacks on schools in an internet video post, citing military raids on Islamic schools in Maiduguri.
2. Between November, 2011 and October 2012, 209 government school buildings (classrooms, hostels, labs, and admin buildings) were burnt down by BH.

124

detonated the explosive device after mingling with a crowd of final year students who had gone to collect their call up letter for the National Youth Corps Scheme.[48]

On November 12th, 2014, another female suicide bomber attacked the Federal College of Education Kontagora, Niger State, killing one student. Two hundred students taking their examinations in the school auditorium were at risk.[49]

The training school of the Department of State Services in Bauchi also came under attack in April 2012.[50] Two of the attackers were killed.

The list of school attacks is endless. Let us now look at another threat faced by schools in the North East.

Seizure of Chibok Girls

This mass abduction event occurred on April 14th, 2014 as the girls were preparing for their school certificate examination. The terrorists used subterfuge in this mass kidnap. They brought several trucks to the school and were dressed in military fatigues. They told the students that there was an imminent terror attack and that they were there to evacuate them to safety. They placed 276 girls into the trucks and then drove off. The trucks broke down a few times and 51 girls escaped. However, 219 girls ended up in the BH camp in Sambisa Forest.

Two weeks after the seizure of the girls, a former education minister, Dr. Oby Ezekwesili, and Hadiza Usman formed a group called **#Bring Back Our Girls** (BBOG) which through marches, protests and meetings kept the captivity of the 219 girls on the front burner of national consciousness.

The BBOG campaign went viral and the former First Lady of the USA, Mrs. Michelle Obama also held up a Bring Back Our Girls poster. The BBOG group holds daily meetings at the Unity Fountain in Abuja where the members strategize.

In October 2016, 21 girls were released by Abubakar Shekau to the delight of Nigerians. The freed girls told a grim tale of servitude in Boko Haram captivity. About half of the school girls converted to Islam, married the BH fighters and some joined the insurgency as fighters. The other half refused to renounce their faith, so they were turned into slaves for the terrorists – washing, fetching water, cooking.[51]

As we wrote in Chapter 5 of this book, Boko Haram had a good payday prior to releasing the girls – a cash-for-girls deal. In May 2017, another set of 82 girls was released from Boko Haram captivity. In a statement, after the release of the 82 girls, this author advised:

The Federal Government should probe the Chibok kidnap incident . . . The panel should determine what vulnerabilities resulted in the security breach. The culpability of the school authorities, the Borno State government and the security agencies in the seizure of the girls would be determined. . . . This would help the government punish those whose negligence contributed to the kidnap of the girls and deter such reckless behavior in future.[52]

Dapchi Kidnap

In another dramatic mass kidnap incident, 110 girls were seized by Boko Haram fighters on February 19th, 2018 from Dapchi, Yobe State. In what appeared to be a replay of the Chibok school girls seizure, Boko Haram fighters dressed in military fatigues drove to the Government Science and Technical Secondary School in Dapchi and told the girls that there was an imminent attack and that they had to be evacuated. The terrorists came in a convoy of trucks. Some girls escaped into the bush while 110 girls were seized from the school.

The federal government negotiated the prompt release of the girls. One hundred and four girls were let go while the only Christian in their midst was given the option of converting to Islam to regain her freedom or else remain a Boko Haram captive. Leah Sharibu chose to defend her faith, refusing to convert. As at September 2019, Leah was still in Boko Haram captivity.

Nigeria's government announced that the release of the Dapchi girls was brokered by the Swiss Government, the International Committee of the Red Cross and other negotiators The government insisted that no ransom was paid. However, this was contradicted by a UN report submitted to the United Nations Security Council (UNSC) which disclosed that a ransom of several million dollars had been paid for the release of the girls.[53]

The Dapchi incident also raised concerns about a metastasis of the insurgency due to the splintering of the BH sect. It has been confirmed that the mass abduction was carried out by the Islamic State of West Africa (ISWA) which is a Boko Haram faction led by the son of the murdered leader of Boko Haram. Abu Musab Al-Barnawi was appointed by ISIS leader Sheikh Ibrahim Al Baghdadi. Understandably, Abubakar Shekau refused to release the reins of power which has led to a splintering of the terror group. Nigerian intelligence officials have reported frequent clashes between members of the two factions.

CONCLUSION

The targeting of schools and school children by Boko Haram has continued to drive the narrative that the terrorists hate Western education. However, the problem with school security in Nigeria is the inadequacy of countermeasures that would prevent threats from exploiting the assets. Boko Haram has observed these vulnerabilities and is exploiting them to terrorize school children. It should be stated that children who are sent to school deserve competent protection from murderers and kidnappers.

The terrorists have bombed students, burnt down schools, shot students and kidnapped school boys and girls in their relentless rampage. It is hoped that the Nigerian authorities will strengthen the security of schools in the conflict zone to mitigate the risk of attacks. After the Dapchi mass abduction in February 2018, President Muhammadu Buhari ordered police personnel and officials of the Nigerian Security and Civil Defence Corps to protect schools. The deployment of these uniformed security personnel in schools would serve as a deterrent to incessant school attacks.

NOTES

1. Uja Emmanuel. "Boko Haram Threatens to Invade Schools in Makurdi" *The Nation* (May 18th, 2014): Page 9.
2. Olatunji Omirin. "UNICEF to Enroll 1 million Children Affected by Insurgency" *Daily Trust* (April 13th, 2017): Page 10.
3. Okechukwu Nnodim. "B'Haram Displaced 800,000, Burnt 254 Schools" *The Punch* (January 14th, 2015): Page 7.
4. Dr. Ona Ekhomu. **Protection of National Critical Infrastructure: An Imperative in the War on Terror**. Paper Presented at the Counter-Terrorism Seminar Held at the Armed Forces Command and Staff College, Jaji, Nigeria (March 12th–13th, 2013).
5. Elizabeth Pearson and Jacob Zenn. "How Nigerian Police Also Detained Women and Children as Weapons of War" *The Guardian – UK* (May 6th, 2014). https://theguardian.com/world/2014/may/06/how-nigerian-police-also-detained-children-as-weapons-of-war
6. Olaleye Aluko. "Expert Advises Schools on Security" *The Punch* (September 23rd, 2014): Page 6.
7. Pearson and Zenn (2014).
8. Adam Nossiter and David D. Kirkpatrick. "Abduction of Girls an Act Not Even Al Qaeda Can Condone" *New York Times* (May 7th, 2014).
9. Yinka Ajayi. "What We Know about Boko Haram New Leader, Abu Musab Al-Barnawi" *Vanguard* (August 17th, 2016).

10. "Our Ordeal in B'Haram's Den – Female Abductees" *The Punch* (March 25th, 2014).
11. Duku Joel. "Fire and Fury as Boko Haram Kills 43 Pupils" *The Nation* (February 26th, 2014): Pages 1, 4.
12. Ibid.
13. Saxone Akhaine et al. "Death toll in Yobe School Attack Hits 59" *The Guardian* (February 27th, 2014): Page 1.
14. Sam Eyoboka et al. "Yobe Massacre: How My Mates Were Killed – Survivor" *Vanguard* (February 27th, 2014): Pages 1, 5.
15. Ibid.
16. Duku Joel. "Pupils' Massacre: Parents Storm Hospital for Kids" *The Nation* (February 27th, 2014): Page 1.
17. Njadwara Musa. "Gunmen Invade School, Kill 29 Students, Others in Yobe" *The Guardian* (February 26th, 2014): Page 1.
18. Ibid.
19. Editorial Page Comment. "When Innocent Students Become Sitting Targets" *This Day* (March 2nd, 2014): Page 8.
20. Adamu Abuh et al. "Terrorists Invade Bayero Vasity, Kill Don, 14 Others" *The Guardian* (April 30th, 2012): Page 1.
21. "BUK Attacks: Two Professors, 13 Other Shot Dead" *The Punch* (April 30th, 2012): Page 8.
22. John Atechenu et al. "Police Find Time Bomb Inside Bayero Varsity" *The Punch* (May 1st, 2012): Page 8.
23. "Security Expert Condemns BUK Killings" *Daily Sun* (May 3rd, 2012): Page 6.
24. Ibid.
25. "Mubi Massacre and Rising Insecurity" *The Punch* (October 18th, 2012): Page 18.
26. Madu Onorah et al. "Troops Search Houses for Students' Killers" *The Guardian* (October 4th, 2012): Page 1.
27. "Boko Haram Denies Mubi Killings" *The Punch* (October 10th, 2012): Page 11.
28. "School Massacre: I Thought the Killers Would Come for Us Next – Lecturer Who Witnessed Mubi Massacre" *Daily Sun* (October 4th, 2012): Page 6.
29. "Boko Haram Threatens to Bomb UNIMAID, Others" *The Punch* (December 13th, 2013).
30. Falaiye Kola Oluwaseun. "Tension in UNIMAID Over Attacks on Borno Villages" *The Guardian* (May 10th, 2014): Page 26.
31. Njadwara Musa. "Military Repels Terrorists from Maiduguri Varsity" *The Guardian* (May 4th, 2014): Page 1.
32. Charles Abah et al. "Even in Varsities, Fear of Boko Haram Is Real" *The Punch* (May 6th, 2014): Page 43.
33. Njadwara Musa. "Boko Haram Activities Scare Lecturers, Students Others from University of Maiduguri" *The Guardian* (June 5th, 2014): Page 56.
34. Ibid.

35. Michael Olugbode. "Again, Bomb Explosions Hit University of Maiduguri" *This Day* (May 20th, 2017).

36. Victor Izekor. "The Implications of UNIMAID Bombings" *The Nation* (July 22nd, 2017): Page 10.

37. "Shettima Donates N50m to secure UNIMAID Against B'Haram Attacks" *The Guardian* (June 28th, 2017).

38. Ibrahim Sawab. "Bomb Attacks: Army Assures UNIMAID of Support" *Daily Trust* (July 12th, 2017): Page 7.

39. "Three Female Suicide Bombers Die in Failed Attacks in Maiduguri – SEMA." *The Punch* (November 18th, 2017).

40. Duku Joel. "Trying Times for University of Maiduguri" *The Nation* (August 6th, 2017): Page 9.

41. Mohammed Abubakar et al. "52 Die, 79 Injured in Potiskum School Blast" *The Guardian* (November 11th, 2014): Page 1.

42. Ibid.

43. Yusuf Alli et al. "Boko Haram Kills 20 Students in Fresh Attack" *The Nation* (July 7th, 2013): Page 2.

44. Kayode Idowu. "14 Injured in Yobe School Suicide Bomber Attack" *The Punch* (May 9th, 2015): Page 9.

45. Fidelis Soriwei et al. "Kano College Blast Kills 20" *The Punch* (September 18th, 2014): Page 2.

46. Ibrahim Shaibu. "Explosion Rocks Kano Kills Eight" *This Day* (June 24th, 2014): Page 1.

47. Ibid.

48. "Bombers Attacks Kano Poly, Potiskum Mosque, Kill 16" *The Punch* (July 31st, 2014).

49. Akin Alofetekun. "Female Suicide Bomber Hits Niger School Kills One" *Daily Sun* (November 13th, 2014): Page 14.

50. Mudiaga Affe. "SSS Kills Two Gunmen in Bauchi School Attack" *The Punch* (April 9th, 2012): Page 13.

51. Chris Stein and Dionne Searcey. "21 Chibok School Girls, Reuniting with Parents, Tell of Boko Haram Slavery" *New York Times* (October 16th, 2016).

52. "Ekhomu Lauds President on Chibok Girls' Release" *The Nation* (May 9th, 2017): Page 42.

53. Imoh Umoren. "After the UN Accused the Nigerian Authorities of Paying Ransom to the Blood Thirsty Boko Haram, Nigeria Federal Government Insists No Dime Was Paid" *Nigeria Serve* (August 17th, 2018).

9

Infrastructure Attacks

INTRODUCTION

The Boko Haram insurgency has taken aim at Nigeria's infrastructure – targeting trophy buildings such as the UN Headquarters, Emirs' palaces, District Head palaces, Local Government Secretariat buildings, transportation facilities, entertainment centers, the hospitality industry, telecoms facilities, power stations, etc. It has been an all-out assault against Nigerian infrastructure with a design to take Nigeria back to the Stone Age – reminiscent of Afghanistan under Taliban rule.

The attacks on national infrastructure assets went far beyond the epi-center of the insurgency in the North East. The biggest of these was the suicide bombing of the United Nations building in Abuja (Figures 9.1a and 9.1b), which had reverberations around the world. After that August 2011 attack – only the second suicide bombing attack by Boko Haram – Abubakar Shekau claimed that BH had 100 suicide bombers ready to martyr themselves for the insurgency. At the time, Nigerian security officials found that claim to be unbelievable. However, eight years later (2011–2019), it has proven to be shockingly true. Boko Haram has deployed suicide terrorists at will. The terrorists have resorted to the use of women and girls – some as young as 10 years old – to carry out suicide attacks.

Figure 9.1 (a and b) Still images of the August 26th, 2011 UN car bomb explosion in Abuja.

WHY TARGET INFRASTRUCTURE?

The logical question to ask at this juncture is: why target infrastructure assets? To the warped logic of BH insurgents, causing wanton destruction is both a means and an end. If an attack could result in the deaths of large numbers of people, then it is well worth it. In the Nyanyan Abuja transportation center bombing in April 2014, 75 people were killed, while the First Tarzan bus bombing of March 18th, 2013 in Kano City killed 25.

Let us explore some reasons the insurgents attack infrastructure assets.

a. **Strategic value of assets:** Boko Haram attacks infrastructure assets as a way of crippling the Nigerian economy and its war efforts. An infrastructure attack is a strategic attack as it affects many areas of the economy and society. For example, destroying a telecommunications mast will result in loss of telephone and internet services to customers in the area. In attacking the UN building, the sect got noticed by the international community. BH is not particularly concerned about cultivating a good image. It is interested in killing, maiming and destruction in the name of God.

b. **Anti-Westernization:** The name of the sect, Boko Haram literally means that Westernization is forbidden. It has also been translated to mean Western education is forbidden. By attacking infrastructure assets, the sect is carrying out its mission of rejecting Western values, civilization and artifacts. Infrastructure facilities such as telecoms masts, bridges, hotels, motor parks, palaces are products of Westernization and destroying them might enable the insurgents to achieve victory.

c. **Mass casualty potential:** BH attacks on transportation centers, hotels, football viewing centers and commercial centers were aimed at killing a large number of people – mass casualty and mass fatality events. The Nyanya bombing and several motor park bombings were intended to maximize the kill factor.

d. **Sharia enforcement:** Targeting such facilities as beer gardens, hotels and other entertainment centers was intended to punish the patrons for drinking alcohol, consorting with prostitutes or just having a good time. To BH fighters it is immoral to live a good life. To them the Sharia code is superior to the Nigerian Constitution – metropolitan law – and has to be enforced by the warriors of God.

e. **Communication blackout:** In September 2012, BH insurgents knocked down several telecoms masts in the North East in order to gain a tactical advantage – communications blackout against the military. This infrastructure target was chosen to cripple command and control capability among Nigerian forces which their strategists believed rode on the backbone of GSM telephony.

f. **Poor risk assessments:** Most attacks on infrastructure assets succeed because they are poorly defended. There are generally not enough security risk assessments being carried out to identify infrastructure assets at risk, the type of risk, the level of the risk, and the mitigation measures that would address the risk. Nigeria has always operated as an open country with friendly peace-loving people. However, with the advent of this determined enemy, government and military thinkers have been slow to make a mental adjustment and become proactive. Ten years into this jihad with BH, this knee-jerk reaction mentality still pervades most official thinking. The favored Nigerian phrase is: "By the grace of God, they won't attack us." However, if we are all pleading that same grace, then who gets attacked? The most vulnerable target.

    As a way of cost reduction and profit/income maximization, owner-operators or managers of infrastructure assets are unwilling to make investments in suitable countermeasures that will mitigate the risk of terror attacks. However, after suffering a crippling bombing or active shooter attack, they promptly seek security advice and implement necessary countermeasures. In Chapter 15 of this book, a risk mapping tool is provided that can enable infrastructure asset managers to identify the risks to their assets and develop countermeasures for risk mitigation.

g. **Targets of opportunity:** BH can choose infrastructure assets to attack as they are everywhere, mostly unprotected and represent targets of opportunity. The terrorists would conduct surveillance, obtain ordnance and then attack as the targets are just there, and their vulnerabilities are observable and exploitable. If a petty thief would exploit a target of opportunity, to a determined terrorist such a target of opportunity is a gift from God.

THE UN HOUSE ATTACK

At 11:00 AM on Friday August 26th, 2011, Mohammed Barra rammed the exit gate of the UN House in Abuja. His car smashed into the reception area of the building. He was temporarily dazed by the impact of hitting the wall. He quickly recovered, and then manually detonated the bomb payload in his car. He died instantly, killing 23 others. Over 68 people were injured in the blast – most by glass fragments and projectiles.[1]

The bomb caused significant devastation to the lower floors of the building. One wing of the building collapsed, while the ground floor was badly damaged. The attack on the UN House was the first suicide bombing in Nigeria to target an international organization.

Even though the bomb blast occurred in Abuja, its sound echoed around the world. President Barack Obama called it a horrific and murderous act, while UN Secretary General Ban ki Moon described the bombing as an attack on helpers. Nigeria's President Goodluck Jonathan described the bombing event as barbaric and senseless.

The UN Security Chief Gregory Star disclosed that the UN had a month earlier received "general threats" against Nigeria operations and these were discussed with Nigerian officials.[2] However, nothing was done beyond that. The Deputy Secretary General of the United Nations, Dr. Asha-Rose Migiro, who led an assessment team to Nigeria, said that cleaners, security guards, UN humanitarian partners and an official of the Nigeria Federal Ministry of Health were among the dead. She remarked: "Such attacks will neither deter us in our work, nor win any new sympathies to whatever cause might be the motivation. Hunger and disease and the need to promote human rights does not stop or allow us to pause."[3]

The UN building is located in the Diplomatic Zone in the Central Business District (CBD) off the airport road. It is a four-storey concrete cement block and glass construction. It is located in the vicinity of the US Embassy.

Providing justification for the attack, the spokesman of BH Abu Qaqa said:

> All over the world, the UN is a global partner in the oppression of believers. We are at war against infidels. In Nigeria, the Federal Government tries to perpetuate the agenda of the UN. . . . We have told everyone that the UN is a bastion of the global oppression of Muslims all over the world. As such, we have warned everyone to steer clear of such places that we have mentioned in the past. The battle has changed.[4]

General Muhammadu Buhari who was a Presidential candidate in 2011 and was formerly a Military Head of State of Nigeria expressed doubt about the authorship of the crime:

> It is unprofessional and incompetent for our security agencies to surrender to the omnibus Boko Haram as the only clue to every security challenge. What that means is that even foreign interests can enter Nigeria today and wreak havoc and issue statement in the name of Boko Haram and we will bury our heads and life continues.[5]

In September 2011, the Department of State Services named Mamman Nur as the mastermind of the UN bomb. The intelligence service placed a bounty of N25 million on his head. In January 2018, the Nigerian military announced that Mamman Nur had been fatally injured in a military bombardment in the Lake Chad region. No corroborative evidence has been provided.

In a predictable knee-jerk reaction, in August 2011 President Jonathan promised to rebuild the UN House in Abuja. This promise partly explains the lack of vigor in protecting infrastructure assets from harm. The government appears not to mind rebuilding destroyed assets. However, Nigeria government financial resources are lean. From a security vantage point, it is more prudent to prevent the compromise of the asset in the first place than to allocate resources for rebuilding. President Jonathan did not only volunteer to assist with the reconstruction of the UN House, he also offered to provide temporary accommodation for the UN in Abuja so that the UN may "continue doing the good humanitarian work you have been doing."[6]

TRANSPORTATION CENTERS

The insurgents have repeatedly wreaked havoc at transportation centers – bus parks, motor parks, taxi parks. With land transport as the dominant mode of inter-city and interstate travel, transportation centers usually have large crowds of people traveling to and from a variety of destinations. Let us examine a few of these attacks.

Nyanya I Bombing

On April 14th, 2014, the same day that 276 school girls were seized from Chibok, BH fighters executed a massive bomb attack at the Nyanya Mass

Transit Park in Abuja. The Nyanya park is a transit point for residents of Mararaba, Nasarawa State and satellite communities of the Federal Capital Territory. The park is used by vehicles belonging to the Abuja Mass Transit Company and other inter-city transporters.

The explosion affected 16 high-capacity buses as well as smaller commercial vehicles – some of which had passengers onboard and were ready to depart.[7] Seventy-one people were killed in the blast according to the police authorities.[8]

Other sources placed the death toll at over 200.[9] One survivor of the blast said: "the first bus had about 47 passengers, the second bus about 59 passengers while a Marco Polo bus had 50 passengers at the time of the incident."[10] The discrepancy in body count is understandable as most victims were heavily dismembered by the blast energy or fragmentation. Additionally, the post-blast fire ball which was fueled by petrol in the vehicles burnt many victims beyond recognition.

The VBIED was brought to the crime scene in a red Volkswagen Golf car, parked up and then left. The two bombers separated themselves from their weapon before activation of the bomb which might have been done by remote control.

In an opinion article written after the Nyanya attack, Gen. Muhammadu Buhari (Rtd) counseled the federal government on the need to be proactive and prevent terror plots. He also called for good governance. His words:

> I call on the government to improve and redefine its strategy in the light of this expanding menace. Clearly, its intelligence gathering needs to be improved so that it can break terrorist plots before they hatch. Moreover, it needs to enact social and economic reforms in the blighted areas of the nation to win the hearts and minds of the people. Give the youth a viable alternative and they will not be duped by the lure of extremist dogma.[11]

The Punch newspaper lamented the brutality of the bombing attack and called on the political elite to stop politicizing the war on terror:

> Most of the victims of the Abuja bombing met their untimely death while attempting to take a ride to the city center where their offices are located. These terrorists are displaying a greater appetite for blood, cruelty, adventure, confidence and sophistication. . . .
>
> Despite this increasing demonstration of the destructive capacity of Boko Haram, the government has continued to show a lack of political will to tackle the problem. . . .

Boko Haram is not a political movement but an evil group. It is regrettable that many of our elite have chosen to politicize the war against it.[12]

A post-mortem analysis of the Nyanya bombing by this author concluded that there was a need to provide security awareness programs on IEDs that would enable citizens to identify suspicious objects, suspicious vehicles and suspicious behaviors of bombers. He called on the federal government through the Office of the National Security Advisor (ONSA) to design and implement the National Improvised Explosive Device (IED) Prevention Initiative. The initiative should comprise IED recognition awareness, reporting channels when citizens observe suspicious objects, vehicles or persons, and the establishment of call centers that will receive the calls and direct competent authorities to provide the necessary response.

Top government officials were advised against racing to blast scenes for inspection visits as this hampers the work of first responders and post-blast investigations, and there is the risk of secondary devices which could target VIPs. He advised that blast scenes should be left to police bomb detectives to render safe before executive assessment visits.[13]

Nyanya II Bombing

Two weeks after the Nyanya I bomb which targeted early morning commuters in the transportation center, another bomb explosion claimed 30 lives on May 1st, 2014. The May Day bombing which occurred at 8:45 PM was detonated on the opposite side of the road, a few meters from the scene of the April 14th bombing. The VBIED was detonated by terrorists who had queued to be inspected at a military checkpoint in the Nyanya area, but later disembarked and fled from their car.[14]

Gombe Line Attack

On October 31st, 2014, the busiest motor park in Gombe was targeted. The bombers drove a vehicle into Gombe Line motor park pretending to drop off passengers and then left the bomb-laden vehicle in the park. At 10:00 AM, the vehicle detonated in the midst of a huge crowd. Thirty people were killed and many more injured in the blast.

The transportation center is located in Gombe city center and serves thousands of passengers who transit to Adamawa, Bauchi and Yobe States, and to destinations within the state including Biliri and Kaltungo.

The explosion destroyed several vehicles, shops and nearly buildings. An eyewitness reported: "Come and see corpses, blood and fear everywhere. It was horrible. It was really sad."[15]

Dukku Bus Station, Gombe

In another transportation center attack in Gombe State, the Dukku bus station was hit with an IED attack killing 20 with a further 25 left injured. The device was planted near a parked bus which had passengers onboard. At 10:50 AM on December 22nd, 2014 the device detonated. A woman was said to have brought the device concealed in a bag. The woman left the bag and disappeared among the crowd of travelers before the bomb detonated. An eyewitness said: "Suddenly we heard a loud noise of the blast from one of the vehicles. Then we saw human flesh flying in the air and blood on our bodies."[16]

Other Transport Center Attacks

On February 24th, 2015, 15 people died and 53 others were injured in Potiskum, Yobe State, when a female bomber boarded a bus at the Tashan Dan Borno motor park on Kano Road pretending to be a passenger. The driver of the bus was waiting for more passengers at the park when the bomber detonated the explosives strapped to her at 11:45 AM. The explosion was accompanied by a huge ball of fire.[17]

Five people died and eight were injured when an IED hidden inside a refrigerator detonated at the New Road motor park in Kano on July 24th, 2014. A bomb-laden refrigerator, disguised as luggage was brought into the car park by a cart pusher. While the refrigerator was being loaded onto a stationary vehicle, the device exploded.[18]

Two BH fighters attacked the Borno Express Terminus park in Maiduguri on July 11th, 2015 detonating IEDs, killing two and injuring three others in the early morning bombing.[19]

On February 24th, 2015, three suicide terrorists attacked the Kano Line motor park in Kano. The youthful terrorists aged between 17 and 18 years were carrying backpacks laden with bombs unbeknown to the transport operators. Two of the bombers stood by the side of the Urvan bus which was loading passengers at the time of the explosion. Ten people and the two suicide bombers died. The third suicide terrorist escaped.[20]

MARKET ATTACKS

Another large crowd target that BH frequently attacks is markets. BH has bombed markets, shot up markets and robbed markets to replenish supplies. Let us consider some high-fatality market attacks.

Borno State

On February 16th, 2018, three suicide terrorists attacked Kondugha fish market in Borno State.[21] The 8:30 PM attack cost 18 lives and those of the bombers. Twenty-seven other people were injured in the suicide attacks. The market had a huge crowd of travelers, shoppers and others at the time of the attack which was carried out by two female and one male suicide bombers.

Mai Fadawu market on the outskirts of Maiduguri was hit by two suicide bombers on January 17th, 2018.[22] Twelve people were killed and 48 wounded in the heinous attack. The female bomber attacked inside the market while the male bomber outside the market took his own life.

Sabon Gari weekly market in Maiduguri was also hit on August 11th, 2015 with explosives concealed in a crop-spraying backpack. The device was left in the market and later exploded killing 50 people and injuring 57.[23] The terrorist detonated the device at about 1:15 PM while the market was packed with shoppers and merchants. An eyewitness gave the following description of the blast scene: "The market was littered with all sorts of articles. The mobile phone section was a mess with many dead bodies, pieces of flesh and blood splattered all over."[24]

In another market suicide bombing, two female terrorists attacked the Baga fish market in Maiduguri on June 22nd, 2015. They surreptitiously entered the market and detonated their PBIEDs causing 35 deaths and over 50 injuries. The first bomber struck at 3:40 PM when the Muslims were observing the *Ishai* prayers. The second female bomber was targeting the mosque in the market, but her PBIED prematurely exploded killing her instantly.[25] The Baga fish market is a few meters from the headquarters of 7 Division Nigerian Army located in Maiduguri.

On Tuesday June 2nd, 2015, an intentional bombing occurred at the Maiduguri abbattoir claiming 25 lives. On Wednesday June 3rd, 2015 at 5:14 PM, another bomb exploded at the Baga Road fish market killing 14 people and seriously injuring 19.[26]

Multiple bomb blasts hit the Maiduguri Monday market, Baga Road fish market and Borno Express motor park on March 7th, 2015 killing over 60 people and injuring 38. At the Monday market, a male suicide bomber who was wearing a concealed suicide vest stopped by, exchanged pleasantries with members of the Civilian JTF who were providing security at the market, and then detonated his vest.[27] It was a calculated murder/suicide.

A 10-year-old female suicide bomber hit the Maiduguri poultry market on January 10th, 2015 killing 20 persons and injuring 18.[28]

Maiduguri main market was targeted on November 25th, 2014 by two suicide bombers – male and female. The attack which occurred at 11:28 AM killed 59 people and injured 92. In a coordinated double-tap strike, the female suicide bomber detonated her payload killing a few people near her. However, when a large crowd gathered to gawk at the grotesque remains of the deceased female terrorist, her male counterpart who had mingled with the crowd struck, killing even more people.[29]

On September 19th, 2014, Boko Haram insurgents attacked Mainok market (56 km west of Maiduguri) killing scores of traders and shoppers with automatic gunfire.[30] After the traders had fled to a safe distance, the BH insurgents proceeded to loot foodstuffs for their sustenance. The terrorists initiated the attack on Mainok market by first firing a rocket-propelled grenade (RPG) into the crowd, then raining AK-47 rifle fire into the crowd of people who were fleeing for dear life.

Potiskum Cattle Market Attack

BH insurgents armed with 20 IEDs and assault rifles attacked the Potiskum cattle market killing 60 and injuring 29 according to Abdullahi Bego, the spokesman for Yobe State Governor Ibrahim Geidam. In the May 3rd, 2012 attack, a member of the BH sect caught attempting to steal a cow was killed by the traders in the largest cattle market in West Africa. The insurgents came on a revenge mission. They locked the gate of the market and shot indiscriminately, setting fire to the market, killing people and livestock.[31]

WATER INFRASTRUCTURE

The United Nations Children's Fund in March 2017 announced that BH insurgents have destroyed 75% of the water infrastructure in the North East. UNICEF Director of Emergency Programs Manuel Fontaine said that 3.8 million people in the North East are threatened by lack of water. He said that Boko Haram damaged 75% of the water and sanitation infrastructure.[32]

Table 9.1 Selected Market Attacks

Date	Market	State	Ordnance	Deaths	Injuries
15/6/14	Daku Market	Borno	AL-47,IEDs Petrol Bombs	15	Unknown
25/5/14	Kamuya Market	Borno	AK-47 Petrol Bombs	24	Unreported
2/3/14	Shopping Mall Ajilari Bintu Sugar Maiduguri	Borno	IEDs	Scores	Unreported
4/4/12	Monday Market Maiduguri	Borno	AK47	12	Not Reported
31/2/10	Abacha Barracks Mammy Market Abuja	FCT	IED	13	13
25/6/14	Emab Plaza Abuja	FCT	IED	21	17
4/12/14	Bajoga Market	Gombe	AK-47	Scores	Not Reported
4/2/14	Ngalda Market	Yobe	AK-47 (Ambush)	18	
22/4/12	Bauchi Central Market	Bauchi	IED	26	
16/11/14	Kasuwan Jagal Azare	Bauchi	IED	31	30
4/6/15	Jimeta Modern Market Yola	Adamawa	IED	32	53
19/5/15	Garkida Market	Adamawa	IED	8	14

ATTACKS ON BRIDGES

The insurgents also destroyed some bridges as part of their war against infrastructure facilities. On July 12th, 2014, the Madafuma Bridge linking the Biu–Damboa–Maiduguri federal road in Borno State was blown up using IEDs. The bridge was destroyed at around 2:00 AM.[33]

In another bridge attack in May 2014, BH insurgents destroyed the bridge linking Nigeria with Cameroon killing 30 people in the process.[34] The bombing occurred on the outskirts of Gamboru Ngala, Borno State.

TELECOMMUNICATIONS MASTS

Beginning from September 2012, the insurgents commenced attacks on telecommunications infrastructure. Hamza Idris of the *Daily Trust* newspaper reported on September 7th, 2012 that BH insurgents had claimed responsibility for the attacks on telecommunications facilities in the North East on September 6th. The insurgents accused the telecoms companies of assisting the security agencies in tracking and arresting their members.

In an attack on Shani Town, Shani LGA, Borno State, on November 30th, 2014, the telecoms mast was burnt down. The insurgents numbering about 20 attacked the town on motorcycles at 8:00 PM. Upon the detonation of IEDs, panic ensued as residents fled for cover. The terrorists shot dead many fleeing residents.[35]

In addition, on December 22nd, 2014, BH burnt down the MTN and Airtel telecoms masts in Geidam, Yobe State.

ATTACKS ON HOTELS

The hospitality industry is the backbone of culture, tourism and business travels. The terrorists bomb hotels in the North East as a way of fighting a holy war against "immoral acts" – relaxation, alcohol consumption, prostitution, etc. On May 7th, 2012, People's Hotel, Bayan Gari, Bauchi City was hit with an IED attack. Four people were injured. The hotel is always busy due to patronage by commercial sex workers.[36]

The hotel was hit again on June 27th, 2014. This time the IED attack resulted in 13 deaths and 14 injuries. The attackers, who came on motorcycles, fired several shots at the survivors of the bomb blasts, increasing the death toll. The hotel's patrons were watching the World Cup match highlights when the facility was attacked.[37]

Analyzing attacks on the hospitality industry by Boko Haram, Mr. Dafe Onojo, a columnist for the *National Mirror* newspaper wrote: "Its fatal assaults on beer parlors and other public drinking joints are more of a moral statement of a rather private nature. It is known, of course, that under strict Sharia jurisdictions alcohol consumption is criminalized."[38]

TELEVISION VIEWING CENTERS

These are similar to bars in the USA where large screen televisions broadcast popular programs. Like most Nigerians, Northern youths love soccer and due to the high level of poverty, most homes cannot afford television sets. People congregate at public television viewing centers to watch popular programs such as World Cup soccer matches.

In a ferocious attack on March 1st, 2014, Boko Haram bombed a TV viewing center in Maiduguri killing over 100 people.[39] Two powerful IEDs were detonated at about 6:00 PM at the center. Fans were watching a game of soccer when the initial explosion occurred. When first responders and sympathizers went to the scene to rescue victims, a secondary blast killed more people and injured others. Eyewitnesses said that the secondary device was hidden in two pickup trucks parked in front of the facility.

On April 10th, 2014, BH fighters attacked a packed viewing center in Potiskum, Yobe State, with automatic gunfire, killing two. The center was showing the quarter-final matches of the European Champions League. The aggressors sped off after the attack. Several people were injured in the rifle attack.[40]

In May 2014, three people were killed in Jos, Plateau State, in a bomb blast outside another viewing center showing the European Champions League.[41] Nigerian security agencies have advised citizens in Borno, Adamawa and Yobe States to stay away from viewing centers in order to avoid being killed by insurgents.[42] The police agency has resorted to closing down some viewing centers in the interest of public safety.

GOVERNMENT HOUSE

The BH insurgents have so far recorded only one incursion into Government House. This was the attack on Government House, Damaturu, on December 1st, 2014. The terrorists fought their way into the grounds of Government House prompting the Nigerian Air Force to employ air assets in a counterattack. The President of the Nigerian Senate, David Mark, said he was troubled that the hoodlums had attempted to take control of Yobe Government House.[43]

EMIRS' PALACES

Emirs are revered religious and social leaders in the Muslim North. The BH insurgents have identified the palaces of these leaders as legitimate targets. In August 2014, the palace of the Emir of Gwoza, Borno State, was attacked and burnt down.[44] On February 15th, 2015, the palace of the Emir of Askira in Askira-Uba LGA of Borno State was also burnt down and several people killed.[45]

LG SECRETARIAT

Local government secretariats – which house government operations at the grassroots level – have borne the brunt of insurgent attacks. In January 2015, the insurgents attacked Babban Gida town, the headquarters of Tarmuwa LGA of Yobe State, and burnt the LG Secretariat building and the Governor's Lodge.[46]

On October 18th, 2012, the LG Secretariat in Potiskum, Yobe State, was also burnt down by insurgents when they laid siege to the city.[47]

Geidam in Yobe State, located about 180 km from Damaturu, was hit on December 21st, 2014. The LG Secretariat and the Government Lodge were burnt down[48] along with other targets. Geidam is the hometown of the Governor of Yobe State Alhaji Ibrahim Geidam. Many civilians were killed in this violent take over of the city.

CONCLUSION

This chapter has analyzed Boko Haram's relentless assault on public infrastructure in Northern Nigeria. It appears that the intention has been to return Northern Nigeria to the Stone Age. A telecoms executive captured the implication of the attacks on telecoms assets this way: "This money (i.e. one trillion naira worth of damage to telecoms assets by BH) that ought to go into expanding and optimizing existing infrastructure will now go into replacing damaged facilities."[49]

NOTES

1. John Alechenu and Adelani Adepegba. "We Informed Govt of Threat – UN" *The Punch* (August 29th, 2011): Page 12.
2. Ibid.
3. Dirisu Yakubu. "UN Bombing: Al-Qaeda or Boko Haram?" *Politico Magazine* (September 19th, 2011): Page 14.
4. Ibid: Page 16.
5. Ibid.
6. Chesa Chesa et al. "Nigeria Offers to Reconstruct Bombed UN Building" *Daily Independent* (August 29th, 2011): Page I.
7. Azimazi Momoh et al. "71 Feared Killed, 124 Injured in Abuja Terrorist Bombing" *The Guardian* (April 15th, 2014): Page 1.
8. Ibid.

9. Romanus Ugwu et al. "200 Bombed to Death in Abuja" *Daily Sun* (April 15th, 2018): Page 6.

10. Ibid.

11. Muhammadu Buhari. "Nyanya Bomb Blast and the Fight Against Terrorism" *The Punch* (April 25th, 2014): Page 22.

12. Editorial Page Comment. "Abuja Terror Attack: Need for Fresh Thinking" *The Punch* (April 16th, 2014): Page 20.

13. Ishola Balogun. "Bomb Prevention Initiative Is Long Overdue – Ekhomu" *Saturday Vanguard* (April 26th, 2014): Page 14.

14. See Niyi Odebode et al. "Fresh Abuja Blast Kills 30" *The Punch* (May 2nd, 2014): Page 12. See also Romanus Ugwu et al. "Nyanya Bombed Again" *Daily Sun* (May 2nd, 2014): Page 6; Soni Daniel et al. "May Day Tragedy: Scores Die in Fresh Abuja Bombing" *Vanguard* (May 2nd, 2014): Page 1.

15. Paul Orude. "Bomb Blast Kills Over 30 in Gombe" *Saturday Sun* (November 1st, 2014): Page 5. See also Kayode Idowu. "Boko Haram Kills 30 in Gombe Blast" *The Punch* (November 1st, 2014): Page 9.

16. Vincent Ohonbamu et al. "Boko Haram's Explosion in Gombe Bus Park Kill 20" *The Nation* (December 23rd, 2014): Page 4.

17. "Dozens Killed in Nigerian Bomb Blast" *Al Jazeera* (December 22nd, 2014).

18. "27 Killed in Kano, Potiskum Explosions" *The Punch* (February 25th, 2015).

19. Njadwara Musa. "Suicide Bombers Kill Two, Injure Three at Borno Park" *The Guardian* (July 12th, 2015): Page 5.

20. John Alechenu et al. "Explosion Rocks Kano, US, Canada Flay Kaduna Attacks." *The Punch* (July 25th, 2014): Page 2.

21. Michael Olugbode. "Multiple Suicide Bombings Kill 18 in Borno Market" *Thisday* (February 18th, 2018): Page 1.

22. Njadwara Musa et al. "Suicide Bomb Attack Killer, Wounds 48 in Maiduguri Market" *The Guardian* (January 18th, 2018): Page 3.

23. "Villagers Describe Horror of Borno Market Bombing" *This Day* (August 13th, 2015): Page 10.

24. Ibid.

25. Ndahi Marawa. "Twin Explosions Kill 35 in Maiduguri Market" *Vanguard* (June 23th, 2015): Page 54.

26. Madu Onuorah et al. "Another Maiduguri Blast Kills 14, Injures 19 Others" *The Guardian* (June 4th, 2015): Page 70.

27. Ahmed Miringa et al. "60 Feared Dead in Multiple Borno Blasts" *Sunday Telegraph* (March 8th, 2015): Page 5.

28. Ejikeme Omenazu. "20 killed in Maiduguri Poultry Market Suicide Bombing" *Sunday Independent* (January 11th, 2015): Page 2.

29. Kayode Idowu. "Suicide Bombers Attack Maiduguri Market, Kill 59" *The Punch* (November 26th, 2014): Page 2.

30. Timothy Olanrewaju. "Scores Killed as Hungry Boko Haram Insurgents Attack Borno Market" *Saturday Sun* (September 20th, 2014): Page 7.

146

31. Ibrahim Mshelizza and Mike Oboh. "Gunfire in Nigerian Cattle Market, 60 Killed" **Reuters** (May 3rd, 2012).
32. "Boko Haram Destroys 75% of Water Infrastructure in Northeast Nigeria" **The Punch** (March 29th, 2017). www.punchng.com/boko-haram-destroys-75-of-water-infrastructure-in-northeast-nigeria/
33. Sodiq Oyeleke. "Boko Haram Bombs Bridge in Borno" **The Punch** (July 14th, 2014): Page 26.
34. Kayode Idowu. "30 Killed as B'Haram Bombs Nigeria–Cameroon Bridge" **The Punch** (May 9th, 2014): Page 13.
35. Timothy Olanrewaju. "Again, Boko Haram Attacks Borno Town" **Daily Sun** (December 1st, 2014): Page 14.
36. Jude Owuamanam. "Four Injured in Bauchi Explosion" **The Punch** (May 9th, 2012): Page 9.
37. Paul Orude. "Bauchi Bombed: 13 Killed, 34 Injured in Blast, Shootings in Hotel" **Sunday Sun** (June 29th, 2014): Page 4.
38. Dafe Onojovhwo. "Bombing Out Beer Parlors" **National Mirror** (July 1st, 2011): Page 56.
39. Ndahi Marama. "Boko Haram Bombs Maiduguri: Over 100 Feared Dead" **Sunday Vanguard** (March 2nd, 2014): Page 1.
40. "Gunmen Kill Two Watching Champions League in Yobe" **This Day** (April 11th, 2014): Page 9.
41. "Averting Tragedies at Football Viewing Centres" **Saturday Sun** (June 21st, 2014).
42. Ibid.
43. Bridget Onochie et al. "Government Imposes 24-Hour Curfew on Damaturu Over Security" **The Guardian** (December 3rd, 2014): Page 5.
44. Njadwara Musa. "Suspected Boko Haram Insurgents Capture More Borno, Yobe Towns" **The Guardian** (August 11th, 2014): Page 9.
45. Mustapha Isa. "Boko Haram Razes Borno Emir's Place, Kills Residents" **Peoples Daily** (February 18th, 2015).
46. "Boko Haram Fighters Battle Nigeria Troops in Yobe Town" **Daily Sun** (January 4th, 2015).
47. "Scores Die, Schools LG HQs Burnt in Maiduguri Potiskum Terror Attacks" **The Punch** (October 20th, 2012): Page 8.
48. Duku Joel. "Boko Haram: Explosions in Gombe Bus Park Kill 20" **The Nation** (December 23rd, 2014).
49. Prince Osuagwu. "Terrorism: The New Frontier for Telecoms Sector" **Vanguard** (September 12th, 2012).

10

Divine Targets

INTRODUCTION

Boko Haram's insurgency has taken aim at churches and mosques in a vigorous manner and with delight. The fatalities are high, and the attacks have provoked strong emotions. Nigerian Christian leaders argue that Boko Haram chooses only Christians for massacre. However, the insurgents have killed thousands of Muslim faithfuls. The Kano Central Mosque bombing of November 2014 killed over 200 people, while the Kodugha Mosque attack in August 2013 killed over 50.

In an advertorial in December 2011, the Pentecostal Fellowship of Nigeria decried the onslaught of BH against the church.[1] It asserted that BH insurgents and their apologists "continue to wage war against Christians in furtherance of their Islamisation agenda." The advertorial concluded:

> We believe that when Muslim clerics, political leaders and leaders of thought from Northern Nigeria publicly condemn and denounce the activities of Boko Haram it will go a long way to quelling this threat to our future peaceful coexistence. If these unprovoked attacks continue and Christians remain unprotected by the security agencies, then we will have no choice but to defend our lives and property.[2]

The Maiduguri Catholic Archbishop added:

> We told the Christians to be prayerful but physically defend themselves if need be, while praying for those persecuting them. What it means is

that they should not just wait and watch somebody coming to kill them because they are Christians. They must physically and spiritually defend themselves, but if in the course of such defence, they were killed, then they would die as religious martyrs.[3]

The Chairman of the Northern States Christian Elders' Forum Olaiya Phillips said that Boko Haram had declared war on Christians:

The most vicious attacks have been reserved for our Christian brothers and sisters, precisely because Boko Haram has declared war on our (Christian) community. That said it should be remembered that both Christians and Muslims have suffered at the hand of Boko Haram, and only when both Christians and Muslims join hands to resist the public menace that Boko Haram represents will their mutual suffering end.[4]

The attacks on places of worship, particularly churches have threatened the fault lines of Nigeria. The country has a religious divide (Christian/Muslim) and a geographical divide (North/South). There are constant tensions along those dichotomies. Boko Haram, an extremist Islamist group attacking and killing Christians at will, assumes a religious coloration. This author describes BH as an "Equal Opportunity Killer." They kill Christians, Muslims, Pagans – all. If you do not belong to their Sunni Salafi sect, then you are fair game.

THE MIND OF BOKO HARAM

It is hard to comprehend how individuals could strap explosives onto their bodies, go into places of worship and then detonate the explosives to kill worshippers. To understand the extremely warped and sick mind of the Boko Haram fighter, we must understand the philosophy of Boko Haramism.

The stated mission of BH is jihad. Shekau has demanded that strict Sharia code be put in effect throughout Nigeria. Under Mohammed Yusuf, the mission of Boko Haram was to institute strict Sharia code in Borno State.

In January 2012, Shekau issued a quit order to all Southerners/Christians in the North to leave or be killed.[5] The problem with that order is that there are millions of Northern Christians who would then have no homes. Yobe, Borno and Adamawa States all have indigenous Christian populations. So, when Shekau says all Christians should move away from the North, is he also referring to Northern Christians?

Boko Haramism is an ideology without a knowledge foundation. Yusuf had a destination for jihad, but Shekau did not. BH is lacking in deep thought and cerebral underpinning. It is a philosophy/ideology which is based upon the one pound of finger pressure logic – to pull an AK-47 rifle trigger or to activate a bomb. It is ideology without intellection.

The spokesman for the Governor of Borno State, Malam Isa Gusau, tried to explain Boko Haramism in an interview on Channels Television on March 31st, 2018.[6] Boko Haram believes that in a holy war all infidels (that is Christians, non-Muslims, traditionalists, Pagans, atheists, etc.) should die or be killed by the warriors of Allah. Muslims who are not Sunni Salafists are not true Muslims and deserve to die.

A Boko Haramist who dies in a bombing attack or in a firefight will be fast-tracked to heaven. Martyrdom is the highest form of transition to heaven. Dying in a holy war is preferable as heaven (*Al jannah*) is assured. Martyrdom by suicide is considered the will of Almighty Allah and is therefore justifiable and acceptable.

This fatalistic, nihilistic, militaristic mindset which exhibits a "loss–loss" suicidal stroke is what is driving the murderous attacks on places of worship. The insurgents cannot be said to be rational and moralistic. In fact, this author has often described Shekau as a lunatic because of the indiscriminate choice of targets – especially places of worship.

So, what type of human being will follow such demented suicidal logic? Thousands of young and vulnerable Nigerians who have been seduced and radicalized by the daring escapades of Boko Haram. In the Muslim North, Mohammed Yusuf recruited from the *almajiris*. In a June 2018 interview with Voice of America (VOA), the mother of Imam Abubakar Shekau, Mrs. Falmata Abubakar, said that her son was an *almajiri* who had left Shekau village as a boy to continue his Islamic education in Maiduguri. That is where he met Mohammed Yusuf who brainwashed him that Western education is sinful.

There are millions of Out of School Children (OSC) who, for the most part, do not know their parents and follow a teacher who sends them out to beg for a living on a daily basis. *Almajiris* who were 12 years old when Yusuf took over leadership of *Jama'atu Ahlus-Sunnah Lidda'Awati Wal Jihad* in 2002, were then youths (19 years old) when Yusuf was later murdered in 2009. By April 2010, when Shekau took over Boko Haram, that same cohort of *almajiris* would have turned 20. These

151

are the warriors of God that believe all that Imam Abubakar Shekau is telling them, and are doing his bidding. Every year, the ranks of the insurgents swell as Shekau's exploits make him a role model for youths.

A public commentator and psychologist, Law Mefor, wrote.

> Conventionally, the world over, would-be terrorists are typically the Almajiri kind of people, for the simple fact that they are impressionistic and pliable and can be bent to any cause, especially religious terrorism. . . .
>
> Even the aim of Boko Haram to Islamise 12 states in the North is still a fulfillment of this assumption that they are pushing to carve out an enclave to impose their own way of life. This makes Boko Haram insurgency a very dangerous religious, political and economic terrorism all rolled in one.[7]

The real danger of religious extremism in Nigeria is that it is capable of destroying the nation. This author has been providing a narrative that, statistically, BH has killed more Muslims than Christians and attacked more mosques than churches – contrary to the popular misconception of the opposite. This difference relates to the reporting of such incidents. Due to beliefs and sensibilities, Christians repeat stories of attacks or casualities in churches. BH attacks on Christians have also made more headlines. So, churches provide the terrorists with larger targets for attacks which will make bigger news headlines.

WHY CHURCHES?

Why does Boko Haram attack churches?

1. **Churches are agents of Westernization:** Boko Haram by its name abhors anything Western. Churches are a key element of Westernization. Churches have proven to be a good mechanism for promoting Western culture. Therefore, attacking churches will root out this key ingredient of Western civilization.
2. **Holy war:** Boko Haram is fighting a holy war, or a war for God. The major protagonists in Nigeria are Christians versus Muslims. Attacking a church or killing a Christian is therefore thought to be divinely ordained.
3. **Vulnerable targets:** Churches are ubiquitous but vulnerable. The open, welcoming, friendly atmosphere facilitated suicide

bombings. After St. Theresa's Catholic Church in Madalla, Niger State, was hit along with a number of churches in Jos, Plateau State, Kaduna, Maiduguri, Kano, etc., there was a learning curve. Countermeasures like stand-off distance between vehicles and church buildings, concrete bollards, dedicated church security personnel, magnetometer devices for weapons searches, predictive profiling of visitors to churches, restriction of packages in churches, and undercarriage search mirrors all became standard procedures.

The Easter Day bomber in Kaduna 2012 was on a suicide mission – a journey of no return. He tried to gain entrance into the First ECWA Goodnews Church on Gwari Road, but he was denied access. The plan was to ram the church building and detonate the explosives. He drove off in frustration and detonated his payload near a group of Okada riders (mostly Hausa Muslims). The bomb crater measured 60.96 cm (2 feet) by 152.4 cm (5 feet) radius. In the wake of the bomb attack, this author wrote: "The Easter bomb blast proved that security enforcement in places of worship was effective and useful. It achieved the physical security goal of denying the suicide agents the opportunity to detonate the explosive payload."[8]

4. **Crowd crowd crowd:** Churches present a delightful target to BH insurgents because of the crowd factor. Churches operate as big businesses in Nigeria using good marketing techniques, evangelical outreach programs, practical Christianity such as free medical clinics, free food programs and free apparel to attract people. When people congregate, a crowd forms. BH, in a bid to maximize the kill factor, needs a crowd. This author wrote the following about the Easter Day 2012 bomb in Kaduna: "The bombing incident also showed that any crowd was potentially a target of Boko Haram bombers. The Okada riders were fair game because they formed a crowd and the suicide bomber found it too tempting to resist."[9]

5. **Ubiquity of churches:** Churches are everywhere to make them easily accessible to members. However, evil people like Boko Haram bombers will also find it easy to attack nearby churches. In one church attack in Kondugha, the terrorists surrounded the church and poured automatic gunfire into the building. Fifty-two people lost their lives in the attack.

153

SELECTED MOSQUE ATTACKS

The Boko Haram insurgents have attacked a large of number of mosques in their campaign of violence. Let us examine a few.

Kano Central Mosque

This attack occurred on Friday November 28th, 2014 while Muslim faithfuls were observing the *Jummat* prayers. The Kano Central Mosque has a capacity of 10,000 people. The mosque is an iconic edifice built about 500 years ago. It is a trophy building in the ancient city of Kano, and is located close to the Palace of the Emir.

A suicide bomber forced his way into a row of worshippers and detonated an IED.[10] After the blast, two gunmen who coordinated their attacks with the suicide bomber opened fire on the worshippers raising the overall death toll dramatically to over 200. Three bombing attacks occurred at the mosque.

> The first went off when one of the suicide bombers sped past worshippers recklessly in a Toyota Space Wagon vehicle, attracting attention.
> The second one exploded at a different location near a line of worshippers while the third one exploded right inside the mosque.[11]

The third device was the most deadly. An eyewitness reported: "Apart from the pieces of human bodies on the floor of the mosque . . . human flesh was glued to the high rising frames of mosque."[12]

The Emir of Kano, HRH Alhaji Sanusi Lamido Sanusi, advocated self-defense against the terrorists citing portions in the Holy Koran to remind Muslims that "whoever dies while defending his territory, protecting his property and children is considered a martyr."[13]

In an editorial on the Kano Central Mosque bomb attack, *The Nation* newspaper wrote: "In the course of their murderous activities, nothing is seen as sacrosanct! Schools, hospitals, churches and mosques are simply fair game in their warped vision to create their Islamic enclave."[14]

While calling for all-source intelligence to help defeat the BH insurgency, *The Nation*[15] wondered how the Emir of Kano knew that the Kano Central Mosque attack had been planned in two months. How had the Emir come by this information and what use had he made of this information? Did the traditional ruler inform security agencies when he got the information? The newspaper said that these interrogatories were critical to harnessing useful intelligence in the fight against insurgency.[16]

Reacting to the Kano Central Mosque attack, the Sultan of Sokoto Alh. Mohammed Abubakar Saad III said that the Boko Haram insurgents are not Muslims.[17]

Adamawa State

On Tuesday May 1st, 2018, a deadly bomb blast destroyed 50 lives during the morning prayers at the Modina mosque in the Ungwar Shuwa area of Mubi. The suicide bomber mingled with worshippers and detonated a PBIED while the prayers were going on. Emergency officials described the blast as "devastating."[18]

In a 2015 mosque attack in Yola, Adamawa State, 27 people were killed when a young suicide bomber detonated his PBIED while in a crowd of people. This deadly bomb attack occurred on a day when the new mosque located near the old Hajj camp in Jambutu, Yola, was being commissioned.[19] Yusuf Osama of the first aid group of *Jama'atul Bid'a Wa Ikhanatus Sunnah* said:

> It was a gory scenario. Many people were killed in the blast and we are busy evacuating dead bodies and injured victims to the hospital. The suicide bomber wanted to get access to the main bowl of the mosque so that he will cause massive havoc but before he reached the building, the bomb detonated. The decapitated head of the suicide bomber was lying among the mangled bodies of the victims.[20]

Yobe State

The Emir of Fika, HRH Alhaji Mohammed Ibn Abali Idris, was attacked by a suicide bomber at the Potiskum Central Mosque on Friday August 3rd, 2012.[21] The bomber was pushed down by a policeman as he tried to get close to the Emir. A PBIED exploded killing the bomber and injuring five policemen and two civilians. The Emir escaped unhurt. Police EOD personnel later defused the second unexploded bomb still strapped to the body of the dead suicide bomber.

In another mosque attack in Potiskum, 13 people were killed when insurgents threw IEDs at the Shakafa mosque on July 29th, 2014.[22] A worshipper who survived the bombing said: "Immediately after our Imam completed the reading of the Holy Koran, we were about to continue with our prayers, when we suddenly heard a blast that shook the entire building."[23]

Borno State

Deadly mosque attacks have been quite frequent in Borno State. On July 13th, 2012, a suicide terrorist detonated a bomb at the Maiduguri Central Mosque located in front of the palace of the Shehu of Borno. The blast killed five people but the Shehu, HRH Alhaji Abubakar Garbai, and the Deputy Governor of Borno State, Alh. Zanna Mustapha, both narrowly escaped with injuries.[24]

Six people, including the soldier who saved the lives of the VIPs by intercepting the suicide bomber, were also injured. The blast occurred after the *Jummat* prayers.[25] The Deputy Governor of Borno State, Alhaji Zanna Mustapha, described the bomber as a 15-year-old male.[26]

On June 17th, 2017, the apocalyptic insurgents attacked a mosque in the Jiddari Polo area of Maiduguri. Invading the area, the insurgents sporadically fired anti-aircraft (AA) guns. The intense firing from the terrorists set several surrounding buildings on fire. The military repelled the insurgents' attack. Thirteen people died.[27]

About 200 BH terrorists surrounded a mosque in Kondugha, Borno State, on Sunday August 11th, 2013 and opened fire indiscriminately. Forty-three people died in this horrific attack.[28] The terrorists attacked the villages of Kireno, Nuru and Naforu in Marte LGA of Borno State on May 23rd, 2014 leaving behind a trail of death. The terrorists brought automatic weapons, IEDs and petrol bombs to their assault on Kireno. They set the local mosque on fire and killed 31 villagers.[29]

On May 30th, 2015, 16 people were killed when a bomb detonated inside a mosque near the Maiduguri market.[30] An insurgent mingled with worshippers pretending to be praying. He later detonated his deadly pay-load injuring, maiming and killing all those around him in the mosque.

Monguno and Kukawa Local Government Areas also came under insurgent attack in July 2015. The insurgents attacked Muslim worship-pers in mosques in Kukawa town as they were observing the *magrib* prayers. They shot the worshippers to death right inside the mosque. The total death toll in the attacks on Monguno LGA and Kukawa LGA was 145.[31]

A mosque in Damboa was attacked by a lone wolf bomber in July 2016. The aggressor mixed with worshippers and then detonated his bomb killing six worshippers and himself. A second bomber tried to pen-etrate Damboa Central Mosque but was deterred by the stringent security checks in place.[32] This again proves that situational crime prevention measures can mitigate the threat of IED attacks.

In another suicide terrorism attack, two female suicide bombers attacked the Juddumuri Mosque of Polo General Area in Maiduguri on April 6th, 2017. The blast killed the two terrorists and injured five people.[33] The two girls aged 10 and 13 were dropped off in a Volkswagen Golf car at 5:10 AM and then walked to the mosque.[34] As they approached the place of worship, alert worshippers who observed them alight from the vehicle predictively profiled them as suicide bombers. They raised an alarm and the young girls detonated their suicide bombs prematurely, hence the low casualty figure.

A vigilante at a Maiduguri mosque gave his life in the line of duty as he interdicted a male suicide bomber trying to attack a mosque in Dalori Quarters in Maiduguri.[35] The Civilian JTF man succeeded in preventing the bomber from accessing the mosque, but the determined terrorist detonated the device killing himself and the vigilante.

CHURCH ATTACKS

The Boko Haram insurgency is religion based. It demands the institution of Sharia in the Muslim North and the expulsion of all Christians from Northern Nigeria. Ironically, Northern Nigeria has millions of indigenous Christian populations while Southern Nigeria has millions of indigenous Muslims.

While we have recorded a number of horrific terrorist attacks against mosques and Muslims' praying grounds, Boko Haram unleashed its full ferocity in attacks on churches. The good news is that church organizations have recognized the threat and taken steps to mitigate them. Since 2015, the number of successful attacks against churches has diminished. This is mainly due to increased security awareness on the part of church clerics and parishioners, risk reduction countermeasures that have been strictly observed and, most importantly, the overall reduction of the Boko Haram threat which commenced with the General Kenneth Minimah's spring offensive in 2015 shortly before the 2015 general elections and was perfected by General Tukur Buratai's Operation Zaman Lafiya and later Operation Lafiya Dole which took the fight to BH, and forced them to transform back into a guerrilla threat rather than an invading "army."

In June 2014, the Pentecostal Fellowship of Nigeria announced that the group "had lost over 700 churches in the North since the terrorist activities started."[36] The Maiduguri Diocese of the Catholic Church announced that 54 Catholic churches were burnt down by Boko Haram between 2009 and April 2014.[37] Going beyond the statistics, let us now examine a few spectacular attacks.

St. Theresa's Catholic Church Attack

Christmas Day 2011 turned tragic for parishioners of St. Theresa's Catholic Church in Madalla near Suleja, Niger State. A massive VBIED attack killed 34 people and injured 62.[38] The bombing occurred after morning mass as parishioners were exiting the church sanctuary into the church compound. The *Daily Sun* newspaper described the bombing as "one of the most gruesome attacks yet by the fundamentalist sect."[39] Nigeria's Minister of Health, Prof. Onyebuchi Chukwu announced that the federal government had set up a psychological support and grief counseling committee for survivors of the attack and relatives of the deceased.[40]

The St. Theresa's bomb was a wake-up call to all churches in Nigeria about the dangers of a VBIED. Prior to the Christmas Day bomb, there had been two VBIED attacks in Nigeria – the FHQ bomb in June 2011 and the UN House bomb in August 2011. Although there had been attacks on churches in the North East using AK-47 rifles or throwing IEDs, the VBIED threat against a church in Nigeria was unprecedented. So, with the St. Theresa's bomb everyone took notice. The large carnage was due to the huge explosive payload that only VBIEDs can deliver.

The learning curve was sharp. Many churches installed concrete bollards, ramped up their security programs, hired security guards, introduced new access control procedures, purchased vehicle undercarriage search mirrors and purchased and deployed magnetometer device for weapons searches. It was a knee-jerk reaction. Suddenly, churches realized that they were under attack and they worked hard at risk mitigation. This author gave several press interviews, lectures and consultancy intervention all aimed at target-hardening churches against criminal explosions. The worshippers killed and injured at St. Theresa's on Christmas Day 2011 paid the price for Nigerian Christians to learn how to survive the BH insurgency threat to churches.

COCIN Church Bombing

By repeatedly attacking the headquarters of the Church of Christ in Nigeria (COCIN) Jos, Plateau State, Boko Haram fighters were indirectly attacking then Governor David Jonah Jang who worshipped at that church. At 7:15 AM on Sunday February 28th, 2012, a suicide VBIED hit the church. Five people including two suicide bombers died in the attack. Three commercial motorcycle riders were lynched by a mob of angry youths near the Hill Station junction on suspicion of being Boko Haram fighters.[41]

The terrorists struck again two Sundays later on March 11th, 2012 at the same COCIN church. In this attack, nine people were killed. The St. Finbarr's Catholic Church, Jos, was hit by two suicide bombers on the same day. The Deputy Governor of Plateau State was a parishioner at the St. Finbarr's Church.[42] Two suicide terrorists were killed in the St. Finbarr's attack.

Deeper Life Bible Church, Okene

March 6th, 2012, some members of this church were holding a prayer session inside the sanctuary in Okene, Kogi State, when BH fighters surrounded the building and opened prolonged gunfire. Twenty worshippers laid dead after the attack. Acting on a tip, police personnel in Kogi and Delta States raided their hideout and engaged the terrorists in a heated gun battle. The police overpowered the terrorists, arresting a woman, seizing some arms and ammunitions and later capturing the leader of the cell, Yekini Isah, in Ibillo, Edo State, where he had gone for treatment for gunshot injuries he had sustained in the fire-fight with police.[43]

Commenting on the Deeper Life Bible Church, Okene, attack, then President of the Christian Association of Nigeria, Pastor Ayo Oritsejafor said:

> The enemies of Christians and Christianity in Nigeria have changed tactics from their Sunday attacks on to everyday onslaught. I urge the leadership of the various churches in Nigeria to step up security around their churches as they hold their daily devotions, crusades and vigils while also being security conscious at all times.[44]

RCCG Potiskum

On Sunday July 5th, 2015, a suicide bomber attacked the City of David Parish of the Redeemed Christian Church of God (RCCG) in Potiskum, Yobe State, detonating a PBIED. The aggressor entered the church and headed for the altar where he was intercepted by the pastor of the church and some church members. He manually activated the device killing himself, Pastor Dotun Okerinola and four others. Eyewitnesses credited the low death toll to the fact that worshippers were just arriving for service when the bomber struck.[45]

Reacting to the RCCG Potiskum attack, President Muhammadu Buhari "wholly condemns the resumption of attacks by terrorists on places of worship, which are highly revered places of prayer and communion with God for most Nigerians."[46]

St. Rita's Catholic Church, Kaduna

A suicide car bomber rammed the fence of this church in Malali during Sunday morning mass October 28th, 2012, but was unable to get to the church building as the Virgin Mary shrine stood in the way of the bomb-laden Mercedes Benz SUV. The impact actuated the bomb and about 1,000 people inside the church were spared. Eight people were killed by fragments from the blast. Church security personnel had denied the bomber entrance into the compound. However, he had reversed his vehicle and charged forward, determined to complete the mission. The okada driver who brought the bomber to the church was lynched by irate Christian youths. Military and law enforcement's quick intervention prevented the incident from becoming another Christian versus Muslim confrontation.

Churches in Borno State

Churches in Borno State have been hit hard by BH insurgency. In the heyday of church attacks, the acts of violence were quite frequent and brutal. On June 29th, 2014, terrorists attacked churches near Chibok during service. They shot and killed many worshippers in Kautikiri, Nguragili and Kwali villages. The churches attacked included: Church of Brethren Nigeria (EYN), Deeper Life Bible Church and Church of Christ in Nigeria (COCIN).[47] Some sources estimated that 48 people were killed in these multiple terrorist attacks.[48] The churches were razed by the terrorists.

In a June 2nd, 2014 terror incident, BH insurgents attacked a church in Attagara, Gwoza LGA, and killed nine worshippers. The terrorists arrived the EYN church at about 9:30 AM and immediately opened fire. The villagers organized themselves and delivered violence on the Boko Haram terrorists killing 37 of their members.[49]

Two churches in the Hrazah and Hembe communities came under attack on Thursday May 30th, 2013 at 7:45 PM. The terrorists torched the two churches killing three people.[50] In Uba/Askira LGA, BH fighters invaded Dille village and set three churches ablaze including the Church of Brethren in Nigeria (EYN) in July 2014.[51]

Other Church Attacks

Boko Haram fighters armed with automatic weapons and explosives killed 22 people in an attack on a Catholic church during service in Waga Chakawa, Adamawa State, on January 26th, 2014.[52] The EYN church in Jilang village in Mahia LGA, Adamawa State, was attacked on May 5th, 2013 killing ten people and injuring 12.[53] Boko Haram gunmen attacked the church at about 11:00 AM during service. Entering the church, they opened fire on the congregation as the pastor was preaching at the pulpit. Eyewitnesses said that the killers who came in two Toyota Hilux pickups were not challenged by anyone. After carrying out the killings, they drove away.[54]

St. Charles Catholic Church in Nomansland, Sabon Gari, Kano was also attacked with an IED on July 27th, 2014. Five people were killed and eight injured.[55]

In coordinated attacks BH insurgents deployed IEDs on June 17th, 2012, at two churches in Zaria and one in Kaduna killing 20 people and injuring 90 others. ECWA Church in Wusasa, Zaria; Christ the King Catholic Church Cathedral in Zaria and Shalom Church in Trikania, Kaduna were all bombed. In addition, the attacks also triggered reprisals by Christian youths against Muslims resulting in 68 deaths. These bombings brought Nigeria even closer to religious war.[56]

CONCLUSION

This chapter has examined the dynamics and cases of attacks on places of worship. As a deeply religious people, matters of faith are treated with great sensibilities in order not to insult. However, the BH insurgency has tried its best to exploit the religious card by building disaffection on a national scale and eventually creating a spark that could lead to an outbreak of religious war in the country.

We cannot conclude this discourse on attacks on places of worship without examining the effects on churches, as they initially bore the brunt of BH attacks.

1. There was a huge cost in human lives that prompted a mass exodus of Southerners to their home states. Northern Christians merely avoided church services or strengthened their defenses in order to ward off BH attacks.
2. Many Church buildings were torched. This was a morale dampener.
3. In places like Madagali LGA in northern Adamawa State and southern parts of Borno State, BH converted churches into mosques.[57] The residences of priests were shared out to BH commanders. The auditoriums in cathedrals were turned into sleeping areas for BH foot soldiers. This report was issued in August 2014 when the insurgents controlled over 30 local governments in Borno and Adamawa States. It should be mentioned that the desecration of church properties must have hurt the feelings of Christians throughout Nigeria. It was such a vile and vicious affront to have a mentally deranged man like Abubakar Shekau dictate what would be done with church property. However, that is the nature of war.
4. Reprisals occurred in some instances in relation to attacks on churches. Plateau State was a good example of where repeated attacks on churches sometimes sparked the killing of Muslims. In June 2012, the bombing of three churches in Zaria and Kaduna sparked reprisals against Muslims. The National Security Advisor, Gen. Owoye Azazi (Rtd.) condemned the reprisals as "criminal."[58] "In certain parts of the country today and I will give an example like Kano, they are more proactive. So you find that you are able to arrest the situation before it gets to this level."[59]
5. The abattoir effect. Given the regularity of Sunday attacks on churches which usually produce mass casualities, a writer cautioned that Nigeria should not be turned into an abattoir by the Boko Haram insurgency.[60]

Protecting Places of Worship

The Boko Haram insurgency is not over. In May 2018, there was the massive bomb blast in a mosque in Mubi which killed at least 50 Muslim worshippers. The threat of Boko Haram has mutated from an insurgency in control of territory to hit and run guerrilla tactics. Either way the threat remains.

Hot Tips

- Security awareness training for clerics, volunteer staffers and parishioners.
- Conduct background checks for all paid staffers. This is a risk mitigation strategy. "Insurgent" is not inscribed on the forehead of anyone, but through background investigation, you can make a risk mitigation decision.
- Implement a search policy with magnetometer devices on worship days and other days. You don't want a device to be emplaced and later detonated when the house of worship is filled with worshippers.
- Deploy a CCTV surveillance system.
- Enforce a stand-off distance between the church auditorium and a VBIED threat. You could use concrete or mechanical bollards or simply parking enforcements.
- Train the wardens to recognize signs of threat. And have clear procedures on actions to take.
- Let all parishioners be their brothers' and sisters' keepers. Look out for one another.
- Establish protocol for dealing with suspicious packages.
- Develop an emergency plan for all places of worship – including emergency preparedness.
- Always prepare for a fire threat and how to safely evacuate your building population.
- Remember the four Ds of security – Deter, Detect, Delay, Deny.
    - **Deter:** Place armed police personnel on patrol to deter the terrorists. If you are in the North East, get military or Civilian JTF to cover your place of worship for the period of time the worship is in session.
    - **Detect:** Ensure through K-9 dogs, security guards or alert parishioners that you are able to detect a threat and respond to it.
    - **Delay:** If you detect a threat, you must ensure that response forces can get there and engage the threat before they can cause harm or escape.
    - **Deny:** You must have the capability to obstruct an attack on places of worship. For the case of BH insurgency, a house of worship must carefully design its plan to deny the terrorists success in the event of a terror plot.
- If you see something suspicious, do say something.Finally, do your best and leave the rest to God.

NOTES

1. Advertorial by Pentecostal Fellowship of Nigeria. "Boko Haram and Its Onslaught Against the Church" *Vanguard* (December 28th, 2011): Page 41.
2. Ibid.
3. "Boko Haram Attacks. Christians Must Defend Themselves – Maiduguri Catholic Archbishop" *Saturday Sun* (May 19th, 2012): Pages 13–14.
4. Allwell Okpi. "B'Haram Declared War on Christians – NOSCEF" *The Punch* (January 26th, 2014): Page 12.
5. "Is Nigeria on the Brink After North-South Clashes?" *BBC News* (January 13th, 2012). www.bbc.com/news/world-africa-16544410
6. Malam Isa Gusau. Television Interview. *Sunrise Daily* Program. Topic: Amnesty for Boko Haram *Channels Television* (March 31st, 2018).
7. Law Mefor. "Nyanya Tragedy and Surviving Asymmetry Terrorist War (I)" *The Punch* (April 16th, 2014): Page 24.
8. Simon Utebor. "States Should Install CCTV – Expert" *The Punch* (April 10th, 2012): Page 8.
9. Ibid.
10. Murtala Muhammed and Abba Anwar. "Bomb Blast in Kano Central Mosque" *The Guardian* (November 29th, 2014): Page 1.
11. Ibid.
12. Ibid.
13. Ibid.
14. "Kano Bomb Blasts" *The Nation* (December 5th, 2014): Page 19.
15. Ibid.
16. Ibid.
17. Adeola Yusuf. "Kano Mosque's Attack: Boko Harams Are Non-Muslims, Sultan Insists" *New Telegraph* (December 5th, 2014): Page 36.
18. "At Least 50 Dead in Adamawa Mosque Bombing" *The Guardian* (May 1st, 2018).
19. "27 Dead, 96 Injured in Yola Mosque Bomb Attack – NEMA" *Premium Times* (October 23rd, 2015).
20. Ibid.
21. David Attah. "Another Emir Escapes Mosque Suicide Bombing" *Saturday Punch* (August 4th, 2012): Page 7.
22. "Bombers Attack Kano Poly, Potiskum Mosque, Kill 16" *The Punch* (July 31st, 2014).
23. Ibid.
24. "Emir Escapes Death as Suicide Bomber Kills Five in Maiduguri Mosque Bombing" *Premium Times* (July 13th, 2012).
25. Ibid.
26. Ibrahim Msheliza. "Suicide Bomber Kills 5 at North East Nigerian Mosque" *Reuters News Agency* (July 14th, 2012).

27. "13 Dead as Boko Haram Terrorists Attack Mosque, Others in Borno – Police Confirm" *Vanguard* (June 8th, 2012).
28. Chuks Okocha et al. "Borno Attacks: Survivors Recount Ordeal as Police Launch Investigation" *This Day* (August 14th, 2013): Page 1.
29. Njadwara Musa. "Gunmen Kill 31 Villagers in Fresh Borno Attack" *The Guardian* (May 24th, 2014).
30. Fidelis Soriwei et al. "Boko Haram Kills 16 in Fresh Attacks on Maiduguri" *The Punch* (May 31st, 2015): Page 5.
31. Kayode Idowu. "B'Haram Kills 145 in Borno Mosque, Village" *The Punch* (July 3rd, 2015): Page 3.
32. Kingsley Omonubi. "Suicide Bombers Hit Mosque, 6 Killed" *Saturday Vanguard* (July 9th, 2016): Page 8.
33. Njadwara Musa. "Two Female Suicide Bombers Killed in Maiduguri Mosque Attack" *The Guardian* (April 9th, 2017): Page 4.
34. Ibid.
35. Olawale Ajimotokan et al. "Suicide Bombers Kill Vigilante at Maiduguri Mosque" *This Day* (February 1st, 2017): Page 46.
36. Chris Irekamba. "We've Lost Over 700 Churches to Insurgency, Says PFN" *The Guardian* (June 16th, 2014): Page 8.
37. Timothy Olanrewaju. "Boko Haram: 523 Christians Killed, 54 Churches Burnt, 90,000 Displace in N'East Since 2009" *Daily Sun* (May 16th, 2014): Page 10.
38. "34 Died, 62 Wounded in Madalla Bombing – Health Minister" *The Punch* (December 29th, 2011): Page 14.
39. Editorial Page Comment. "Stop the Killings" *Daily Sun* (January 13th, 2012): Page 18.
40. "34 Died, 62 Wounded in Madalla Bombing – Health Minister" *The Punch* (December 29th, 2011).
41. Seriki Adinoyi et al. "8 Killed as Bombers Target Jang's Church" *This Day* (February 27th, 2012): Page 1.
42. Ahamefula Ogbu et al. "Suicide Bombers Hit Another Church in Jos" *This Day* (March 12th, 2012): Page 1.
43. Success Nwogu et al. "Police Arrest Woman, Two Others for Kogi Attacks" *The Punch* (August 9th, 2012): Page 10.
44. Ibid.
45. Kayode Idowu et al. "Suicide Bomber Kills Six Inside Redeemed Church" *The Punch* (July 6th, 2015): Page 2.
46. Ibid.
47. "Boko Haram Kills Scores in Attacks on Churches" *The Nation* (June 30th, 2014): Page 1.
48. Njadwara Musa. "48 Feared Killed in Attack on Churches Near Chibok" *The Guardian* (June 30th, 2014): Page 1.
49. John Alecbenu et al. "B'Haram Kills Nine During Church Service" *The Punch* (June 3rd, 2014): Page 9.

50. Njadwara Musa. "Gunmen Torch Churches, Kill Three in Borno" *The Guardian* (June 1st, 2013).
51. Kingsley Omonobi and Ndahi Marama. "Boko Haram Invades Borno Villages" *Vanguard* (July 15th, 2014). Page 16.
52. "Boko Haram Kills 74 in Church, Village" *The Punch* (January 28th, 2014).
53. Michael Olugbode and Daji Sani. "Gunmen Kill 14, Injure 12 in Adamawa, Borno State" *This Day* (May 6th, 2013): Page 1.
54. Ibid.
55. Desmond Mgboli. "5 Worshippers, Suicide Bombers Killed in Multiple Bomb Attacks in Kano" *Daily Sun* (July 12th, 2014): Page 6.
56. Kingsley Omonobi et al. "Kaduna Church Blast/Reprisals: Death Toll Rises to 68" *Vanguard* (June 19th, 2012).
57. Owolabi Adenus. "Boko Haram Turns Annexed Churches into Mosques" *Saturday Newswatch* (August 30th, 2014): Page 68.
58. Vincent Ikumola. "Azazi Condemns Reprisals" *The Nation* (June 20th, 2012): Page 63.
59. Ibid.
60. Nnamdi Ebo. "Suicide Bombing as Sunday Sunday Medicine" *This Day* (June 24th, 2012): Page 19.

11

Targeted Assassinations

INTRODUCTION

Boko Haram, named the world's deadliest terror group of 2014, is probably also the leader in assassinations. The group assassinated several members of the political class, district heads and moderate clerics in a narrative that saw Wahabi extremism attempting to muscle moderate Islam. The assassins targeted five first-class emirs.[1] The Emir of Gwoza, HRH Alhaji Idrissa Timta was shot dead. The insurgents also attempted to assassinate a former head of state, Major General Muhammadu Buhari (Rtd.) who is now the President of Nigeria.

Boko Haram assassinated Zakariya Isa of the Nigerian Television Authority (NTA) whom they accused of broadcasting uncomplimentary reports about them.[2] At the height of BH's power, most political actors and elected officials from the North East fled the region to sojourn in Abuja or Maiduguri out of fear of being killed.

It takes a very sick mind to surveil a subject, move in on the subject and then without provocation, cold-bloodedly terminate the life of the victim. Such callous, heartless, cruel and sinful acts are usually the handiwork of "extreme" or "way out" criminal elements in society. Yet the BH insurgents have turned assassination into common currency.

Assassination is defined as the intentional targeting, selection and killing of a VIP or other significant figure in society such as religious leaders, traditional rulers, top government functionaries, military or

167

political chieftains, former and serving CEOs of complex organizations, celebrities, foreign expatriates and others. The killing of military or law enforcement in the line of duty is not considered assassination. Setting off an IED in a crowded marketplace, in a place of worship, or at a school is considered a homicidal terrorist attack but not an assassination.

Assassination is so vile a crime that it can actually change destinies. For example, the assassination of Alhaji Fanami Gubio, the All Nigeria Peoples Party (ANPP) gubernatorial candidate in the 2011 general elections, changed the course of events for Borno State.[3] Alhaji Kashim Shettima might not have become governor if Boko Haram had not killed Alh. Fanami Gubio.

The targeting of General Buhari in July 2014 might have sparked generalized violence in Nigeria as Buhari had a cult-like following in Northern Nigeria.[4] Fortunately, his security detail managed to protect him and save his life during the VBIED attack in Kaduna. The protection detail took the bullet for the principal – as they should have.

The question now is why does Boko Haram carry out targeted assassinations?

1. **To silence people:** Boko Haram insurgents have used assassination as a tool of settling scores with people who criticize them. People who have made strong statements against them have been attacked and terminated to permanently silence them. Many moderate clerics who spoke up or preached against Boko Haramism were targeted. Sheikh Auwal Adam Albani was trailed and killed in Zaria along with his wife and son on February 1st, 2014.

   Seven members of the BH sect were arrested years later by the Department of State Services (DSS) for the assassination of the renowned Muslim preacher. DSS spokeswoman Marilyn Ogar said:

   > Investigation and confession made by the suspects revealed that Albani's pro-western posture and his preachings were contrary to the Boko Haram ideology. . . .
   > It was this hatred that Albani's preaching generated that culminated in a meeting by the members of the sect, under the leadership of Yakub Abdullahi in Rigasa area of Kaduna where the sect's Shura Council declared that Albani must be killed.
   > On 1st February 2014 he was tracked down at Markaz Salafiya Centre where they waited for him till the end of the programme and eventually murdered him, his wife and son.[5]

168

2. **Fear factor:** Assassinations by Boko Haram are intended to spread fear – the contagion effect. By trailing and deliberately killing a prominent person in a cruel manner, the zealots strike fear into the hearts of others. Family members were forced to watch the execution of district heads in Borno State.[6]

3. **Impunity:** The biggest driver of assassinations is an ability to do the crime and get away with it. The ability of law enforcement to detect and arrest Boko Haram assassins is low. The zealots can kill without fear of getting caught. It is apparent that the insurgents do not respect the institutional capacity of Nigeria's law enforcement agencies to detect them and bring them to justice. It should, however, be stated that Sheikh Albani Adam's killers were caught as were those of Major General Muhammed Shuwa (Rtd.). Unfortunately, most Boko Haram assassins were never detected, prosecuted or punished.

4. **Counter-narrative:** One important goal of Boko Haram is to offer its Islamist ideology and practice as the right form of worship. Assassination is employed as a draconian tool of the counter-narrative that extremism is superior to mainstream Islam. Those who get assassinated are not true followers of the Islamic faith and their just dessert is death. This is enforcing the fundamentalist narrative of "conversion or death."

5. **Evilry:** The Boko Haram ideology is based on Salafi Wahabism. Due to the relative underdevelopment of its philosophical/ideological underpinnings, BH has interpreted conflict in savage and evil terms. Any act is justifiable as long as Allah allows it. Evil has substituted morality. The assassins cold-bloodedly killed Sheikh Adam Albani, his wife and son without compunction. Evil is the creed of Boko Haramism.

SELECTED CASES OF ASSASSINATION OR ATTEMPTS

Boko Haram has carried out so many assassinations that it could be considered the terror group with the largest number of kills. One factor is that its victim pool is rather large. BH has targeted emirs, retired generals, political office holders, district heads (monarchs), clerics, academics, expatriates and journalists. This author has received death threat calls from persons claiming to be BH insurgents because of his media contribution on the BH threat.

Let us now consider some attacks by these terrorists.

169

Gen. Muhammadu Buhari (Rtd.)

The former military head of state was targeted in Kaduna on July 23rd, 2014, the same day a prominent Muslim cleric Sheikh Dahiru Bauchi was targeted in a bomb blast.[7] The Gen. Buhari assassination attempt occurred near the headquarters of 1 Division Nigerian Army in Kawo, Kaduna. Gen. Buhari was traveling in a private convoy when the suicide bomber attacked his vehicle. The plan of the assassins was to pull alongside the politician's car and then detonate their explosives. However, the executive protection officials following in the chase car behind sensed that the car trying to overtake might have sinister plans and therefore refused to let it through. Near the populated area the VBIED detonated massively destroying the general's follow-up car and his armored Prado Jeep executive transport. Two of his bodyguards and an aide were severely injured while he escaped unhurt. Between the Gen. Buhari attempted assassination and the Sheikh Dahiru Bauchi attack, 70 people died.

Speaking of the incident, General Buhari said:

> I was personally involved in a clearly targeted bomb attack today (Wednesday) at about 2:30 PM on my way to Daura. . . .
>
> The unfortunate event, clearly an assassination attempt, came from a fast-moving vehicle that made several attempts to overtake my security car, but was blocked by my escort vehicle. . . .
>
> We reached the market area of Kawo where he took advantage of our slowing down and attempted to ram my car and instantly detonated the bomb which destroyed all the three cars in my convoy.[8]

The general described the crime scene: "Unfortunately, when I came out of my vehicle, I saw many dead bodies littered around. They were innocent people going about their daily business who became victims of mass murder."[9]

A military patrol that arrived at the crime scene arrested a young man dressed as a woman and named him the suspected mastermind of the attack[10] without adducing any hard evidence linking him to the crime.

The Guardian newspaper described the Buhari and Sheikh Bauchi twin bombing incidents as "unconscionable acts of malevolence and sadistic fury perpetrated by the enemies of Nigeria."[11] The editorial explained that Gen. Buhari had recently become outspoken against Boko Haram. The editorial said: "His recent invectives against the murderous sect prompted the Federal Government to take pro-active measures for his security."[12]

Post-Mortem Analysis

The General Buhari attempted assassination is an excellent case study in executive protection. Several things were done that ensured that the VIP survived that roadway attack on July 23rd, 2014.

1. **Risk assessment:** The federal government took proactive steps in beefing up security around the former head of state once he began to speak out against the BH sect. The security officials correctly assessed that the risk rating had risen to critical. Incidental to the risk assessment, his personal security was increased.
2. **Armored transport:** Being a very ascetic, frugal and non-flamboyant personality, it was fortunate that the general was traveling in his recently provided armored transport at the time of the VBIED attack. If he had been in a regular vehicle, it might have been a different outcome.
3. **Executive protection specialist:** The bodyguards of the general were the real heroes on July 23rd, 2014. They are the reason the general remained alive to become the president of Nigeria. What did they accomplish?
   a. **Counter-surveillance:** The close protection agents were sharp enough to detect the surveillant agency.
   b. **Blocking maneuver:** The driver in the chase car (the escort car following in the three-car convoy) used his vehicle to physically deny efforts by the bombers to pass.
   c. **Taking the bullet:** When at Kawo market the bombers decided to ram the executive transport. The chase vehicle drove into the path of the bomb-laden vehicle thereby protecting the VIP's vehicle from blast damage. The chase vehicle bore the full brunt of the VBIED. The executive transport was damaged, but the general survived.
   d. **Evacuation:** Upon alighting from the vehicle, the security details swiftly evacuated the general from the blast scene. This move probably saved the VIP from a secondary attack. The security details took the general to the other side of the road, stopped a random oncoming vehicle and removed him from the scene to his house in Kaduna.

Given the heroic protection that the security details gave on that day, this author urged the authorities to reward the security details for saving the life of the VIP as a way of encouraging others in the executive protection field.[13]

171

HRH Alhaji Ado Bayero

There was an assassination attempt by Boko Haram insurgents on the amiable and revered then Emir of Kano, HRH Alhaji Ado Bayero in January 2013. The emir's convoy was attacked along Zoo Road, near Sahad Stores Kano as he was returning from a Koranic graduation ceremony which took place at Masallacin Murtala. The emir's driver, police orderly and his traditional bodyguard were killed in the roadway ambush where AK-47 rifles were used. Two of the emir's sons were injured, as was the royal father.[14]

HRH Alh. Idrissa S. Tinta

On May 30th, 2014, the Emir of Gwoza, HRH Alhaji Idrissa Shehu Tinta was assassinated by Boko Haram insurgents after ambushing him on the Biu–Garkida road in Borno State. The first-class traditional ruler was in the company of two other monarchs – the Emir of Uba, HRH Alhaji Ali Ibn Ismaila Mamza II, and the Emir of Askira, HRH Alhaji Abdullahi Ibn Muhammadu Askirama – while on the way to Gombe for the burial of the Emir of Gombe.[15]

The attack on the royal personage occurred at about 9:00 AM at Tashan Alade. The assassinated emir and his brother kings were on their way to pick up the Emir of Biu before proceeding to Gombe when they were ambushed by BH fighters who mounted a roadblock with their Hilux pickup vehicles. As the royal convoy came to a halt, the terrorists opened fire on the executive transport and the security details returned fire.[16] They were quickly overpowered by the terrorists who killed two policemen. The Emir of Uba and Emir of Askira escaped into the bush. Troops deployed in Garkida responded to their distress call and rescued the emirs from the crime scene. They also recovered the body of the slain royal father. Vehicles stricken at the crime scene by the terrorist attack were torched by the insurgents.[17]

The Guardian newspaper reported that the slain emir had been earmarked for assassination since April 13th, 2014 "when he publicly castigated the group for making life unbearable for his people by turning his domain into a base for carrying out such terrible and horrendous activities, as well as for crippling the economy of his embattled region."[18]

The emir had excoriated the sect over its near destruction of the Gwoza Emirate, and the sect promptly issued a *fatwa* on him. Boko Haram is such a transactional insurgency. For example, in June 2011 when the Inspector General of Police Hafiz Ringim declared that the sect's days were numbered, BH delivered a VBIED to his office two days later with

172

the apparent intention of knocking down the FHQ building and causing mass deaths. Similarly, when Gen. Buhari made strong statements against Boko Harm, they replied with the attempted roadway assassination at Kawo, Kaduna. HRH Idrissa Tinta had lamented the excesses of BH just a few weeks before he was killed.

Maj. Gen. Mohammed Shuwa (Rtd.)

A hero of the Nigerian Civil War was shot dead in his home by BH insurgents on Friday November 2nd, 2012. General Shuwa, aged 79, was assassinated at his Gwange I Maiduguri residence along with a guest by a four-man execution squad as he was preparing for *Jumaat* prayers. A native of Kala-Balge LGA, Borno State, General Shuwa was a frontline military officer who had fought for Nigeria's unity during the civil war (1967–1970). He later served on the Federal Cabinet.

Then Chairman of the Northern Governors' Forum, Alhaji Babangida Aliyu of Niger State described General Shuwa's assassination as callous and one death too many. He said "no grievance can justify such a dastardly act against innocent people."[19]

Analysis of Shuwa Killing

The assassination was made possible by poor risk assessment. In November 2012, BH insurgents were killing without hindrance in Maiduguri. The prevailing security situation should have resulted in raising the general's security profile.

The general represented a target of opportunity to the insurgents. The Gwange I neighborhood had witnessed a large number of attacks. The terrorists were carrying out more savage and shocking acts to grab media attention and apparently could not resist the temptation to target the elder statesman, even though he had not uttered provocative words against them. He was targeted because he was a VIP and killing him would increase their notoriety.

The Attempted Assassination of Gov. Nyako

On February 28th, 2014, then Governor of Adamawa State Vice Admiral Murtala Nyako (Rtd.) was on a condolence visit to Madagali LGA when his convoy came under fire. The governor had planned to visit Shuwa, Gulak and Michika which had been attacked on February 27th, 2014 by Boko Haram.[20]

The insurgents killed 37 people in the attacks on the villages which are located about 90 km from Yola, the Adamawa State capital. Upon hearing approaching heavy gunfire, the security details determined that the governor's life was being threatened. They swung his car around and fled the area, aborting the visit. There was pandemonium as members of the entourage also tried to flee the approaching gunfire.[21]

Gov. Nyako's roadway encounter might well have been a case of nerves. Gunshots were heard, and a military truck warned the entourage that the insurgents were approaching – hence the flight. It is not clear whether the insurgents knew that the governor was inbound to Madagali LGA and had made a decision to attack him. While the governor's security detail reacted prudently, and out of an abundance of caution, there is no evidence that the state chief executive and former chief of naval staff had been targeted for elimination. Playing devil's advocate, it could be argued that someone familiar with the governor's itinerary could have informed Boko Haram to enable the ambush of the executive.

Was the governor's life in danger? Was the governor threatened? Did the executive protection detail act properly? The answer to all these three questions is yes. With the uncertain security situation at that time, they were not overreacting when they turned the convoy around and returned to base in Yola.

The Attempted Assassination of Emir Sanusi III

The Emir of Kano, HRH Alhaji Sanusi Lamido Sanusi invoked the wrath of BH insurgents in October 2014 when he charged the people of Kano to arm and defend themselves against the sect. The emir, who was formerly Governor of the Central Bank of Nigeria before ascending the royal throne, urged religious and community leaders to reinvent courage in their people, particularly the youths in preparation for self-defense against Boko Haram attacks.

On Friday November 28th, 2014, the insurgents bombed the Kano Central Mosque (*Massalachi Sarki*). Several IEDs detonated and there was rifle attack claiming over 200 lives (see Chapter 10 of this book).[22] The Kano Central Mosque attack targeted the emir. Fortunately, the king was out of the country. The pre-attack surveillance was sloppy.

174

Emir Sanusi's words:

> People must stand resolute in the face of attack and not abandon their town, women and children. These people, when they attack towns kill boys and enslave girls. People must not assume that the crisis will not reach their area . . . If it comes, we are asking God to give us fortitude, but if He wishes to take martyrs from among us, we should be ready to give up our lives. People must not wait for soldiers to protect them.[23]

Upon return from his overseas trip, Emir Sanusi visited the attacked mosque and reaffirmed that the Kano people will not cower in the face of Boko Haram's threats.

Replying to the Emir of Kano in a 20-minute video, BH leader Imam Abubakar Shekau said his group was very pleased to fight and kill anyone who challenged its ideology, and all non-Muslims and "fake" Muslims like the emir. He said:

> Now listen to me Emir of Kano. I am talking to you and only you because of your recent utterances. . . .
>
> Let me inform you now that you are late, you are. You should know that only but the King of Kano, King of Central Bank, King of Money, you are only Sanusi Lamido. Because you are made the Emir of Kano that is why you called on the vigilante groups and hunters to attack us, but the hunters and vigilante groups will fail you. We would kill you and take your people as hostages.[24]

Shekau denounced the emir's religion as one based on constitution, idol worship and homosexuality. Emir Sanusi dismissed Shekau's threat to his life anchoring his confidence on divine protection from evil. He said that nothing, except if it is willed by Allah would happen to him.[25]

VIPs

Aside from emirs and generals, the insurgents also targeted other VIPs including active duty or retired CEOs of major organizations, civil commissioners and police executives.

The retired Comptroller General of the Nigerian Prisons Service, Ahaji Ibrahim Jarma was shot by BH insurgents in front of a mosque in Azare, Bauchi State, on September 17th, 2012 and died in hospital the next day.

The Borno State Commissioner of Justice and Attorney General, Mr. Zanna Malam Gana, was shot dead in his hometown of Bama on September 18th, 2012.[26] The General Manager of the Borno State Water Board was also assassinated by BH terrorists.

Three North Korean doctors – two men and one woman – working for the Yobe State Ministry of Health at the Potiskum General Hospital were assassinated by religious militants on February 15th, 2013 in their home. The Boko Haram terrorists slit their throats.[27]

On October 31st, 2014, the son of the Emir of Mubi was captured by BH terrorists in Vintim, Adamawa State, and murdered. The prince had fled Mubi due to the attack on the emir's palace on October 29th.[28]

Monarchs

District heads were hit very hard by BH terrorists. To survive the BH onslaught, many district heads had to go into hiding.[29] District heads are traditional rulers of districts under emirs.

The District Head of Gambula village in Biu LGA, Borno State, Alhaji Ibrahim Dani was assassinated with a headshot by BH insurgents on July 22nd, 2014. The assailants also killed the monarch's bodyguards in the terror attack which claimed 11 other lives.[30]

On April 16th, 2014, BH assassins invaded Sabon Kusawa village in Hawul LGA, Borno State, and killed the district head. He suffered gunshot injuries to the head.[31] The Monarch was trailed from the mosque where he had gone for *Ishai* (evening) prayers.

The traditional ruler of Lawanti Ward in Bale, Borno Emirate, was assassinated on April 30th, 2013. The assassins besieged the palace of District Head Alhaji Baba Zarabe at about 2:00 AM. He was shot in the head and his wives and children were compelled to watch the death scene.[32]

In October 2014, Boko Haram terrorists killed Alhaji Dalailu Digil, the acting District Head of Nasaran. Alh. Digil was also the Barade Mubi.[33]

Politicians

The insurgents targeted politicians for elimination. Local government officials, state and federal lawmakers and other politicians succumbed to the assassins' rifles. On September 17th, 2012, the acting Chairman of Maiha LGA in Adamawa State, Alhaji Lawan Datti was shot dead by BH insurgents.[34]

A member representing Garko constituency in the Kano House of Assembly, Hon. Ibrahim Abba Garko, was trailed by gunmen on motorcycles and shot dead in Kano in November 2012. Two people accompanying the lawmaker were also injured in the assassination attack.[35]

The Chairman of the All Progressives Congress (APC) in Kala Balge LGA of Borno State, Alhaji Modu Janga, was assassinated near Mafa Town on the Maiduguri–Dikwa road on April 21st, 2014.[36] The party chieftain was shot dead in a highway ambush after the assailants confirmed his identity.

Clerics

Clerics are another endangered species in Nigeria's North East. In February 2017, BH terrorists killed an Islamic scholar in Mafa village, Chibok LGA.[37]

Secretary of the Christian Association of Nigeria (CAN) in Borno State, Rev. Faye Pama Musa, was shot dead at his house in Maiduguri by two BH fighters on May 14th, 2013.[38]

On July 24th, 2012, a Kano-based Islamic cleric, Malam Shuaibu Gwamaja, was murdered by BH insurgents in the Gwanajo area of Maiduguri.[39]

A 92-year-old Islamic cleric, Malam Goni Mustapha, was also shot dead at his residence in Gwange, Maiduguri, on April 17th, 2012. Four gunmen formed the tactical team that killed Malam Goni.[40]

PROTECTING DIGNATARIES

After the assassination of the Emir of Gwoza, this author declared that given the threat environment, neglecting to provide adequate executive protection for emirs and other traditional rulers "was tantamount to criminal negligence."[41] He advocated the following security measures for traditional rulers:

a. Appointment of competent executive protection specialists to be charged with conducting risk and vulnerability assessments for the VIPs and taking steps to mitigate risks.
b. Provision of armed police personnel and Civilian JTF to protect the rulers.
c. Improving security measures in the palaces. Redesigning some palaces to become blast resistant.

d. Providing a safe haven for the royal fathers inside the palace. This could be a secret room or passageway where the ruler can ride out an assassination attempt.
e. Providing security driving training and retraining for executive drivers.
f. Light armoring of executive transport. If cost is a constraint, then use plastic laminates to strengthen car windows and windshields.
g. Providing security awareness training and retraining to traditional rulers to enroll them as part of the security effort.
h. Improving rapid response to targeted assassination attempts on monarchs and other VIPs. Given enough time, the assassins will find the weak link in the chain of protection. However, with rapid response the life of the VIP may be saved.

CONCLUSION

This chapter has examined the targeting of a wide range of VIPs by Boko Haram insurgents. The Nigerian terrorist group has become the world leader in assassinations. With the recent military onslaught code-named Operation Lafiya Dole, the terrorists no longer control large swathes of land in the North East. They have now adopted lethal guerrilla warfare tactics, which are costing human lives.

Political elites and corporate executives going into the North East region should conduct detailed risk assessments to mitigate or prevent the risk of being targeted by Boko Haram.

The inconvenient truth is that this terror brand will be around for a few more years. So, executives who must travel into or live in the North East region of Nigeria must be aware that assassination is part of the threatscape. Security awareness is the key to staying alive.

NOTES

1. Ndahi Marama and Wole Mosadomi. "Boko Haram Attacks Three Emirs, Kills One" *The Vanguard* (May 31st, 2014).
2. Freedom Onuoha. **Boko Haram: Nigeria's Extremist Islamic Sect**. Doha, Qatar: Al Jazeera Center for Studies (February 2012): Page 4.
3. "Six Killed in Nigerian Political Massacre" *The Telegraph* (January 28th, 2011).
4. Garba Muhammed. "Suicide Bombs in Nigeria's Kaduna Kill 82, Ex-Leader Buhari Targeted" *Reuters* (July 23rd, 2014).

5. Kola Olawoyin. "DSS Parades Seven Boko Haram Suspects Who Murdered Islamic Preacher" *Daily Newswatch* (March 4th, 2014): Page 76.
6. The assassination of the district head of Pulka, Gwoza LGA, Malam, Ali Pulka was carried out in the presence of his wife and children on April 2nd, 2013. See "Suspected Boko Haram Gunmen Kill Borno District Head" *Daily Trust* (April 3rd, 2013).
7. John Alechenu et al. "Buhari in Narrow Escape as Kaduna Blast Kills 70" *The Punch* (July 24th, 2014): Page 2.
8. Ibid.
9. Ibid.
10. Yusuf Alli et al. "Attack on Buhari: Military Arrests Suspected 'Mastermind'" *The Nation* (July 26th, 2014): Page 2.
11. Editorial Page Comment. "Terror and that Attempt on Buhari's Life" *The Guardian* (August 11th, 2014): Page 16.
12. Ibid.
13. Ishola Balogun. "Buhari's Assassination Attempt Intended to Destabilize Nigeria – Ekhomu" *The Vanguard* (July 26th, 2014).
14. "6 Killed in Attack on Emir of Kano's Convoy" *Daily Trust* (January 19th, 2019).
15. Yemi Adebowale et al. "Boko Haram's Relentless Killing Continues, Kills First Class Emir" *This Day* (May 31st, 2014): Page 1.
16. Fidelis Soriwei et al. "Boko Haram Kills Emir of Gwoza, Kidnaps Others" *The Punch* (May 31st, 2014): Page 4.
17. Timothy Olanrewaju. "Boko Haram Attacks Borno Emir" *Saturday Sun* (May 31st, 2014): Page 4.
18. "The Killing of Emir of Gwoza" *The Guardian* (June 23rd, 2014): Page 14.
19. Joseph Abiodun et al. "Shuwa Killing: Tributes as Slain General Is Laid to Rest" *The Nation* (November 4th, 2012): Page 2.
20. Barnabas Manyam. "Confusion in Adamawa Over Alleged Attack on Governor's Convoy" *The Nation* (March 1st, 2014): Page 2. See also John Alechenu et al. "Boko Haram: Adamawa Gov, Guards Flee, Abort Trip" *The Punch* (March 1st, 2014): Page 6.
21. Manyam (2014).
22. Soni Daniel and Abdulsalam Muhammad. "Bomb Blast Kills 200 in Kano Central Mosque" *The Vanguard* (November 23rd, 2014).
23. Olusegun Adeniyi. "Insurgency: The Emir's Prescription" *This Day* (November 20th, 2014): Page 54.
24. Michael Olugbode. "Shekau in New Video Vows to Attack Emir of Kano" *This Day* (December 18th, 2014): Page 9.
25. Ibrahim Shuaibu. "Allah Is My Protector, Sanusi Replies to Boko Haram" *This Day* (December 21st, 2014): Page 7.
26. Kolade Adeyemi. "Gunmen Kill Commissioner in Borno" *The Nation* (September 19th, 2012): Page 1.

27. "Killing of Polio Vaccinators and Korean Doctors" *The Guardian* (February 22nd, 2013): Page 14.
28. "Mubi Attack. Terrorist Kill Emir's Son, Torch Badeh's House" *Saturday Vanguard* (November 1st, 2014): Page 4.
29. Fisayo Falodi. "Tension Rises as Boko Haram Targets District Heads" *The Punch* (June 21st, 2014): Page 10.
30. Ahmed Miringa. "Monarch, 11 Others Killed in Borno" *New Telegraph* (July 25th, 2014): Page 7.
31. Anule Emmanuel and Ahmed Miringa "Boko Haram: Monarch, 18 Others Killed in Borno" *New Telegraph* (April 17th, 2014): Page 1.
32. Michael Olugbode. "Gunmen Kill Traditional Ruler in Borno" *This Day* (May 2nd, 2013): Page 8.
33. "Boko Haram Kills Mubi District Head After Hoisting Flag on Palace" *The Paradigm Online* (November 1st, 2014).
34. Kolade Adeyemi (2012).
35. Njadwara Musa et al. "Gunmen Kill Law Maker, Cleric in Kana, Borno" *The Guardian* (November 19th, 2012): Page 6.
36. Saxone Akhaine and Njadwara Musa. "Suspected Terrorists Kill Borno Council APC Chairman, Youth Leader" *The Guardian* (April 23rd, 2014): Page 3.
37. Nkechi Onyedika – Ugoeze. "Boko Haram Terrorists Attack Borno Village, Kill Islamic Scholar, Injure Boy" *The Guardian* (February 15th, 2017): Page 8.
38. Timothy Olanrewaju. "Gunmen Kill Borno CAN Secretary" *Daily Sun* (May 15th, 2013): Page 9.
39. Kolade Adeyemi et al. "Gunmen Kill Islamic Cleric" *The Nation* (July 25th, 2012): Page 58.
40. "Gunmen Kill 92-Year-Old Cleric in Maiduguri" *Daily Sun* (April 19th, 2012): Page 14.
41. Okosun Okhueleigbe. "Boko Haram: Need for Robust Executive Protection for Emirs' *The Union* (June 3rd, 2014): Page 15.

Part Three

Combating Insurgency

12
The Military Solution

INTRODUCTION

A misapplied military solution produced the unintended consequences of the BH insurgency. In Chapter 1 we narrated the Customs Roundabout massacre of June 11th, 2009. On July 26th, 2009, angry sect members attacked Dutsen Tashi Police Division and they were easily repelled. The military option ensured victories in Kano, Yobe and ultimately in the Battle of Maiduguri which was personally supervised by Maj. Gen. Saleh Maina then General Officer Commanding 3 Division Nigeria Army. Gen. Maina carried out President Umar Musa Yar'Adua's directive to put down the rebellion. Yusuf was captured by the army, questioned in a video-taped session and turned over to the police authorities. Some angry policemen extra-judicially murdered Yusuf and Alhaji Buji Foi on July 30th, 2009. They also murdered another 700 Boko Haram members who were in detention.

This author argues that the extra-judicial murder of Yusuf was a mistake. It is conventional wisdom that you never kill the head of an insurgency when you capture him. You need him to talk down his followers and prevent exacerbating the conflict. However, those policemen apparently did not know this rule.

With Yusuf dead, Abubakar Shekau, his extremely militant second-in-command and head of the military wing, assumed leadership of the group. In April 2010, Shekau vowed to avenge the deaths of Yusuf and the BH members.

By September 2010, BH had attacked Bauchi prison where they killed five people, freed 756 prisoners and torched the correctional facility (see Chapter 6 of this book). The sect carried out a large number of targeted killings of police personnel in the North East. They assassinated clerics who preached against them and their murderous activities spread fear throughout the North East. On Christmas Eve 2010, BH carried out deadly bombings in Jos, Plateau State. On New Year's Eve, they hit the mammy market at Sani Abacha Barracks in Abuja. It became clear at this time that this was a serious foe that the government was up against. The threat was initially poorly defined as a low-risk law enforcement challenge. It was later realized that this was a determined enemy who could strike across the Northern states. This change in threat assessment sent Nigeria's security officials into planning mode to determine how to address the new national security threat.

It is the constitutional duty of the government of Nigeria to protect civilians from the onslaught of BH insurgents. The various lethal bombing and shooting incidents meant that decisive military action had to be taken to safeguard property and the reputation of the Nigerian government.

Although President Umar Musa Yar'Adua gave the order for the routing of Boko Haram in July 2009, he had passed on by May 5th, 2010, and the Vice President, Dr. Goodluck Jonathan, became president. All the security breaches in 2010 happened on Jonathan's watch – Bauchi prison break, the Christmas Eve bombings in Jos (killing 38 people and the reprisal attacks leading to a total of 86 deaths). In Maiduguri, churches and Christian worshippers were also attacked on Christmas Eve. Five worshippers were killed at Victory Baptist Church in Dala Alemderi. The pastor Rev. Bulus Marwa was killed and the church set on fire. BH terrorists also attacked the Church of Christ in Nigeria (COCIN) in Sinmowu, Maiduguri, killing a guard, two parishioners and the pastor. BH insurgents also bombed the mammy market at Sani Abacha Military Barracks on New Year's Eve 2010.

In an internet post claiming responsibility for the two Christmas Eve attacks in Jos and Maiduguri, Shekau said:

> O Nations of the world, be informed that verily the attacks on Suldaniyya (Jos) and Borno on the eve of Christmas was (sic) carried out by us. Jama'atu Alilus-Sunnah Lidda awatil wal Jihad, under the leadership of Abu Mohammed, Abubakar bin Mohammed Shekau (May Allah preserve him), to start avenging the atrocity committed against Muslims in those areas, and the country in general.

184

Therefore, we will continue with our attacks on disbelievers and their allies and all those who help them until Allah's deem triumph by His Grace and Will.[1]

This was Shekau's **"I'm coming out message."** Since then, he has not relented in killing his enemies.

Faced with a mounting body count by the nascent BH insurgency, President Jonathan had to set the broad policy goals for military action that would stop the carnage. However, the president failed to give a clear directive on what he wanted done about the insurgency. He tried to play down the threat and repeatedly claimed that the problem posed by Boko Haram was "temporary."

The president was highly deferential to the views of the Northern elite on the insurgency. At one point, the Borno Elders' Forum asked the federal government to withdraw the Joint Task Force combating the insurgents from their state.[2]

POLICE ACTION

The federal government misread the insurgency as criminality. It felt that if police detectives swung into action, they could detect the perpetrators of these bombings. At this time, several police personnel had been shot dead by Boko Haram. Muslim clerics had been murdered. Churches had been attacked and parishioners/pastors killed. Prison breaks had occurred setting free hundreds of BH sect members. Even the mammy market at Abacha Barracks had been bombed with tragic results.

A pattern of virulent terrorism was apparent. Unfortunately, either President Jonathan did not have good policy/intelligence analysts or the products of their analyses were defective. The president ignored the huge threat and consistently issued similar statements after every mass murder incident, promising "surely" to bring the perpetrators to book.

The federal government was in denial[3] in its response to the insurgency. From 2010 to about 2013, the federal government exhibited "a sad narrative of denial, recrimination and the trading of blames by public officials, politicians and their supporters."[4]

The sustained attacks by then opposition parties on every move President Jonathan made to try and contain the crisis created significant distraction. The president did not have the nation united behind him in the war.

185

The president appeared not to have policy analysts and intelligence analysts who could dissect the information and produce good policy alternatives to deal with the crisis, even in the face of mounting deaths.

Ashindorbe and Owonikoko wrote:

> Whenever there was a terror attack, government officials and political party stalwarts attempt to shift blame, divert attention and reframe the discourse to suit certain narratives.
>
> Open division and needless controversy and blame game principally between the then ruling Peoples Democratic Party and the then leading opposition party, the All Progressives Congress regarding who was responsible for the series of terrorist attacks became a constant theme . . . The inevitable outcome was a lack of coordinated response against the terrorists, resulting in massive casualties in both servicemen and civilians.[5]

Analyzing the political bickering hampering the war on terror, this author wrote in 2014:

> There has been a lot of political interference in the fight. In fact some groups called for the arrest and prosecution of the immediate past Chief of Army Staff. What for? I don't know. Nigerian politicians still do not appreciate the severity of the threat. So they make reckless, opportunistic statements and engage in finger-pointing.[6]

In November 2012, the former governor of Yobe State, Senator Bukar Abba Ibrahim, accused the Joint Task Force (JTF) of killing more people in the North East than Boko Haram. Senator Ibrahim who was the governor of Yobe State in 2003 when the fish pond incident occurred (see Chapter 1 of this book), accused security agencies of mass killings. He said:

> Security agencies are the number one killers in terms of number. I was surprised the other day when the Chief of Army Staff said that Boko Haram killed 3000 people. The security agencies have killed a lot more than 3000 since this thing started.[7]

The senator who then belonged to the opposition political party did not adduce any evidence to substantiate these outlandish accusations.

In April 2014, the Secretary General of the *Jama'atu Nasril Islam* (*JNI*), which is the umbrella body of mainstream Muslims in Nigeria, alleged that there were various cases of massacre of Muslims by the military in Borno, Adamawa and Yobe States under the guise of fighting terrorism. He said:

> The dimension of extra judicial killing of Muslims by the Military on unsubstantiated suspicion leaves much to be desired, which clearly depicts that Muslims have become an endangered species, murdered and maimed indiscriminately under the guise of fighting terrorism. . . .
>
> We can say without any fear of contradiction that there is a grand agenda to destabilize the Muslim Ummah in Nigeria.[8]

The statement issued by the Secretary General of *JNI*, Dr. Khalid Aliyu, referenced an incident at Keana in Nasarawa State. However, given the penchant for unsubstantiated statements, there was a broad allegation of a plan to kill all Muslims in Nigeria. Coming from the pre-eminent Muslim organization in Nigeria, this statement had a chilling effect on the war on terror. There was no shred of evidence to buttress the allegation that Muslims were being killed systematically by the military.

The chairman of then ruling Peoples Democratic Party (PDP), Alhaji Bamaga Tukur, carelessly stated that members of the Boko Haram Islamic sect were fighting for justice. He said that many Nigerians were aggrieved and seeking various means of airing their grievances. He said there was "no way angry people would control their anger when there was nothing in their stomachs."[9] This curious narrative that Boko Haram was fighting for justice gave the impression that the ruling party chairman was justifying the killings by the insurgents.

MILITARY OPERATIONS

The military response to the BH insurgency has been episodic. At the beginning, President Jonathan wrongly diagnosed the threat as a law enforcement matter. However, shortly after the general elections of 2011, which were almost marred by terrorist bombings in Suleja, Maiduguri, etc. and the inauguration day (May 29th, 2011) bombing incidents, the president set up the Joint Task Force – Operation Restore Order (JTF-ORO) on June 15th, 2011. The goal of the JTF-ORO was to provide a multi-service response to the insurgency. Its mission was to restore law and order.

The JTF-ORO was a multi-agency matrix organization led by the Nigerian Army. It comprised the Nigerian Air Force (NAF), the Defence

Intelligence Agency (DIA), the Department of State Services (DSS), the Nigerian Customs Service (NCS), the Nigeria Police Force (NPF) and the Nigerian Immigration Service (NIS).

The NAF 79th Composite Group was given responsibility for aerial reconnaissance. This role later changed to armed attacks. The DIA and DSS were in charge of intelligence gathering. The role of the NCS was to interdict weapons, IEDs and other contraband. The NPF was to provide traditional policing duties for citizens – crime prevention, detection, prosecution and reporting. The NIS was made a part of JTF-ORO to provide border security and control service. The three states affected by the insurgency have borders with neighboring countries such as Cameroon, Chad and Niger.

The 21st Armored Brigade of the Nigerian Army augmented with counter-terrorism trained units coordinated the entire JTF. The operation succeeded in dislodging BH elements from Maiduguri as many BH fighters were caught in the raids. The hunt for insurgents, usually conducted via large-scale house to house searches, prompted an exodus of BH fighters from Maiduguri to Damaturu.

As the military operation went on, it understandably met some resistance from the civil populace. The JTF was stymied by lack of intelligence on the insurgents, and lack of information and cooperation from the local residents. The JTF operatives were literally flying blind so they achieved limited success in interdicting Boko Haram weapons and IEDs.

The operation was also hampered by the extensive land borders with the neighboring countries of Chad, Cameroon and Niger. The Damaturu–Maiduguri axis has about 250 border footpaths. These paths are mostly unknown by security agencies, are unmanned, unprotected and thus serve as leaky routes for arms and ammunitions trafficking into Nigeria.[10]

STATE OF EMERGENCY

The JTF-ORO was established on June 15th, 2011, with its headquarters in Maiduguri. One day after the establishment of JTF-ORO, Boko Haram detonated a suicide VBIED at the Police Headquarters building in Abuja (see Chapter 7 of this book). On August 25th, 2011, Boko Haram expanded its theater of operation to Adamawa State where it targeted banks and police stations in Gombi killing 16 people including seven policemen. Targeting banks is a method of terrorist funding for BH (see Chapter 5 of this book). On August 26th, 2011, BH hit the United Nations

House in Abuja taking the conflict international. The deadlist insurgent operations in this series were the Sallah Day (November 2011) attacks in Damaturu where police facilities, churches and mosques were attacked and over 150 people killed. This was Armageddon as the terrorists took control of the state, killing at will.

Katsina State bore the brunt of BH insurgency on June 20th, 2011, when a deadly gun and IED attack on Kankara town resulted in seven deaths (including five policemen). The targets were a police station and a nearby bank. Cash was seized by the terrorists.

On June 27th, 2011, BH insurgents bombed and shot up a bar (beer garden) in Maiduguri killing 25 people and injuring dozens more. On September 4th, 2011, Muslim cleric Malam Dala was shot dead by BH fighters in front of his house in Maiduguri.

Bauchi State was attacked on September 12th, 2011. Seven men including four policemen were killed in a bombing and shooting attack on a bank and police station in Misau. The BH fighters seized cash from the bank.

In Kaduna State, a policeman and a bank security guard were killed in a combination bombing and shooting attack on a police station and two banks in Saminaka. On October 23rd, 2011, BH fighters opened fire on a market in Katari town in Kaduna State, killing two people.

A shocking attack occurred on October 29th, 2011, against a Muslim cleric. BH fighters assassinated Sheikh Ali Jana'a outside his home in the Bulabalin Ngarnam ward of Maiduguri. The cleric was said to have provided information to security forces about Boko Haram.

The motorcade of Borno Governor Kashim Shettima was hit with a roadside bomb on November 4th, 2011, while on its way from the airport to the governor's residence. The executive was not hurt. However, BH fighters on motorbikes drove beside a protocol officer with the Borno State government on his way home on November 27th, 2011 and shot him dead.

Boko Haram hit Kaduna City Oriapata district on December 7th, 2011 with a bomb attack that killed eight people.

In the ancient city of Kano, a police raid on December 17th, 2011 resulted in a shootout in the Danmanawa area of the city. Seven people including three police personnel lay dead after the armed assault by law enforcement. Police arrested 14 BH fighters and seized a large cache of arms and bombs.

Pomponari area on the outskirts of Damaturu became a war zone on December 22nd, 2011 when BH insurgents engaged JTF troops in a protracted gun battle. About 100 people were killed.

Niger State was hit on April 4th, 2011, when the INEC office was bombed and several National Youth Service Corps members who had reported for election duty were killed.

The broad picture that emerges is that within the final six months of 2011 there were very many terrorist attacks across several states.

The federal government declared the first state of emergency on December 31st, 2011. The emergency covered 15 local government areas (LGAs) in four states – Borno, Adamawa, Niger and Plateau. This emergency declaration was a weak response to the vicious siege that had been laid to Nigeria. The FHQ bomb, the UN bomb and the St. Theresa's Catholic Church bomb were some of the iconic attacks in this period. The four states named in the declaration were highly affected by insurgency violence and should probably have been put under emergency rule. However, choosing local governments as the basis for geographical enforcement of emergency rule watered down the potency of this policy action. The insurgents merely relocated their assets to local governments that were not named in the declaration.

The emergency declaration gave broad powers to security agencies to detain suspects, take possession or control of any property in the emergency area, enter and search any premises and the payment of compensation and remuneration to people adversely affected by the order.

The emergency declaration appeared to have angered the insurgents deeply. The insurgents gave all Christians living in Northern Nigeria three days to leave the region. This order was illegal and unenforceable, yet it caused considerable panic among Southerners living in the North. Some of whom decided to relocate to the South.[11]

In January 2012, the insurgents went on a killing spree in an apparent rebuke of the emergency rule. On January 5th, 2012, six worshippers were killed and ten others wounded in a church attack in Gombe City. The next day, eight worshippers were killed in a shooting attack in Yola, Adamawa State. BH gunmen murdered 17 Christian mourners in Mubi, Adamawa State. The Ibo men were friends and relations of one of five people killed in a BH attack in a hotel the previous day.

The violence played out in Biu, Borno State, on January 7th when three men (Christians) playing cards were shot dead and seven others wounded. It was not clear if they were targeted for being Christians or for playing a game of poker which is also "*haram*" to BH. On January 9th 2012, a secret policeman and his friend were gunned down as they left a mosque in Biu.

The violence moved over to Yobe State where on January 10th BH attacked a beer garden in Damaturu killing eight people including five policemen and a teenager. On January 11th, 2012, four Ibos fleeing incessant BH attacks in Maiduguri to their homes in Southeastern Nigeria were gunned down as they made a fuel stop in Potiskum, Yobe State.

The most spectacular act of violence by BH in January was the series of attacks in Kano City on January 20th, 2012. On that day, Kano saw war. The government death toll of 250 is significantly lower than other estimates of over 800 deaths. BH terrorists sacked the city.

In the six months of the pendency of emergency rule, BH carried out several deadly terrorist attacks. The Easter Day bomb on April 8th, 2012 hit Kaduna City. The April 26th, 2012 destruction of the *This Day* newspaper office in Abuja was ominous. A VBIED attack destroyed the Abuja office of this media organization. There was also a simultaneous attack on the *Sun* newspaper office in Kaduna. Shekau claimed responsibility and released a video taping of the attack as proof. He issued threats against some other media houses portraying the insurgents in a "bad light."

Boko Haram pushed back hard against the emergency initiative showing that it was ineffective. At the expiration of the emergency rule after six months, the national assembly did not renew it.

SECOND STATE OF EMERGENCY

Following more vicious attacks by Boko Haram, sharp criticisms of President Jonathan by the leadership of Christian organizations and Muslim groups and refusal of Boko Haram to come to the negotiating table, the federal government declared a new state of emergency covering Borno, Yobe and Adamawa States on May 14th, 2013.

The new emergency rule was accompanied with significant military assets – 2,000 troops and more air assets and infantry assets. One thousand troops were subsequently deployed to Adamawa State bringing the total troop strength in the theater to 8,000 men. This was described as the largest deployment of the military since the Nigerian Civil War (1967–1970).

President Jonathan justified the state of emergency:

> This is not just militancy or criminality but a rebellion and insurgency by terrorist groups which pose a very serious threat to the national unity and territorial integrity of Nigeria. Already, some northern parts of Borno State have been taken over by groups whose allegiance is to different flags and ideology.[12]

The new state of emergency re-energized the fight against Boko Haram. However, some leaders of opposition parties opposed the declaration. Maj. Gen. Muhammadu Buhari (Rtd.) then leader of Congress for Progressive Change (CPC) and Senator Bola Ahmed Tinubu, then leader of the Action Congress of Nigeria (ACN)[13] were troubled by the Amnesty International Report of November 2012 which alleged widespread abuses against the military[14] in the counterinsurgency operations. The governors of Borno and Yobe States who were from the opposition All Nigeria Peoples Party (ANPP) supported the military deployments and emergency rule. Three years into the insurgency and with thousands dead, Nigeria politicians had still not closed ranks on what the threat was, and what was needed to defeat the enemy. The emergency rule was renewed twice more before it finally lapsed.

Baga Massacre

On April 16th, 2012, a Multinational Joint Task Force (MNJTF) patrol team in Baga, Borno State, came under attack by BH insurgents. The combatants engaged in a firefight overnight and 36 people died. The dead included 30 Boko Haram fighters and six civilians. One soldier, Lance Corporal Aramaja Olaleja, who was shot in the eye in the initial encounter, later died of his injuries.[15]

While retreating, the insurgents torched houses in Baga. The facts were later misrepresented by local politicians. It was said that the military committed massacre of civilians and razed 2,600 houses. Then Chief of Defence Staff, Admiral Ola Saed Ibrahim ordered a full investigation. When Maj. Gen. Lawrence Ngubane's investigation panel visited the scene, the local grave diggers gave testimony that 36 graves were dug to bury the dead.[16] A physical search of the town did not reveal any mass graves. Yet, the allegation of a "Baga massacre" would not go away. The media seized upon it and there were calls for action by the International Criminal Court (ICC).[17] This author was invited by Defence Headquarters to conduct an independent investigation and render an impartial opinion. The findings were as follows:[18]

1. There was no massacre in Baga. There was a fire-fight that resulted in 36 deaths.
2. Satellite imagery that the Human Rights Watch interpreted to conclude that over 2,000 homes were burnt down did not have ground verification. The number of houses razed was in fact 115.

3. NIGCOMSAT satellite photographs provided direct rebuttal of the HRW satellite interpretation.
4. The intentional torching of homes is the trademark of Boko Haram and occurred incidental to the use of incendiaries in the firefight.
5. An independent televised investigation by Al Jazeera television on the matter did not uncover any massacre.
6. The District Head of Baga, Dr. Shettima, who misinformed the Secretary to the State Government of Borno State about the casualty figure, later recanted as he never came to Baga. The casualty figure was a fabrication.

Confirming this author's investigation findings and conclusions, the Nigerian Senate Joint Committee that investigated the alleged Baga massacre discovered nine fresh graves and 115 houses torched contrary to the fabricated figures. The District Head had long since relocated to Maiduguri due to fear of assassination.[19]

The so-called Baga massacre is an indicator of the dilemma the Nigerian military faced under President Jonathan. There was a tendency to manufacture untruths and peddle them as facts. A section of the Nigerian press (the South West press) would propagate the stories with sensational headlines and little or no verification. The deck of cards was stacked against the military and President Jonathan.

CIVILIAN JTF

During the second emergency rule, some youths in Maiduguri came together to differentiate law-abiding youths from Boko Haram elements as the military crack usually followed the pattern of arresting all the young men within a cordon for screening. Some of the arrests were indiscriminate and was a source of complaint about rights violations.

The goal of the "Civilian JTF" is to identify the real Boko Haram and point them out to the military authorities. The young men were armed with sticks, machetes and daggers. The CJTF began by conducting stop and search duties and the local population bristled at the fact that they had no official authority.

Within a short time, the youths gained the trust and confidence of the military and they took on an active role of being spotters of the enemy.

A leader of the CJTF explained their mission thus:

> We are tired of them (Boko Haram) and we want to put an end to it. Since soldiers don't really know who the Boko Haram members are, we who live with them and know them very well, resolved we have no option than to fish them out.[20]

The Civilian JTF has been a major contributor to the relative peace in Maiduguri. The youths successfully identified many BH insurgents for arrest by the military.

The Nation newspaper praised the CJTF as heroes:

> These young men and ordinary citizens are true heroes. Many of them barely could eke out a living. Hardly had any members of their families benefitted anything of the Nigerian State. They rose up and, imbued with patriotism, chose to defend their ancestral homes, ready to die in the process if necessary. . . .
>
> The contribution of the Civilian JTF has shown that there must be partnership between the military and the civilian population if progress is ever to be made in the defence of Nigeria's territorial integrity.[21]

In one dramatic exploit in June 2013, the CJTF in Maiduguri arrested four suspected Boko Haram members including the sect's operations commander and handed them over to the military. The CJTF recovered arms and ammunitions from the suspects. The arrest occurred during a "stop and search" operation by CJTF in the Galtimari Ward, Maiduguri.[22]

In another incident, the CJTF ambushed and killed about 70 Islamist insurgents in Madagali, Adamawa State. The CJTF were tipped off that the insurgents would be coming to Madagali to purchase foodstuff. The vigilantes mobilized and laid an ambush for the militants. About 100 militants showed up for the shopping spree, but the vigilantes opened fire on them with Dane guns.[23]

In 2014, the *New York Times* reported that the vigilantes have been able to clip the wings of Boko Haram to a reasonable extent:

> Boko Haram has been pushed out of Maiduguri largely because of the efforts of a network of youthful informers-vigilantes fed up with the routine violence and ideology of the insurgents they grew up with. . . .
>
> Governor Shettima has recruited the vigilantes for "training" and is paying them $100.00 a month. . . .
>
> The vigilante group's leaders say some of their recruits are repentant former Boko Haram members, making it easier to correctly identify and catch the insurgents.[24]

There was understandable pushback by Boko Haram against the CJTF. The insurgents killed 24 vigilance personnel in Monguno in 2013.[25] In Banisheikh (Borno State), a lack of coordination between vigilance personnel and the military resulted in the killings of several vigilance personnel.[26] Six CJTF members were killed in Damasak. The vigilance operatives had traveled to Damasak to purchase inventory of women's necklaces. They were asleep in a house when four insurgents came in and executed them in their sleep.[27]

In March 2014, Shekau passed a *fatwa* (death sentence) on Civilian JTF members:

> I'm telling you that I have started a war against you. In this world there are two kinds of people; there are those who are with us or those who are against us, and the latter group are those I'll kill once I spot them. From now on, my focus of attack is going to be the Civilian JTF. Let the Civilian JTF know that this is Shekau talking. You will now really understand the person called Shekau. You don't know my madness, right? It is now that you will see the true face of my madness. I swear by Allah's holy name that I will slaughter you.[28]

DISCIPLINE

The Nigerian Army admonished the CJTF to be disciplined. During a visit to CJTF members undergoing training in Borno State, the General Officer Commanding 7 Division of the Nigerian Army, Major General Obidah Ethan, commended their impressive zeal. The GOC also commended the Borno governor for providing the platform for the empowerment training. General Obidah recognized the youths as "formidable partners in the fight against insurgency."[29]

In May 2016, the CJTF asked the federal government to allow them to carry firearms to protect civilians in Borno State. The vigilance group members argued that by using sticks and knives and relying on fire power from the military they succeeded in chasing BH insurgents out of Maiduguri. However, the insurgents resorted to killing civilians in the countryside. Their spokesman Bello Dambata said:

> We have structures in all the 27 local government areas and our members are highly disciplined.
> We want arms so that we can take the fight to the insurgents in the bushes. We also need arms for our members to protect vulnerable civilians who are being attacked everyday.[30]

195

In July 2016, 250 former Civilian JTF members joined the Nigerian Army. Upon completion of military training and induction, the new soldiers paid a thank you visit to Governor Kashim Shettima at Government House in Maiduguri on July 22nd, 2016. The governor acknowledged that "the emergence of the Civilian JTF is a game changer in the fight against Boko Haram."[31]

The CJTF is structured along the lines of a quasi-military organization with a uniform and ID cards. It is the lead helper to the military in the fight against insurgency in Nigeria's North East region.

In January 2016, local hunters in Borno asked to join the fight against Boko Haram.[32] In November 2014, after the military was defeated by Boko Haram in the attack on Mubi, the hunters in Adamawa State mobilized and took the fight to the insurgents and recaptured Mubi from the insurgents. Adamawa State government was so pleased that it announced that it would recruit and train 10,000 local hunters to combat the insurgents.[33] Some analysts have contended that the CJTF and hunters use mystical means (African Science) in battle. It makes them bulletproof and sometimes invisible to the assailants.[34] Prof. Nwolise calls it "Strategic Spiritual Intelligence." However, it has not been subjected to scientific validation.

BURATAI'S LEADERSHIP

On May 29th, 2015, President Muhammadu Buhari was sworn in as the president replacing President Jonathan whom he defeated in the elections held in March 2015. President Buhari changed the military high command in July 2015, appointing Lt. Gen. Tukur Buratai as the Chief of Army Staff (COAS). General Buratai was formerly the Commander of the Multinational Joint Task Force (MNJTF).

The president ordered that the military command and control center be relocated to Maiduguri. It was and is now housed at the headquarters of 7 Division in Maimalari Barracks. Gen. Buratai has served as an effective leader of the Nigerian Army, recovering all territories from Boko Haram and ensuring that the morale of the troops is high.

The respected *Guardian* newspaper wrote about Gen. Buratai:

> His expert management of the army and the role his men have played to save Nigeria from national disgrace and international ridicule are notable. His strategic restructuring of the army is wise and timely just as he was rounding off with combing Sambisa forest in search of insurgents and rescuing the abducted Chibok girls.[35]

196

Buratai practices Management by Walking About (MBWA). He motivates his men with this personal presence, going into places where his life could be at risk. His convoy has been ambushed more than once by Boko Haram, but the chief is not deterred.

Nigerian Air Force

The Nigerian Air Force, which was first fully deployed with significant air assets during the second emergency rule in May 2013, has become a major part of the assault on the insurgents. Given refusal of the United States to sell modern aircrafts to Nigeria because of alleged violations of the United States Leahy Act,[36] President Jonathan acquired modern air assets from Russia,[37] China,[38] Canada[39] and Belarus,[40] These assets are now fully operational and have changed the tide of battle in favor of government forces. The Nigerian Air Force is now equipped with aircraft for flying intelligence, surveillance and reconnaissance missions, a capability that did not exist during the Chibok mass abduction of April 2014.

CONCLUSION

The military solution to the Boko Haram insurgency has been hampered by many factors. Under President Jonathan there was no clear direction and political will to tackle the insurgency. The Jonathan administration has also argued that the lack of a weapons buying program since the tenure of President Shehu Shagari (1979–1983) was a problem. President Shagari was overthrown in a military coup on December 31st, 1983. Successive Nigerian leaders including Gen. Muhammadu Buhari, Gen. Babangida, Gen. Sani Abacha, Gen. Abdulsalami Abubakar, President Olusegun Obasanjo and President Umar Musa Yar'Adua did not attend to the armaments needs of the military. So, when BH declared war on Nigeria, the troops were forced to fight with expired bullets. In Chapter 7, it was narrated how the heavy weapon at Giwa Barracks – the Shilka – had failed to fire when the soldiers had BH insurgents in their gun sights.

In February 2014, Governor Kashim Shettima declared that Nigeria was at war, but Boko Haram was better armed than the Nigerian military.[41]

The Jonathan government was so desperate for arms that it entrusted individuals with large sums of cash to buy spot market arms in South Africa.

197

The South African authorities first seized US$9.3 million and three weeks later seized another US$5.7 million. The South Africans said the huge sums of cash were not declared.[42]

The Buhari government has found the new US government under President Trump to be more cooperative. In April 2017, President Trump promised to sell to Nigeria US$600 million dollars worth of 12 numbers Embraer A.29 Super Tucarno fighter jets.[43] President Buhari's government has recently paid a down payment of US$500 million for the jets which will be delivered in 2020.[44]

Armed with modern equipment and having an inspirational leadership, the Nigerian troops have taken the fight to Boko Haram and recaptured all local governments under their control. BH insurgents have gone back to their playbook of guerrilla warfare. It is hoped that the military will increase its intelligence assets that will enable it to contain the guerrilla tactics being used by the enemy. Despite the impressive prowess of the military under President Buhari and Gen. Tukur Buratai, the BH threat remains existential in the North East. Military thinkers and planners need to invent new ways of dealing with this insurgency.

NOTES

1. Adrian Morgan. "Nigeria: Muslim Massacres of Christians" *Family Security Matters* (December 29th, 2010). http://www.familysecuritymatters.org/publications/detail/nigeria-musim-massacres-of-christians
2. "Borno Elders Call on FG to Withdraw JTF" *Sahara Reporters* (July 14th, 2011).
3. Kelvin Ashindorbe and Saheed B. Owonikoko. "Religion, Radicalisation and Terrorism in Nigeria" in Pius Adejoh and Waziri Adisa (Editors). **Terrorism and Counter-Terrorism War in Nigeria**. Lagos, Nigeria: University of Lagos Press (2017).
4. Ibid. Page 188.
5. Ibid. Page 189.
6. Laolu Adeyemi. "There Has Been a Lot of Political Interference in the Fight Against Insurgency" *The Guardian* (September 6th, 2014): Page 50.
7. Uchenna Awom and Chibuzo Ukaibe. "JTF Killed More Civilians than Boko Haram – Sen. Bukar Ibrahim" *Leadership* (November 9th, 2012): Page 4.
8. "JNI Accuses Army of Killing Innocent Muslims" *The Punch* (April 8th, 2014).
9. Olusola Fabiyi. "Boko Haram Fighting for Justice – Tukur" *The Punch* (May 16th, 2012): Page 8.
10. See Virginia Comolli. **Boko Haram: Nigeria's Islamist Insurgency**. London: Oxford University Press (2015): Page 112.

11. "Bomb Blasts Rock Northern Nigeria" *News24* (January 5th, 2012).
12. Joe Brock and Felix Onuah. "Nigeria Declares Emergency in Areas Hit by Islamists" *Reuters* (May 14th, 2013).
13. Comolli (2015): Page 79.
14. Amnesty International. **Nigeria: Trapped in the Cycle of Violence**. London: Amnesty International Ltd. (2012). www.amnesty.org
15. Vincent Kalu. "Baga Massacre: The Untold Story" *Saturday Sun* (May 18th, 2013): Page 64.
16. Ibid.
17. See the following reports: "Baga Killings May Constitute Crimes Against Humanity, ACN Warns" *The Guardian* (April 26th, 2013): Page 3; "Why International Criminal Court Should Visit Baga – SERAP" *The Punch* (May 6th, 2013): Page 79; Tobi Soniyi et al. "NBA Condemns Baga Attacks" *This Day* (May 3rd, 2013): Page 10; Yusuf Ali, "CPC Blasts Jonathan Over Baga Massacre" *The Nation* (May 6th, 2013): Page 2. "The Mindless Baga Killings" *Sunday Punch* (May 5th, 2013): Page 16. Michael Olugbode and Senator Iroegbu. "Baga Carnage Underestimated, Says Senator Lawan" *This Day* (April 28th, 2013): Page 10.
18. Dr. Ona Ekhomu. **Baga Crisis Disinformation Correction Project – Final Report**. Abuja, Nigeria: Office of Chief of Defence Staff – Defence Headquarters (June 4th, 2013).
19. Taiye Odewale. "Shettima, District Head Lied in Baga Casualties – Senate" *Daily Newswatch* (June 27th, 2013): Page 3.
20. Collins Edomaruse. "Living with the Monsters and Civilian JTF" *This Day* (July 6th, 2013): Page 16.
21. Editorial Page Comment. "Civilian JTF to the Rescue" *The Nation* (October 15th, 2014): Page 19.
22. Njadwara Musa. "Youths Arrest Boko Haram Commander, 15 Others" *The Guardian* (June 29th, 2013): Page 1.
23. Barnabas Manyam. "Madagali Massacre: Vigilance Group Did Not Hand Over Boko Haram Suspects to Us, Say Police" *The Nation* (May 18th, 2014): Page 8.
24. "How Civilian JTF Drove Boko Haram into Bush" *New York Times* reproduced in *The Nation* (October 22nd, 2013): Page 4.
25. Obinna Anyadike. "Updated Timeline of Boko Haram Attacks and Related Violence" *The New Humanitarian – Geneva* (December 12th, 2013).
26. Ibid.
27. Inusa Ndahi. "Insurgents Kill Six Civilian JTF in Borno" *National Mirror* (August 28th, 2013): Page 49.
28. Ola Audu. "Boko Haram. Shekau Claims Responsibility for Attack on Giwa Barracks, Threatens to Attack Universities, Civilian JTF" *Premium Times* (March 24th, 2014). http://www.premiumtimesng.com/news/157374-boko-haram-shekau-claims-responsibility-for-attack-universities-civilian-jtf.html
29. Michael Olugbode. "Army Demands Discipline from Civilian JTF" *This Day* (November 24th, 2013): Page 96.

199

30. Njadwara Musa. "Borno Civilian Task Force Seeks Permission to Carry Arms" *The Guardian* (May 15th, 2014): Page 12.
31. "Former Civilian – JTF Members Join Nigerian Army" *Saturday Sun* (July 23rd, 2016): Page 52.
32. See "Hunters Seek to Join Boko Haram War" *The Nation* (January 4th, 2016): Page 8.
33. Jaji Sani. "Adamawa Got Set to Train 10,000 Local Hunters to Counter Boko Haram" *This Day* (November 18th, 2014).
34. OBC Nwolise. "Military Intelligence, Military Operations and War Against Terrorism in Nigeria" in Pius Adejoh and Waziri Adisa (Editors). **Terrorism and Counter-Terrorism War in Nigeria**. Lagos, Nigeria: University of Lagos Press (2017): Pages 453–474.
35. "The Military and Nigeria's Security" *The Guardian* (January 24th, 2017): Page 14.
36. Senator Iroegbu and Deji Sani. "US Blocks Nigeria's Purchase of Chinook Helicopters from Israel" *This Day* (September 23rd, 2014): Page 1.
37. Olalekan Adetayo. "Boko Haram: Russia to Supply Nigeria Arms" *Sunday Punch* (September 28th, 2014): Page 5.
38. Guy Martin. "Recent Nigerian Military Acquisitions" *Defence Web* (March 30th, 2015). www.armscor.co.za
39. "Boko Haram: Canada Tops Countries Selling Arms to Nigeria" *This Day* (March 17th, 2015): Page 7.
40. "Belarus to Supply 12 Helicopters to Nigerian Air Force" *The Nation* (September 26th, 2014): Page 2.
41. Augustine Ehikoya. "Boko Haram: Nigeria at War, Says Governor" *The Nation* (February 18th, 2014): Page 1.
42. "Bad Arms Deal: Nigeria Loses $5.7m More to South Africa" *The Nation* (October 7th, 2014): Page 1.
43. Olaleye Aluko. "B'Haram: Trump to Sell $600m Fighter Planes to Nigeria" *The Punch* (April 11th, 2017): Page 15.
44. Marcel Mbamalu. "Nigeria Takes Delivery of 12 Tucano Warplanes in 2020" *The Guardian* (April 23rd, 2018). www.guardian.ng/news/nigeria-takes-delivery-of-12-tucano-warplanes-in-2020/

13

Negotiations

INTRODUCTION

The Nigerian government exhibits a pattern of behavior in its management of conflicts. It confronts any major crisis with the use of force. Usually, this quells the conflict. Then it attempts to soothe frayed nerves with the constitution of a judicial commission of inquiry.[1] A new conflict resolution methodology is being experimented with by the government – negotiations and amnesty programs. Negotiations/amnesty was first used after the Nigerian Civil War (1967–1970) when the federal military government led by General Yakubu Gowon declared "no victor, no vanquished." It was again used skillfully by President Umar Musa Yar'Adua in 2009 to end an armed insurgency in the Niger Delta that crippled oil mining operations. Oil production is the economic mainstay of government revenues providing up to 90% of foreign currency earnings.[2]

The response to the Boko Haram insurgency has followed the government's conflict and peace management architecture. The response to the Customs Roundabout massacre was a crackdown. If the federal, state and local governments had established effective risk mapping tools that would have resolved the conflict, then perhaps Nigeria might have avoided this insurgency. Unfortunately, the conflict was poorly managed setting off a chain reaction that created an insurgency. Consequently, by September 2019 the insurgency had claimed about 35,000 lives, displaced 4.2 million people and destroyed the economy of the North East.

In April 2018, Nigeria's President Muhammadu Buhari announced that his government was willing to grant amnesty to Boko Haram members willing to surrender their arms. He said the government was ready to rehabilitate penitent members of the sect and reintegrate them into society. His words:

> While efforts are being made to release every abducted citizen . . .
>
> In Nigeria, government is ever ready to accept the unconditional laying down of arms by any member of the Boko Haram group who shows strong commitment in that regard . . . We are ready to rehabilitate and reintegrate such repentant members into the larger society . . . This country has suffered enough of hostility. Government is therefore appealing to all to embrace peace for the overall development of our people and the country.[3]

The negotiations approach to solving the BH insurgency did not commence with the statement above made by President Buhari. As far back as April 2013, President Jonathan bowed to pressure from influential Northerners including the Sultan of Sokoto, the Northern Elders' Forum and the Northern Governors' Forum to set up the 26-member Turaki Committee formally known as the Presidential Committee on Dialogue and Peaceful Resolution of Security Challenges in Northern Nigeria.[4] President Jonathan had previously described BH fighters as "faceless" and "ghosts," saying that the government could not negotiate with "ghosts."[5]

The offer of amnesty to Boko Haram is argued in tribal silos. While proponents of amnesty maintain that there is precedent and parallel between Boko Haram and Niger Delta militancy which was resolved through amnesty, opponents maintain that the crimes of Boko Haram are too many – with over 35,000 kills to their credit including video-taped beheadings of civilians and soldiers and sundry atrocities.

The greatest difficulty with negotiations and perhaps amnesty for BH insurgents is that the insurgents have not asked for it and are not interested in it. While some BH fighters have on their own surrendered to government security forces,[6] and many others have been captured and taken off the battlefield, the leadership of BH personified in Imam Abubakar Shekau is unrepentant and says the Islamists do not need amnesty. Rather, it is the federal government that should be granted amnesty.[7]

This author holds the position that until Boko Haram is defeated in battle, there can be no negotiation because the insurgency is ideology based. It is based upon extremism, radicalism, nihilism and fatalism. His words after the 2014 fraudulent negotiation:

> Well, I personally feel that the Federal Government knows very little about the sect. If government had good understanding or intellection, then it would have known that you cannot negotiate with these people until they are defeated. The only good terrorist is a dead one or one in custody. Yet the government feels it can convince them to lay down their arms. Boko Haram is about religious extremism. . ..
>
> Understanding the sect is a job for intellectuals. These are people we can refer to as "Boko Haramologists" and the Federal Government is not consulting them.[8]

IMPEDIMENTS TO NEGOTIATIONS

The BH insurgency has been going on for ten years now (as at September 2019), with tens of thousands of deaths and considerable ruin to the economy of the North East region. A negotiated settlement would have been desirable such that the job of rebuilding could then begin. However, this conflict has been different. There have been several impediments to negotiations including:

1. Ideological constraint
2. Leadership of BH
3. Wanton killings and destruction
4. Nihilism, fatalism and cultism
5. Negotiation fraud
6. Best and brightest.

Ideological constraint

The BH insurgency is not a garden variety insurgency aimed at righting some societal ill. The insurgency is built on Wahabi Salafi ideology and its method is conversion or death. Frequent reference is made to the Niger Delta insurgency which was about environmental degradation and lack of employment opportunities for youths in the Niger Delta. Once the Yar'Adua government agreed to address the issues, the combatants laid down arms and went through a program of disarmament, deradicalization and reintegration into society. It worked like a charm because the insurgency was aimed at solving a social ill. In the BH insurgency, the Nigerian government would not be able to institute strict Sharia code throughout the country as demanded by Abubakar Shekau. This was illustrated in 2013 following the aborted dialogue by the Turaki Committee. Shekau's words:

> We are stating it categorically that we are not in dialogue or ceasefire agreement with anyone. And we have never asked anybody in the name of Abdulazeez to represent me, Abubakar Shekau, the leader of this movement. . . ..
> I swear by Allah that Abdulazeez or whatever he calls himself did not get any authority from me to represent me in any capacity. . . . .
> What we are doing now (the jihad) is what is prescribed for us by Allah and his holy prophet. We are workers in the vineyard of Allah.[9]

Leadership of BH

The insurgency is led by the battle-hardened and bloodthirsty Shekau. Shekau has so much hatred and venom for Nigerian authorities and non-members of his death cult. He is a psychopath, a sociopath and a man of base morality who often covets the wives of his commanders and kills them in order to "marry" their wives (see Chapter 3 of this book).

Shekau explains his excesses: "We are not out to cause destruction, but to correct the ills of the society. And Allah is more powerful than all, and He has the might. Allah will surely assist us to victory."[10]

The young leader of the BH splinter group, Abu Musab Al-Barnawi, whose group is now called Islamic State in West Africa (ISWA), is probably more amenable to negotiation with the federal government. If Al-Barnawi, the son of slain BH leader Mohammed Yusuf, was in charge of the main BH group, there might be hope for a negotiated settlement.

Wanton Killings and Destruction

The BH insurgency is not being prosecuted in a manner that will facilitate negotiations and peace. The insurgency has cost tens of thousands of lives and massive destruction of whole towns, villages, schools and homes. In April 2013, BH fighters engaged in a firefight with troops of the MNJTF in Baga. Retreating BH fighters set fires to homes. The burning of homes was replicated in Bama on April 2013[11] and in so many other towns and villages. In the second attack on Baga in January 2015,[12]

BH killed 2,000 people. That was murder on a genocidal scale. See more statistics of BH killings in Table 13.1. In the last three years, the sect has killed over 18,000 people. There is no insurgency anywhere in the world that has produced so many fatalities.

Vanda Felbab-Brown wrote in *Foreign Affairs*: "Boko Haram stands out in predatory behavior and failure to deliver the most rudimentary public services in the communities it controls."[13]

In April 2018, *The Punch* newspaper wrote about amnesty for BH: "But we draw a red line where blood-stained mass killers are concerned. There should be no blanket amnesty. The responsibility of the state is to apprehend and prosecute criminals as demanded by natural justice and the law."[14]

In March 2018, four United Nations aid workers providing humanitarian aid in Rann IDP camp were killed and a female nurse abducted by Boko Haram. A UN spokesman said that aid workers put their lives on the line every day to provide emergency assistance to vulnerable women, children and men. He said:

> Over 7.2 million people are in need of humanitarian assistance this year in the worst affected states of Borno, Adamawa and Yobe, and 6.1 million targeted for humanitarian assistance. The BH insurgents killed a medical doctor, two employees of the International Organization of Migration (IOM) and an aid worker with the International Committee of the Red Cross (ICRC).[15]

Rann, a town in Kala Balge LGA of Borno State, is located 175 km north of Maiduguri. It hosts a camp for over 55,000 internally displaced persons (IDPs).

Table 13.1   Boko Haram Scorecard for the Last Three Years

Year	No. of Attacks	Deaths
2017	500	3,329
2016	417	3,484
2015		11,500
Total		**18,313**

Source: Compiled by another from Vanda Felbab-Brown, "Nigeria Troubling Counterinsurgency Strategy Against Boko Haram" Foreign Affairs.com.

With over 30,000 murders to its credit, the Boko Haram insurgency is the deadliest conflict Nigeria has faced aside from the Nigerian Civil War.

Nihilism and Fatalism

The insurgents have exhibited nihilistic and fatalistic behaviors since the jihad erupted in 2009. The group has questioned the religious beliefs of other Muslims and rejected the leadership of the Sultan of Sokoto. The group attempted to assassinate the late Emir of Kano, HRH Alhaji Ado. Bayero, and has made death threats against the current Emir of Kano, HRH Alhaji Sanusi Lamido Sanusi.

The sect has questioned the fundamental beliefs of Islam in its wrong-headed interpretation of jihad. Muhammed Alli who converted Mohammed Yusuf was a student of the Taliban. Al Qaeda and Talibanism are kindred ideologies. Yet Al Qaeda has since disavowed the BH insurgency because of its bestiality and blood-spilling ways. Recently, ISIS, to which Shekau pledged *bayat*, attempted to relieve Shekau of his leadership of the sect. Shekau refused to hand over to Al-Barnawi the newly appointed leader. Shekau's intransigence has led to the splintering of the group where Al-Barnawi now heads the Islamic State of West Africa and Shekau heads Boko Haram.

A May 2018 report by *Reuters* asserted that the Islamists have not been defeated as the Nigerian government claims. The report states that ISWA, which is less extreme than BH, has become the dominant group. The report claimed that on some occasions ISWA protected residents of Borno State from BH fighters. It also stated that following a model of benign Islamism, ISWA would insist on locals following its rules and not hurt them. The report said: "They don't touch civilians, only security personnel."[16]

It should be noted here that ISWA is not a harmless jihadi group. They killed about 70 people in the attack on University of Maiduguri researchers and Nigerian National Petroleum Corporation (NNPC) officials in search of oil in the North East. They abducted two lecturers and a driver, releasing them only after ransom had been paid. It was also ISWA that seized the 110 school girls from Dapchi in February 2018.

They released the girls in April 2018 after collecting an undisclosed ransom. ISWA is a deadly and dangerous insurgent group. However, it appears slightly less bloodthirsty and bestial than Shekau's Boko Haram. Another faction of Boko Haram is the Mamman Nur group. Although its leader is in federal custody, the sect is still executing insurgency attacks in the North East and in Kogi State.

The BH insurgency is an apocalyptic death cult driven by its doomsday ideology. Its mission is to kill and destroy or be destroyed. It defies logic to assume there can be repentance in this group. Yet the conflict must be brought to an end not only militarily, but also through negotiation.

Negotiation Fraud

Negotiation with Boko Haram has been fraught with a lot of fraud. President Jonathan was averse to negotiations. However, he was prevailed upon by the Northern elite to dialogue with the jihadis.

In December 2014, the Department of State Service arrested seven associates of an Australian negotiator, Stephen Davis, who claimed that they were Boko Haram commanders and organized a phantom ceasefire with the federal government. The men collected millions of naira from the federal government while giving the impression that they were members of the Islamist militancy group interested in a ceasefire.[17]

The Saminu Turaki Amnesty Committee's work in 2013 also ended up with false representations which discredited the work of the committee. To meet its 90-day performance deadline, the committee reported that it had met with the suspected mastermind of the St. Theresa's Church bomb – Kabiru Sokoto. However, this was contradicted by the captured terrorist. He said that the alleged secret meeting between the Amnesty Committee and he had never been held. He described the assertion as a "blatant lie."[18] Amnesty Committee Chairman and Minister of Special Duties Alh. Saminu Turaki had announced that the committee held a parley as a confidence-building measure between Boko Haram and the committee. Turaki claimed that the meeting had been held at Kuje prison in Abuja. Sokoto's lawyer revealed that the terrorist (Sokoto) had been in the custody of the State Security Service all along, and had never been in Kuje prison.

The fact that BH leadership was not communicating directly with government officials made it easy for fraudsters to come forward and claim connections to the group. The presumed leader of the group that brokered the phantom ceasefire in the fall of 2014, Junaid Khadi, was an aide to Borno governor Kashim Shettima. He was believable and acted the role of a Boko Haram commander during negotiations that were led by the principal secretary to President Jonathan, Ambassador Hassan Tukur. The con men received a fortune in cash.

207

Another fraudulent negotiation was initiated in August 2012. A so-called deputy leader of BH, Habu Mohammed, announced in Mecca, Saudi Arabia, on August 13th, 2012 that the sect was in talks with the federal government represented by then National Security Adviser Col. Sambo Dasuki (Rtd.). Habu Mohammed claimed that the sect agreed to negotiations in response to peace moves by a cross section of Nigerians.[19]

On August 17th, 2012, the Minister of Information, Mr. Labaran Maku, disclosed that the federal government was reviewing the demands by the fundamentalists which included:

a. Release of their members currently being detained and prosecuted
b. President Jonathan's conversion to Islam
c. Payment of compensation (*Diyya*) for their members whom they considered were killed "unjustly" by security forces.[20]

On August 22nd, 2012, a Boko Haram spokesman said the sect was not involved in any talks with the federal government. He said that the sect had two sessions of dialogue with the federal government in 2011 and they were both aborted halfway through.[21]

Abu Qaqa warned those parading themselves as fake negotiators to desist or face the consequences. He warned the federal government in the email statement that the negotiation was a scam. He said:

> We wish to unequivocally distance ourselves from one Abu-Muhammad who is wittingly disguising himself as the next in command to our leader Mallam Mohammed Shekau. . ..
> We believe that the purported Abu Muhammed is the creation of the Nigerian government in order to mislead Nigerians on the crusade we are waging and they by the grace of Allah will not succeed.[22]

NEGOTIATING POWER

From 2011 to 2015, BH insurgents seriously terrorized the North East. They attacked targets at will and took over large swathes of territory. In 2012, the jihadis raised a negotiation wish list which they later discarded. Then, in 2013, the Turaki Amnesty Committee was rejected by Shekau. In 2014 some fraudsters obtained millions of dollars from the federal government promising to release the Chibok girls and prevailing on the government to observe a ceasefire. However, this was a hoax. BH was at the height of its power under President Jonathan and had no incentive to negotiate with the federal government.

Under President Buhari, BH has now lost physical control of all major towns in the North East. The insurgents have relocated to the countryside from where an asymmetric campaign is being carried out on a daily basis with attacks on mosques, IDP camps, highway ambushes, etc. While BH does not rule over any major city in the North East, it is still able to cherry-pick targets and strike at will. BH also has heavy presence in the Lake Chad area.

Notwithstanding the political realities of the 2019 general elections, the Buhari government did not suddenly become obsessed with amnesty and negotiations as the Jonathan government did in 2014 in the run up to the 2015 general elections.

The question now is: What does BH want?

1. Establishment of an Islamic Republic or caliphate in Northern Nigeria
2. Full implementation of Sharia law in Northern Nigeria
3. Fair share of the nation's wealth, particularly the redistribution of oil revenues
4. Eradication of poverty in the impoverished North
5. Restitution for the numerous injustices inflicted on Muslims by the Nigerian government.[23]

Boko Haram insurgents have simply shunned the various negotiation efforts of the federal government because the only thing the government could offer – money – does not hold a high value for the insurgents. Abu Musab Al-Barnawi, an AQIM-trained terrorist/operative, is adept at kidnapping for ransom, but he is not interested in living an opulent materialistic life. The ransom income funds the insurgency.

MAJOR NEGOTIATION INITIATIVES

There have been four negotiation initiatives with Boko Haram since the inception of the jihad. In 2012, BH presented a list of impossible demands to the federal government. In May 2013, the Turaki Amnesty Committee got to work but produced no results. In the fall of 2014, there was the major fraudulent negotiation-cum-ceasefire in which the president's principal secretary played a leading role along with the chief of defense staff, Air Chief Marshal Alex Badeh. The Buhari government now has an ongoing initiative which has thrice been productive for the government: a) release of 21 Chibok girls (b) release of 82 Chibok girls and c) release of 104 Dapchi girls. President Buhari has stated that repentant jihadis who lay down their weapons will be deradicalized and reintegrated into society.

November 2012 Dialogue

The presidency announced on November 12th, 2012 that the government was holding talks with Boko Haram. Confirming the talks, presidential spokesman Dr. Reuben Abati said the dialogue was not being carried on in the way Nigerians would expect.[24]

The sect asked for compensation for its killed members and for the rebuilding of the Ibn Tiamiyya Mosque in Maiduguri which was destroyed in 2009.[25]

Speaking through Abu Mohammed Ibn Abdulaziz, the second-in-command to Shekau, the sect named some trusted Nigerians it would be ready to negotiate with in a list:

1. Former head of state Gen. Muhammed Buhari (he rejected the nomination)
2. Dr. Shettima Monguno
3. Former Yobe governor Bukar Ibrahim
4. Ambassador Gaji Galtimari
5. Aisha Alkali Wakil (known as Mama Boko Haram)
6. Mr. Wakil (Aisha's husband).[26]

After the assassination of civil war hero and former Federal Transport Commissioner Maj. Gen. Mohammed Shuwa in Maiduguri in November 2012, the federal government concluded that BH was not observing the ceasefire which it claimed would accompany the negotiation. On November 18th, 2012, President Jonathan confirmed that there was no dialogue going on with the Boko Haram sect.[27]

According to President Jonathan: "They (Boko Haram) are still operating under cover. They wear a mask. They don't have a face. You don't dialogue with people you don't know. We don't have anybody to dialogue with. There is no dialogue going on."[28]

This botched dialogue was suspected to be a ploy to buy time for the jihadis. They were aware that public opinion favored dialogue and the offer was made to freeze the government in place while the insurgents were hatching the next brutal terrorist plot. In the fourth quarter of 2012 when the dialogue/discussion was ongoing, Boko Haram killed three Chinese workers in Maiduguri (October 6th) and bombed St. Rita's Catholic Church in Kaduna (October 28th), which sparked reprisals against innocent Muslims. Gen. Shuwa was then murdered in his Gwange Maiduguri home (November 2nd).

Amnesty Committee

President Jonathan bowed to the Sultan of Sokoto to grant amnesty to the Islamists. The entire Northern elite campaigned vigorously for the amnesty program. The thinking was that amnesty would bring Boko Haram fighters in from the cold and cause them to lay down their arms, creating an opening for the cessation of hostilities and peace.

To give context to what President Jonathan was dealing with – following the declaration of Operation Serval by France in Mali, Nigerian troops who were on their way through Kogi State were ambushed by Ansaru, a splinter group of BH, in the first quarter of 2012. Then, in February 2013, nine female polio vaccinators were shot dead by BH in Kano. In Potiskum, Yobe State, three North Korean medical doctor employees of the Yobe State Health management Board had their throats slit in their home by BH fighters. BH also extended its operations beyond Nigeria's borders when it kidnapped a French family in the Northern region of Cameroon. On March 16th, 2013, seven foreigners working for the Lebanese construction company Setraco who were earlier kidnapped by Ansaru in Bauchi were executed. There was also the New Tarzan bus terminal bombing in Kano on March 18th which killed 26 people.

It was under this difficult security environment that President Jonathan introduced the Presidential Committee on Dialogue and Peaceful Resolution of Security Challenges in Northern Nigeria. The Committee was headed by Alhaji Saminu Turaki.

The terms of reference of the Amnesty Committee included considering the feasibility or otherwise of granting amnesty to the Boko Haram fighters. Another objective was the collation of the clamor arising from different interest groups that wanted the federal government to administer clemency, and the modalities of granting the amnesty.

The Amnesty Committee was applauded by many Nigerian leaders including former head of state, Gen. Muhammadu Buhari, former governor of Kaduna State, Alhaji Balarabe Musa, the leader of Jama'atul Izalatul Bida'a Waikamadul Sunna (JIBWIS) Izala sect, Sheikh Usman Abubakar Mabera, Katsina State Governor, Dr. Ibrahim Shema and Jigawa State Governor, Alhaji Sule Lamido.[29]

On April 11th, 2013, Shekau rejected the amnesty offer from the federal government. He said that the sect had done no wrong and that it was the government that needed to be pardoned by the sect. Shekau said that his sect had: "not committed any wrong to deserve amnesty. Surprisingly, the Nigerian government is talking about granting us amnesty. What wrong have we done? On the contrary, it is we that should grant you pardon."[30]

The Christian Association of Nigeria (CAN) which had all along opposed the idea of granting amnesty to Boko Haram, condemned the group for rejecting the amnesty offer, saying that it was an indication that the sect was bent on Islamizing Nigeria. CAN President Pastor Ayo Oritsejafor challenged Northern Nigerian leaders seeking amnesty for Boko Haram to bring Shekau to the table.[31] This author advised the government that unless and until Abubakar Shekau personally approved a negotiation, there could not be one as the jihadi leader was a megalomaniac.[32]

House of Representatives member Hon. Bitrus Kaze described the rejection of the amnesty as "humiliating, indescribably sickening and ridiculing. In my honest view granting amnesty to remorseless and unrepentant terrorists is the weirdest policy ever contemplated."[33]

Despite the rejection of the amnesty offer, the federal government urged the Amnesty Committee to continue its work and render its report.[34] The government said that the Amnesty Committee was part of bringing the Boko Haram crisis to an end.

The Executive Secretary of the Civil Rights Congress, Mr. Shehu Sani (who served as a member of the Nigerian Senate from 2015 to 2019)), said that the sect rejected the amnesty proposal because they saw through the "charade." He said that the amnesty program was intended to defraud the federal government by some individuals. He stated: "The sect has never made any demand, so attempting to entice them with money will simply not work. The process of finding lasting peace should begin with building confidence."[35]

The curtain was drawn on the committee's work after it was unable to get Boko Haram to the table. It concentrated on negotiating with sect members in prison custody. The false statement by the committee that it had met with Kabiru Sokoto in Kuje prison seriously dented its credibility.

In July 2013, the federal government announced a cease fire with Boko Haram.[36] Shekau promptly denied that the sect had signed any peace deal with the Turaki Amnesty Committee.[37] Evidential proof of the fraudulent ceasefire deal was the massacre of 52 students at the Government Secondary School (GSS) in Mamudo, Yobe State, on July 6th, 2013.

October 2014 Ceasefire

In October 2014, Chadian President Idris Deby brokered a ceasefire between the federal government and Boko Haram. The Principal Secretary to President Jonathan, Ambassador Hassan Tukur, led the federal government's delegation. The focus of this ceasefire was the release of the 214 Chibok school girls seized on April 14th, 2014.

The federal government acceded to the ceasefire but the girls were not released. The Chief of Defence Staff, Air Chief Marshal Alex Badeh, who announced the ceasefire on October 17th, 2014 said that hostilities would cease on all sides.

Within 24 hours of the ceasefire announcement by the Chief of Defence Staff, BH insurgents stepped up attacks in the North East.[38] They attacked Maikadiri village in Abadan Local Government Area, Borno State, and two villages in Adamawa State – Sina and Grate villages in Michika LGA. Scores of the villagers were killed. They tried to recapture Damboa town but were repelled by the military. BH insurgents also kidnapped ten girls in Wagga Mangono and Gana villages in Adamawa State.

The October 2014 peace deal signaled the naivety of the federal government and its anxiety to get the Chibok girls back. Some fraudsters put together a fraud scheme and were able to get paid for intermediation while an obviously angry Boko Haram lashed out at communities killing as many people as it could.

Another factor responsible for the lack of due diligence by the federal government on the representatives of Boko Haram was the looming 2015 general elections. The ruling party, the Peoples Democratic Party, knew that the electorate would punish it if the Chibok girls were not found. The abduction and captivity of the girls showed the federal government as ineffective. The party lost the presidency to the opposition in the March 2015 elections.

Buhari's Amnesty Program

President Buhari had publicly counseled his predecessor to grant amnesty to the insurgents. On May 29th, 2015, Buhari was sworn in as Nigeria's president. In April 2018, President Buhari announced that insurgents who were willing to surrender their arms could be granted amnesty. The president pledged to rehabilitate and reintegrate repentant Boko Haram sect members.

The effectiveness of this amnesty policy has not been seen. The insurgent attacks have continued unabated. One hundred and six Chibok girls are still in captivity. One Dapchi girl, Leah Sharibu, who refused to convert to Islam to gain freedom, is still with her ISWA captors as at September 2019.

The Buhari administration must be given credit for skillfully and expeditiously negotiating the release of 104 Dapchi school girls from ISWA captivity. The girls were seized in February 2018 and released in April 2018.

The Dapchi negotiations had significant inside track. Given that it was an ISWA job, there wasn't too much arrogance and intransigence as might have been the case under Shekau.

The point here is that offering amnesty to BH or ISWA is a necessary but not sufficient condition for peace. There must be something that will convince the insurgents that the time for peace is now.

CONCLUSION

The Jonathan administration made several peace efforts but they were a flop because Shekau did not believe that BH should show remorse or repentance. The federal government repeatedly acted as though it was on a mission to appease the insurgents.

Given the scale of destruction of lives and physical assets in the BH insurgency, the authorities must sort the leaders and ideologues who wantonly spilled human blood from those fighters who joined the insurgency under duress or were simply brainwashed. While stiff punishment should be meted out to the culpable sect members, the fighters on the periphery should be pardoned and allowed to resume their lives.

The victims of BH excesses that are still alive would be extremely offended by an act that simply sweeps all the transgressions of Boko Haram fighters under the carpet. The federal government should put a peace architecture in place which would provide backing for negotiations and eventual forgiveness programs. Without a peace plan, it will be easy to lapse into violent behavior.

It is not the prediction of this author that Shekau would ever adopt the negotiation option. His ego and his atrocities are too expansive. He is therefore on a suicide mission. Appeals for dialogue should be addressed to his lieutenants and fighters. If he can somehow become isolated, then he can be captured dead or alive. In October 2018, a commander of the Mamman Nur faction of BH was on the verge of surrendering to the federal government with 300 fighters. As a result, he was arrested by his superiors and executed.

The leader of ISWA, Sheikh Abu Musab Al-Banawi, is the son of the late Sheikh Mohammed Yusuf. Since it is Yusuf's blood that runs through his veins, diplomacy is part of his DNA. He could be targeted and convinced to come to the bargaining table. His forces who are right now protecting Borno villagers from marauding BH fighters can be left in place as village vigilantes to defend the homeland. Slowly, they would be absorbed into the deradicalization and reintegration program. With Sheikh Al-Barnawi already in the program, others might buy into it. The federal government can rebuild the Ibn Tiamiyya Mosque which was so rashly demolished in 2009. And Al-Barnawi should be compensated for the extra-judicial murder of his father. His example would become a powerful one against jihad.

Negotiation with BH insurgents is definitely an option but it should be done skillfully to achieve the desired results. The Buhari government should avoid the pitfalls of the Jonathan administration where garden-variety fraudsters scammed the government in the name of dialogue.

NOTES

1. See Isaac Olawale Albert. "Rethinking Conflict, Peace and Sustainable Development in Nigeria" in Isaac Olawale Albert et al. (Editors). **Peace, Security and Development in Nigeria**. Abuja, Nigeria: Society for Peace Studies and Practice (2012): Pages 1–18.
2. Ifeanyi Onuba. "Oil Still Accounts for 92% of Nigeria's Earnings – Investigation" *The Punch* (September 17th, 2017).
3. "Buhari Offers Amnesty to Repentant Boko Haram Members" *The Nation* (March 24th, 2018).
4. "Boko Haram: Jonathan Gives Committee Three Months" *The Nation* (April 24th, 2013). https://thenationonlineng.net/boko-haram-jonathan-gives-committee-3-months/

5. "Nigerian President Goodluck Jonathan Rejects Boko Haram Amnesty Call" *Africa Outlook* (March 8th, 2013).
6. See Michael Olugbode. "132 Boko Haram Terrorists Surrender to Nigerian Military" *This Day* (May 28th, 2018) and "1050 Boko Haram Insurgents Surrender, Many Flee – Army" *The Punch* (February 7th, 2018).
7. "Shekau, Boko Haram Leader Slams Amnesty Offer" *P.M. News* (April 11th, 2013).
8. Laolu Adeyemi. "Government Negotiators Did Not Apply Enough Savvy in the Ceasefire Deal" *The Guardian* (October 25th, 2014): Page 50.
9. "No Pact with FG – Shekau" *The Nation* (July 14th, 2013): Page 9.
10. Ibid.
11. Ola Audu. "17 Persons Killed, Over 200 Houses Burnt in Another Boko Haram – JTF Battle" *Premium Times* (April 29th, 2013).
12. Monica Mark. "Boko Haram Deadliest Massacre: 2000 Feared Dead in Nigeria" *The Guardian* (January 10th, 2015). https://theguardian.com/world/2015/Jan/09/boko-haram-deadliest-massacre-baga-nigeria
13. Vanda Felbab-Brown. "Nigeria's Troubling Counterinsurgency Strategy Against Boko Haram" *Foreign Affairs* (March 30th, 2018). https://www.foreignaffairs.com/articles/nigeria/2018/03/30/nigerias-troubling-counterinsurgency-strategy-against-boko-haram
14. "Boko Haram: No Amnesty for Mass Murders" *The Punch* (April 18th, 2018): Page 22.
15. Budget Chiedu Onochie and Njadwara Musa. "UN, EU Condemn Killing of Aid Workers, Civilians in Borno" *The Guardian* (March 3rd, 2018): Page 1.
16. "Claims and Counter Claims" *The Nation* (May 6th, 2018): Page 19.
17. Adelani Adepegba. "DSS Parades Seven Alleged Fake Boko Haram Negotiators" *The Punch* (December 17th, 2014): Page 3.
18. Ibid.
19. Ade Alade. "FG, Boko Haram Hold Talks Outside Nigeria" *Saturday Sun* (August 18th, 2012): Page 13.
20. Olalekan Adetayo. "Presidency Considers Boko Haram's Terms" *The Punch* (August 19th, 2012): Page 2.
21. Yusuf Alli. "Boko Haram Disowns Dialogue with Govt" *The Nation* (August 23rd, 2012): Page 9.
22. Ibid.
23. "Boko Haram as Freedom Fighters" *This Day* (April 15th, 2013): Page 16.
24. Olalekan Adetayo. "Govt in Talks with Boko Haram – Presidency" *The Punch* (November 13th, 2012): Page 2.
25. Ibid.
26. Ibid.
27. Madu Onuorah et al. "No Dialogue with Boko Haram, Says President" *The Guardian* (November 19th, 2012): Page 2.
28. Ibid.

29. "US Views Amnesty Option with Cautious Optimism" ***This Day*** (April 6th, 2013): Page 1.
30. Olawale Olaleye. "Roadblock to Peace Path" ***This Day*** (April 15th, 2013): Pages 18–19.
31. Ibid.
32. See "Ex-Army Chiefs, Don, Security Expert, Politicians, Others Unite Against Negotiations" ***The Nation*** (May 15th, 2014). See also Laolu Adeyemi. "Government Negotiators Did Not Apply Enough Saavy in the Cease-Fire Deal" ***The Guardian*** (October 25th, 2014): Page 50.
33. Jude Onwuamanam. "Rejection of Amnesty, Humiliation to FG" ***The Punch*** (April 14th, 2014): Page 4.
34. John Alechenu. "Boko Haram Amnesty Committee Will Go Ahead – Presidency" ***The Punch*** (April 14th, 2013): Page 4.
35. Ibid.
36. Clifford Ndujihe et al. "Boko Haram, FG Sing Ceasefire Deal" ***The Vanguard*** (July 9th, 2013): Page 1.
37. Okechukwu Uwaezuoke et al. "Shekau Denies Boko Haram Ceasefire" ***This Day*** (July 14th, 2013): Page 1.
38. Ayomide Oluokun. "The Curious Peace Deal" ***The News*** (November 3rd, 2001): Pages 12–14.

14

International Assistance

INTRODUCTION

The Boko Haram jihad broke out into an armed conflict in July 2009. Relying on the quick-fix military model, President Yar'Adua called out the military and after four days of fighting in Maiduguri, the military vanquished the jihadists. What government security officials failed to grasp at the time was that Yusuf's deputy was alive, and that the Boko Haram jihadi ideology of extremism and hate had crossed Nigeria's borders into neighboring Niger, Chad and Cameroon. It was a failure of Nigerian intelligence agencies that they did not connect the dots between the emirs in the neighboring countries and their value to the insurgency. After Boko Haram's defeat, an injured Shekau relocated to the Niger Republic where he escaped the military crackdown.

The situ of the conflict was Nigeria. However, the ownership resided in four countries in the Lake Chad Basin – namely Nigeria, Niger, Chad and Cameroon. So, the conflict was instantly regional and not national. Intelligence analysts apparently missed this important element of the conflict. In April 2010, Shekau released a video proclaiming himself the new leader of the jihadi group, vowing to avenge the death of Yusuf and their sect members.

To effectively combat the BH insurgency in its infancy, the government would have had to understand these variables and addressed them vigorously. A menu of actions available to the Nigerian authorities included:

a. Hot pursuit of Boko Haram fighters into those neighboring countries to incapacitate the jihad.
b. Enlist the help of the neighboring countries in defanging the snake.
c. Enlist the help of colonial powers such as France and Britain in addressing the threat of the insurgency decisively.
d. Identify financiers and backers of the sect and investigate the level of support to the jihadis.
e. Investigate the source of weapons recovered from the sect – such as the munitions in Dutsen Tashi, Bauchi State.
f. Conduct a judicial inquiry into the activities of the sect and the violent conflict. The panel should have determined if the military use of force was proportionate to the threat. The panel should have determined if the extra-judicial murders of over 700 people in Borno Police SHQ was justified use of deadly force.
g. Compensation for wrongful deaths should have been paid to survivors of victims along with sincere apologies.
h. Security officials who exceeded their authority should have been punished – prosecuted and dismissed from the service. The Operation Flush team that was at the customs market round-about on June 11th, 2009 should have been prosecuted for mass murders.
i. The Ibn Tiamiyya Masjid at Railway Quarters in Maiduguri should not have been demolished.

The actions by the government on July 30th, 2009 were hasty and were not the product of deep thought. The actions were arbitrary. The government was mistaken in the following assumptions that it made:

a. That it had solved the problem of Boko Haram by winning the Maiduguri battle.
b. That Abubakar Shekau, the deputy leader of the sect was dead. This was characteristically negligent thinking as there was no *corpus delicti*.
c. That the military crackdown had succeeded and BH would never rise again.
d. That an ideology can be suppressed under the jack boot of the military.
e. That if you don't see a foe, then maybe he doesn't exist.

In intelligence analysis and policy analysis, there is reference to the application of more vigor and creativity in the analytic process.[1] The catastrophic mistakes made here by the federal government (under President Yar'Adua) showed that there was probably inadequate intelligence analytic products forming the basis of important security policy decisions. When President Jonathan succeeded Yar'Adua on May 5th, 2010, the products of analysis (if any) did not improve significantly. There was frequent recourse to intuitive thinking.

Had the government's decisions been the product of structured analytical thinking; had the government appreciated the complexity of the problem of religion-based insurgency; had the government asked key intelligence questions (KIQs) of its analysts; had the analysts conducted deep analysis of the BH insurgency, then perhaps we would not have been where we are today (with a score card of 35,000 deaths, 4.2 million displaced persons, the economy of the North East in ruins and continuing attacks by suicide bombers).

The government merely heaved a sigh of relief, and life went on. It was an ostrich approach to governance, with the ostrich burying its head in the sand while its backside remained exposed. Denial is simply not a solution to a problem; it is a postponement of the evil day.

A careful and thoughtful dissection of the problem would have enabled the government to realize that since the BH insurgency was based in a border area with populations that speak Hausa, Kanuri, Arabic and other languages, that the membership of the sect involved citizens from four countries making it an international jihadi group. Since the sect was international in nature, the Nigerian authorities would have to involve its neighbors in solving the problem.

At the early stages of the conflict in July 2009 to August 2011, it was a local affair and was well within the capacity of localized response. However, the sophisticated bomb that destroyed the UN House on August 26th, 2011 was not a locally made IED. The target that was chosen, the weapon that was employed, the method of delivery of the ordnance to target and the declaration by the sect that it had intentionally targeted the humanitarian workers showed that the conflict was global. After the UN House bomb, the US Federal Bureau of Investigation (FBI) conducted blast scene forensics. The purpose was to determine the size of the ordnance, its chemical composition and other properties. The investigation by the US FBI was an international assistance.

The Nigerian government under President Goodluck Jonathan did not request such international assistance. The neighboring countries

221

were known to be safe havens for BH. However, President Jonathan did not insist that they must not give assistance to the insurgents. As has been said elsewhere in this book, President Jonathan assumed that they were "misguided youths," or "our brothers" and so handled the insurgents with kid gloves. By May 2011, he instituted a half-hearted state of emergency in 15 local governments across four states including Borno, Yobe, Plateau and Niger. Jonathan mixed up the ethnic violence that was occurring in Plateau state with Boko Haramism that was located in the North East. After six months, the emergency rule was not renewed by the Nigerian legislature (see Chapter 12 of this book).

INTERNATIONALIZATION OF CONFLICT

Aside from the geographical location of the insurgency in the Lake Chad Basin area connecting four nations, Boko Haram's operations provided other early indications of the international character of the conflict. Some instances are given in this section:

On May 12th, 2011, British citizen Chris McManus and Italian Franco Lamolinara were kidnapped in Kebbi State by BH splinter group, Ansaru. They were later killed by their captors in March 2012 in Sokoto during a botched rescue attempt by the British Special Boat Service, the Department of State Services and the Nigerian Army.

On August 26th, 2011, the UN House was attacked killing 23 and injuring over 100 people. In January 2012, German engineer Edgar Fritz Raupach was kidnapped in Kano by Ansaru and later murdered in May by his captors.

The United States Department of State on June 21st, 2012 designated BH leader Abubakar Shekau, Adam Kambara and Khalid Al-Barnawi, the leader of Ansaru, as "Specially Designated Global Terrorists" (SDGT).

Three Chinese workers were murdered in Maiduguri on October 6th, 2012 by BH insurgents. In November 2012, the United Kingdom proscribed Ansaru in response to the murder of Chris McManus.

On December 20th, 2012, a French engineer working in Katsina, Francis Collomp was kidnapped by Ansaru. In February 2013, three North Korean doctors (two males and one female) working for the Yobe State government were butchered in their home in Potiskum. Their throats were slit. On February 16th, 2012, Ansaru kidnapped seven foreigners working for a construction company, Setraco, in Bauchi. The seven men were later executed when the security agencies attempted their rescue.

In February 2013, a French family vacationing in Northern Cameroon was seized by BH insurgents. The family was later released upon payment of ransom in April 2013.

In July 2013, the UK proscribed BH. A French priest, Father George Vandenbeusch, was kidnapped by BH in Northern Cameroon on November 13th, 2013. He was released in December after ransom payment was received.

On November 13th, 2013, the United States Department of State followed the lead of the UK and designated Boko Haram and Ansaru "Foreign Terrorists Organizations." In December 2013, following the lead of the USA, Canada designated Boko Haram a terrorist organization.

Two Italian priests and a Canadian nun were kidnapped by Boko Haram in Northern Cameroon on April 4th, 2014. They were freed on June 1st, 2014 after ransom had been collected.

APPEAL FOR ASSISTANCE

In March 2014, President Jonathan called on France for assistance in the fight against the BH insurgents. This was in addition to the assistance and cooperation that was already in place with the US and the UK in the counter-insurgency operation.

The government had apparently underestimated the threat that BH posed to the country and insisted that a domestic approach was needed for its resolution. The government had tended to rely on the capacity of the military to deal with threats to national security. However, Nigeria's conventional army and military response could not adequately neutralize or control the BH threat. In an armed encounter in Mafa village, Borno State, in 2014, soldiers fled as insurgents attacked villagers with superior weapons.[2]

France

Despite suspicion, acrimony and tension in relations between France and Nigeria,[3] President Jonathan was compelled by circumstances to seek help in intelligence gathering and put pressure on the neighboring Francophone countries to join the fight against Boko Haram.

Regional cooperation with Nigeria's neighbors needed substantial and practical engagements in terms of effective border control, joint military operations, information gathering and sharing.[4]

The international assistance that the Western nations offered did not include combat troops on the ground. It was limited to intelligence gathering and military assistance,[5] such as training in counter-insurgency and counter-terrorism operations.

The French Ambassador to Nigeria, H.E. Jacques Champagne de Labriolle, told *The Guardian* newspaper that subsequent to the pledge by French President François Hollande in Abuja in July 2014 to support the war against Boko Haram, the French will provide "intelligence, intelligence sharing, strategic information and data."[6]

The envoy said:

> Our ideal which is drawn from the lesson we learnt in the Sahel is that for a long time, terrorists have been hiding in neighbouring countries. A deep analysis would now be put at the centre of the thinking that it's a regional wide action that is needed. It is a borderless region.[7]

In April 2015, the United States government announced the investment of the sum of $35 million in the fight against the BH insurgency. The US stated that the $35 million will be in the form of military and defense support services to France in the war against the Islamist terrorist group Boko Haram. The White House said the funding will provide assistance to France which has been actively supporting Nigeria's French-speaking neighbors – Niger and Chad – in their fight against BH insurgents as well as Mali which is also battling Islamist extremism. The three Francophone countries have been at the forefront of the war against the dreaded Islamist group.

United Kingdom (UK)

In August 2017, the UK government approved a £200 million assistance package to help Nigeria with the fight against BH insurgency. In a visit to the epi-center of the insurgency – Maiduguri – then British Foreign Secretary Boris Johnson and International Development Secretary Priti Patel announced a five-year care package. The aid package is targeted at the prevention of famine for 1.5 million people and to help keep 100,000 boys and girls in school.[8] This is an example of development assistance dealing with the effects of the insurgency.

Direct military assistance from the UK has been in the form of training. About 28,000 Nigerian soldiers have been trained in counterterrorism while another 40 UK military personnel have been deployed to Nigeria on a long-term basis.[9]

Chris McManus's Botched Rescue

British citizen Chris McManus was killed by his captors along with his co-hostage Franco Lamonilara on March 8th, 2012 in the Mabera sub-district of Sokoto City. He was executed by Ansaru terrorists, a splinter group of BH.[10]

Twenty commandos of the British Special Boat Service (SBS), which is the equivalent of the US Navy Seals, were deployed into Sokoto in a joint operation with Nigeria's DSS agents and the military. The Nigerian Navy (NN) on December 27th, 2006 established an elite special force unit named the Special Boat Service (SBS). The NN-SBS is dedicated to combating high security threats such as terrorism, insurgency, hostage taking and piracy. The NN-SBS has been playing a major role in the fight against the BH insurgency.

Intelligence about the location of the captives was obtained from the Boko Haram Emir in Zaria, Abu Muhammed, who was captured by the DSS. The intelligence was evaluated by the British authorities and Nigerian intelligence officials and found to be credible. British Prime Minister David Cameron authorized the rescue in conjunction with President Jonathan.[11]

The raid started early in the morning, but the Special Forces personnel found it difficult to breach the compound. The helicopter sound and overhead platform provided by GCHQ gave away the secrecy of the rescue operation. An armored personnel carrier had to be deployed to breach the perimeter fence. In the ensuing firefight the terrorists killed the hostages and some of the terrorists were also killed in action.

The terrorists held the two foreigners for over ten months before executing them. They had demanded a ransom of N150 million for the release of the two engineers.

Reacting to this tragic rescue incident, this author wrote: "The commanders ordered their (McManus and Lamolinara) execution once the security forces stormed their hideouts. The killing further underscored the fatalism and cruelty that epitomizes Boko Haram mentality and world-view."[12]

The author advised the security forces to mount such rescue operations at night time. He said: "In future, such a rescue operation should take place at night using night vision equipment in order to catch the terrorists off guard."[13]

The leader of Ansaru, Mohammed Usman, also known as Khalid Al-Barnawi, and seven other defendants are being tried in 2018 at the

Federal High Court Abuja Division over the murder of Chris McManus, Franco Lamolinara and Edgar Fritz Raupach. Hon. Justice Anwuli Chikere is presiding. The defendants and others at large are accused of conspiring to commit acts of terrorism in Sokoto, Kebbi, Bauchi, Borno, Gombe and other states in the Northern region of Nigeria between 2011 and 2013. The wife of Khalid Al-Barnawi, Halim, is also being prosecuted for having information which she knew to be of material assistance in preventing members of the splinter group from carrying out acts of terrorism but failed to disclose to the relevant security agencies.[14]

Other UK Assistance

After the unfortunate mass abduction of the Chibok school girls in April 2014, the UK government announced in May that it would send military assistance to Nigeria. The words of then Prime Minister David Cameron: "We agreed to send out a team that includes some counter-terrorism and intelligence experts to work alongside the bigger American team that's going out there."[15]

In June 2014, then British Foreign Secretary William Hague announced that the UK will increase its military and educational aid to help Nigeria tackle Boko Haram.[16]

US Assistance

The US government under President Obama provided significant assistance to Nigeria in the fight against extremism and BH insurgency. However, the relationship between Nigeria under President Jonathan and the US government was frosty. The US government, following various reports by Amnesty International on alleged abuses of human rights by the Nigerian military was reluctant to help Nigeria.

Clearly, foreign assistance is driven by national interest rather than altruism. If the BH insurgency was occurring in Nigeria's oil-bearing communities (South-South and South-East), the US might have overlooked some of the alleged infractions of the military and assisted. However, since the US did not have any interest at stake in the North East, the BH insurgency could claim 35,000 lives and not engage the interest of the US government.

For example, in the thick of the conflict, Nigeria was prevented from procuring sophisticated weapons that would have given her a tactical edge in combat. The US government invoked the Leahy Act which prevents the selling of weapons to governments that abuse human rights. The Nigerians promptly turned to the Chinese, the Russians, the Canadians, the Australians and other sources for weapons.

Defending the security forces against the human rights abuse allegations, then Nigerian Ambassador to the United States, Prof. Ade Adefuye (now deceased) described the US as a major pillar in the struggle against terrorists. He said that the US was reacting to claims by media sympathetic to opposition parties in Nigeria. The ambassador insisted that the rights abuses could not be substantiated as many of them were meant to embarrass the government of President Jonathan. He said: "The allegations of human rights violations were based on rumors, hearsay and exaggerated accounts of clashes between the Nigerian forces and Boko Haram members."[17]

President Donald Trump's administration which is more business oriented has been friendly with the President Buhari government. In April 2018, the Nigerian government paid a $469 million down payment for the purchase of Super Tucano aircraft and President Buhari promptly got invited to the White House.

The US government provided a complex mix of assistance to Nigeria in the fight against Boko Haram. In June 2013, the US offered a $23 million bounty for BH leader Abubakar Shekau and four others. Usually reward money produces information about wanted individuals.[18]

In June 2014, the US government placed a bounty of $18 million on the head of Khalid Al-Barnawi,[19] the leader of Ansaru – the Boko Haram splinter group that specializes in kidnapping and killing hostages, especially foreigners. As at May 2018, he was facing justice in a Federal High Court in Abuja for conspiracy, murder, kidnap and terrorism charges.

After the seizure of the Chibok girls, the US deployed search experts to help the Nigerians.[20] The US government provided overhead intelligence platforms to assist in the search. The team flew intelligence, surveillance and reconnaissance (ISR) flights in search of the Chibok girls. Deploying the team to Africa, then US President Barack Obama informed Congress that he had sent 80 armed forces personnel to Chad to help in the search for the Chibok school girls. President Obama wrote: "These personnel will support the operation of intelligence, surveillance and reconnaissance aircraft for missions over northern Nigeria and the surrounding area. The force will remain in Chad until its support in resolving the kidnap situation is no longer required."[21]

These intelligence assets were later diverted to other missions away from the search for the Chibok girls. The spy planes are in high demand for other American military operations from Afghanistan to the West of Africa.

227

Anti-Jihad Radio Station

Another aspect of international assistance provided by the US was the setting up of a 24-hour satellite radio and TV channel in Northern Nigerian to counter the jihadi narrative. The TV channel is being financed by the US Bureau of Counterterrorism at a cost of $6 million.[22]

Termination of CT Training

In December 2014, ongoing training for Nigerian military personnel being conducted under the US Counter-Terrorism Assistance Program to Nigeria was terminated by the Nigerian government. About 600 Nigerian soldiers benefitted from the counter-insurgency training before it was stopped. Nigerian military spokesman, Maj. Gen. Chris Olukolade, explained that it was a "purely strategic action."[23] The American trainers had requested the Nigerians to withdraw some equipment from the battlefield to facilitate the training. The Nigerians refused, saying that they could not withdraw equipment from battle for training.

Post Blast Scene Investigations Training

A team of bomb crime scene instructors with the United States FBI led by Michael Trubenback in September 2016 conducted training for Nigerian bomb detectives drawn from the Nigeria police force, the Nigerian Army, the Nigerian Navy, the Nigerian Air Force, the Office of the National Security Advisor and the Nigerian Security and Civil Defence Corps.

Chief Instructor Trubenback said: "this training is one of the post blast scene processes to help them investigate the post blast scene. They are being trained on how to identify Improvised Explosive Devices, how to collect evidence, among others."[24]

The FBI trainers explained that the skills they were imparting to the participants would enable the police explosives ordnance disposal (EOD) personnel to process terror attacks as crime scenes to gather evidence that would help in detecting and successfully prosecuting the perpetrators of such heinous attacks.

Security Governance Initiative

In August 2014, President Obama announced Nigeria's participation in the Security Governance Initiative (SGI) during the United States–African

Leaders Summit. In the SGI, the US and Nigeria work to improve security sector institution capacity to protect civilians and confront challenges and threats with integrity and accountability. The SGI involves multi-year funding commitments of increased US support and requires sustained, high-level leadership and commitment by partner countries to pursue policies in support of the agreed upon goals.[25]

Trans-Sahara Counterterrorism Partnership

Nigeria is a partner in the Trans-Sahara Counterterrorism Partnership, a US government effort to enhance regional security sector capacity to counter violent extremism, improve country and regional border systems, strengthen financial controls, and build law enforcement and security sector capacity.

Assistance for Affected Populations

The US government provides assistance to affected populations in the North East region of Nigeria. This includes support to health, water and sanitation services; the delivery of emergency relief supplies and protection services – including psycho-social support for survivors of BH violence. The US government also invests in helping to build security and increased opportunity in the North East region of Nigeria through education programs for boys and girls; maternal and child health services; and programs to strengthen democracy and governance, and counter violent extremism by engaging leaders across society, including women.

The US Agency for International Development (USAID) provides trauma counseling for survivors and their families, including those directly affected by the Chibok abduction. In 2014, USAID completed its third training course for psycho-social support teams based in Borno State. The role of the social workers, health care providers, and other community members is to sensitize communities to prevent stigmatization of BH abductees when they return, and to provide psycho-social first aid to girls and their families.

Nigeria Regional Transition Initiative

The Nigeria Regional Transition Initiative is a USAID program aimed at improving stability and strengthening democratic institutions in North

East Nigeria. The initiative focuses on building the resistance of communities vulnerable to the effects of violent extremist organizations, weak governance and insecurity through increased positive engagement between the government and communities; increased access to credible information; and support to reduce youth vulnerability to violent extremist influences.

The Sovereignty Issue

The United States government and other Western nations did not approve of President Jonathan's treatment of the Boko Haram threat as an internal matter – a domestic threat. A US intelligence official described the Boko Haram threat thus: "A persistent, regional threat that has long demonstrated the ability to carry out sophisticated, deadly attacks."[26]

President Jonathan wanted to go it alone. However, the government later relented and asked for foreign assistance, particularly with respect to controlling the borders with Cameroon, Chad and Niger which had hitherto made it easy for BH militants to evade capture by Nigerian forces.

The West accused the Nigerian Army of "heavy-handed tactics, shoddy logistics" and criticized President Jonathan's "preference for unilateral action instead of coordinating with regional governments."[27]

President Muhammadu Buhari in contrast has been more open to international military and humanitarian assistance.[28] President Buhari began his presidency by visiting Nigeria's neighbors in an attempt to forge alliances in the fight against the insurgents. The neighbors came on board with the blessing of France and the military campaign has gone well in favor of Nigeria and her allies.

Unfortunately, due to their military assistance to Nigeria, the neighbors have come under vicious attacks by the regional terror group. For example, Boko Haram carried out over 60 suicide attacks in Cameroon in 2017, making it the country most impacted by the regional extension of the BH insurgency. The over 60 attacks in Cameroon's Far North region represent a 50% increase in attacks over 2016. The UN Under-Secretary-General for Humanitarian Affairs, Ms. Ursula Mueller, said "some 3.3 million people need urgent humanitarian assistance in Cameroon."[29]

The reluctance of President Jonathan to call for foreign assistance was based upon his conception of sovereignty in terms of its conventional Westphalian meaning. Sovereignty relates to a state's monopoly in the legitimate use of force within a territory. It is defined as the "exclusive right of a state to exercise supreme authority over a territory and the people within that territory."[30]

The reality that President Jonathan faced was that sovereignty has become conditional. Political legitimacy at the international level is challenged by human rights principles which are now conceptualized as the basis of state sovereignty. In other words, the rights of the citizens such as the respect, protection and fulfillment of human rights (human security) form the basis of the legitimacy and authority of the state. When states are unable to fulfill this conception of sovereignty, then international human rights principles such as the Responsibility to Protect (R2P), allow the international community to provide assistance and support.[31] The negative local media coverage of the war, which was mainly engineered by the opposition parties, gave the Nigerian military a bad name and by extension the government of President Jonathan.

Western governments largely held back assisting Nigeria and Nigerians in the war against BH insurgency based upon Amnesty International's reports of rights abuses against Boko Haram suspects. Unverified interviews of anonymous victims were the uncorroborated evidence that formed the basis of President Obama's tepid response to the Boko Haram question. Some US lawmakers including Senator Christopher Coons (Democrat – Delaware), Representatives Steve Stockman, Sheila Jackson Lee, Frederica Wilson and Ms. Lois Frankel visited Nigeria on a humanitarian mission and became advocates for the North East and the rescue of the Chibok girls. Representative Sheila Jackson Lee (Democrat – Texas) called on the Nigerian government to set up a National Victims Fund[32] which the Jonathan government implemented in 2014.

Multinational Joint Task Force (MNJTF)

The Multinational Joint Task Force with its headquarters in Ndjamema, Chad, is a military alliance between Nigeria, Niger, Chad and Cameroon. These Lake Chad Basin nations had been suffering from banditry across their national boundaries for some time. In 1998, the MNJTF was created to combat cross-border banditry. This military alliance has become part of the fight against BH insurgency.

The trans-national nature of the BH terrorist organization as it operates beyond Nigerian shores into Niger, Chad and Cameroon has made it a regional threat. The MNJTF can be regarded as falling within the category of Wait's balance of threat theory of military alliance.[33]

President Muhammadu Buhari's regional offensive using the instrumentality of the MNJTF has dislodged Boko Haram from towns and villages that the insurgents had controlled in the North East. The stronghold of the terrorists in Sambisa Forest, near the Cameroon border, and hideouts within Lake Chad's huge maze of small islands and swamp land have been attacked by troops of the military alliance, defeating the insurgents in battle after battle.

Despite their defeat by the military forces, the insurgents have exhibited amazing resiliency in their ability to launch terror attacks at will. The primary method of attack is the use of PBIEDS – typically strapped onto young girls to evade detection.

An 8,500-man Multinational Joint Task Force (MNJTF) has been in hot pursuit of the insurgents. The porous borders have become better secured and the terrorists are no longer able to evade arrest by escaping from one country to the other.

After suffering devastating suicide bomber attacks in 2015, the Chadian authorities arrested, tried and convicted ten members of the BH sect. On Friday August 28th, 2015, the ten men were sentenced to death by firing squad. On Saturday August 29th, the men were executed. Among the ten Islamists executed was Bahna Fanaye (alias Mahamet Moustapha) whom a Chadian official described as the Emir of Boko Haram in Chad.[34]

CONCLUSION

This chapter has examined the role of international assistance in combating the BH insurgency, President Jonathan embraced the traditional orthodoxy of sovereignty and hesitated in seeking international help. His successor President Buhari has skillfully used the augmentation of better secured borders and synergies of the combined armies of the MNJTF to defeat the insurgents in conventional warfare.

The United States has led in the provision of foreign assistance in the fight against Boko Haram. Although President Barack Obama was cold toward the Jonathan government, his government still provided significant non-military assistance to the Nigerian people. After the mass kidnap of the Chibok girls, President Obama sent in intelligence assets, locating them in Chad with the mission of finding the girls through ISR flights.

The US anger against the Jonathan government was as a result of unproven allegations of human rights abuses against the Nigerian military. Several media organizations in Nigeria wrote exaggerated and even concocted stories of rights abuses which polluted the relationship between Nigeria and the West, raising the issue of sovereignty based upon human rights.

The Buhari administration has focused on building alliances with neighboring countries and seeking assistance from the West in combating the BH insurgency. While the government has clearly recovered all territory held by BH, the insurgency is far from over as the government does not appear to have a solution to the guerrilla tactics that the terrorists have adopted.

Substantial humanitarian assistance is now pouring in from the United Nations, European Union, USA, UK, France and other world powers. The BH insurgency has caused 4.2 million displaced persons in the North East – who all need to be fed daily.

The MNJTF needs to be strengthened and funded to keep the Lake Chad Basin area safe from BH elements who are camping out there in large numbers. The MNJTF has been a key asset in the fight against BH as they prevent the cross-border mobility of the terrorists. This has been a threat-based alliance which has been productive in military terms.

It is hoped that the international community will remain engaged with Nigeria for some time to enable the rebuilding of communities and population ravaged by the insurgency.

NOTES

1. See Katherine H. Pherson and Radolph H. Pherson. **Critical Thinking for Strategic Intelligence**. Los Angeles, CA: CQ Press (2013).
2. "Nigeria's Boko Haram Attack Borno State's Mafa Town" **BBC News** (March 3rd, 2014). https://www.bbc.com/news/world-africa-26418161
3. David Zounmenou and Mouhamadou Kane. "Nigeria's Fight Against Boko Haram: How Can France Help?" **ISS Today**. Pretoria: RSA (March 11th, 2014). https://issafrica.org/iss-today/nigerias-fight-against-boko-haram-how-can-france-help
4. Ibid.
5. Mohammed Isa. "Boko Haram and Nigeria's Foreign Relations" **Daily Trust** (August 8th, 2014).
6. Oghogho Obayuwana. "How France Will Support Nigeria's Anti-Terror War" **The Guardian** (August 4th, 2014).
7. Ibid.

8. Patrick Wintour. "UK Government Unveils £200m in Aid to Help Fight Boko Haram in Nigeria" *The Guardian – UK* (August 30th, 2017).
9. Ibid.
10. Madu Onuorah. "Fight Against Terror: Nigeria, Britain, Others, Deepen Cooperation" *The Guardian* (March 11th, 2012): Page 10.
11. Ibid.
12. Sesan Olufowobi. "Expert Suggests Night Raid for Future Rescue Operation" *The Punch* (March 14th, 2012): Page 6.
13. Ibid.
14. Ade Adesomoju. "Expatriates' Murder: FG Re-arraigns B'Haram Suspects" *The Punch* (February 23rd, 2018): Page 9.
15. Olalekan Adetayo. "Abducted Girls. Britain May Send Soldiers" *The Punch* (May 12th, 2012): Page 2.
16. Oghogho Obayuwana. "Another Berlin Conference Over Security in Nigeria" *The Guardian* (June 15th, 2014): Page 60.
17. Laolu Akande. "America Let Nigeria Down in Fight Against Boko Haram" *The Guardian* (November 11th, 2014): Page 6.
18. Paul Ohia. "Boko Haram: US Offers $23 Bounty for Shekau, 4 Others" *This Day* (June 4th, 2013): Page 1.
19. "US Places $18m Bounty on Boko Haram Splinter Group's Leader, Three Others" *The Nation* (June 14th, 2014): Page 5.
20. The experts included military advisers, negotiators and counselors. "US, UK Search Experts Arrive Nigeria" *The Nation* (May 10th, 2014): Page 4.
21. Emma Emeozor. "Chibok Girls: US Deploys Troops in Chad" *Daily Sun* (May 22nd, 2014): Page 15.
22. "US Sets Up Anti-Terrorism Radio in Nigeria" *Sunday Newswatch* (June 8th, 2014): Page 8.
23. "Nigerian Military Training Cancellation Baffles US Experts" *This Day* (December 4th, 2014).
24. Olaleye Aluko. "Probe Terror Attacks FBI Urges Nigerian Security Agencies" *The Punch* (September 27th, 2016): Page 12.
25. White House Facts on US Aid to Nigeria Against Boko Haram (October 14th, 2014).
26. Dan deLuce and Siobhan O'Grady. "US to Boost Military Aid to Nigeria for Boko Haram Fight" *Foreign Policy* (July 16th, 2015).
27. Ibid.
28. "Nigeria and Boko Haram European Foreign Policy Score Card 2016" **European Council on Foreign Relations** (2016).
29. "Boko Haram Carried Out 60 Suicide Attacks in Cameroon" *The Nation* (February 27th, 2018): Page 61.
30. Olajumoke Ayandele. "The Loneliest War" *The Republic* (June/July 2017).
31. Ibid.
32. Damilola Oyedele. "US Lawmakers Urge FG to Set Up Special Fund for Boko Haram Victims" *This Day* (June 16th, 2014): Page 8.

33. Stephen M. Walt. "Testing Theories of Alliance Formation: The Case of Southwest Asia" *International Organization* Vol. 42 No. 2 (1988): Pages 275–316.
34. "Chad Executes 10 Members of Boko Haram by Firing Squad" *The Guardian – UK* (August 30th, 2015).

15

Solving the Insurgency

INTRODUCTION

While most of the violence in this asymmetric conflict has been localized to the North Eastern states of Borno, Adamawa and Yobe, the reverberations of the BH insurgency have reached almost every corner of Nigeria. Many arrests of BH elements have been made in Lagos and the South West. BH has attacked targets in Kano, Gombe, Bauchi, Kaduna, Katsina, Niger, Plateau, Taraba, Kogi and other North West and North Central states.

The insurgency is a complex problem which involves extremist religious beliefs, doomsday ideology, Islamist militancy, apocalyptic cultism, suicide terrorism, nihilism, fatalism and a cruel mentality. The insurgents, like their ISIS "first cousins," are not fighting to build society, but to destroy everything in their path. BH insurgents are driven by Salafi jihad ideology an ultra-conservative type of Sunni Islam that espouses the use of violence to return the world to an ultra-puritanical version of the religion similar to the 7th-century caliphate.

While the spark for BH insurgency was local – corruption, betrayal of the sect by the former Borno governor, Senator Ali Modu Sheriff, official high-handedness by security forces, the extra-judicial murder of Mohammed Yusuf and others, insensitivity by the government, etc. – the inspiration is global jihad. The sect was radicalized in 2002 and has continued to preach radical Islamist ideology ever since. The provocations of June 11th, 2009 finally acted as *causus belli* for the undeclared war which is still ongoing at September 2019.

PROBLEM ANALYSIS

In order to solve the problem of insurgency in Nigeria, we have to accurately analyze the real problem. We argue that this problem has been poorly defined and analyzed hence the inability to solve it. With over 35,000 deaths and billions of dollars in asset destruction, this problem is a major catastrophic event. Figure 15.1 illustrates some of the societal and cultural challenges that Nigeria is facing.

On April 19th, 2010, Abubakar Shekau proclaimed himself the leader of the sect and threatened revenge. This did not portend any danger at the time. However, subsequent events have proven that the self-declaration should have been considered with concern and planning and the expenditure of considerable efforts to design meta-cognitive strategies that would address the looming insurgency. The government should keep the population safe by awareness, anticipation and action.

When the Bauchi prison break occurred on September 7th, 2010, a total of 756 prisoners were released and the facility torched with the deaths of officials. By the end of 2010, BH had launched attacks against churches in Maiduguri and Jos, attacked the mammy market in Sanni Abacha Barracks in Abuja and killed several people in a market in Jos. There was ample evidence of serious terrorist/insurgent activity:

a. The large number of attacks
b. The method of attacks – use of IEDs and automatic rifles
c. The large number of deaths – Bauchi Prison, Jos, Maiduguri, Abuja
d. The claim of responsibility for the attacks
e. The intentional targeting of government security agents and churches.

The Jonathan government should have taken notice of the grave threat that was afoot. There should have been an urgent and deep threat assessment by all security agencies and the nation should have gone on war footing. The nation was already under attack with over 100 killed in terrorist violence in four months, yet government officials hardly took notice. Instead, it was seen as a problem of the Nigeria Police Force. In September 2010, President Jonathan relieved Lt. Gen. Abdulrahman Dambazau of his appointment as Chief of Army Staff and appointed Lt. Gen. Azubuike Ihejirika as his successor. Consequently, Gen. Ihejirika was settling down in his new role, and did not recognize that the nation was under attack by an army of extremist jihadis.

Worriesome Statistics – Nigerian Education

As of 2019:

- 13.2 million out-of-school children (highest in the world)
- 6% of households with children own at least 3 books
- 2 in 3 children do not have access to early childhood education
- 51% of children engage in child labor
- 49% of children move on to secondary school
- 30+% of Nigerians are unable to read and write
- 9 million Almajiri children, out of the total 13.2 million, are out of school
- <8% of the country's budget is allocated to education

Figure 15.1 Education in Nigeria: worrisome statistics (statistics reported by EduCeleb).

Sources: FME, NBS, UBEC, UNICEF, EduCeleb research.

The problem analytic duty was that of intelligence agencies. They had the responsibility to anticipate threats, analyze the threats and present decision alternatives to the executive. When an executive does not or cannot appreciate the threat, it behooves the intelligence agencies to creatively alert the public so that they can protect themselves from imminent harm. The executive will eventually see the problem, and probably respond – hopefully appropriately – but people might have died in the time it took to bring the problem into the consciousness of the executive.

If intelligence agencies take their jobs seriously, then they would go beyond intentions and warning (I & W). They would include some actions that will safeguard the targets of planned attacks.

The threat assessment of the BH insurgency at its inception (April 19th, 2010 – December 31st, 2010) was poor or non-existent as the policy/intelligence/threat analysts missed all the indicators. They did not see a major problem. They wanted to see a minor problem, if at all. The poorly defined policy problem has been described as "the framing effect."[1] It is "the tendency to accept problems as they are presented," even when a logically equivalent reformulation would lead to diverse lines of inquiry not prompted by the original formulation. If the problem is not properly defined, it cannot be accurately and adequately dissected, and it cannot therefore be solved. At best, the analyst would recommend, and the executive would choose a wrong course of action

239

(COA) to solve the problem. Since applying good medicine to the wrong ailment never solves the problem, then it remains. This was the problem with the BH insurgency. If, while it was in its infancy, the government had realized that this was a threat that could claim over 35,000 Nigerian lives, it might have girded its loins and perhaps developed a broad spectrum of responses to the threat. The goal of the government would have been to prevent terrorist attacks, and not merely responding to terror attacks or worse yet – denial. The government has historically been able to use force to solve problems within its borders, so it was lulled into a false sense of security.

In December 2010, the Boko Haram threat did not appear to be anything more than a minor annoyance. The federal government felt that whenever it wished, it could make the problem go away. The politicization of the conflict also did not help matters. Northern leaders felt that the government should handle the terrorists with kid gloves. Despite the December 2010 murder of Alh. Fanami Gubio, the gubernatorial candidate of the All Nigeria Peoples Party (ANPP) in the 2011 elections, the governments – federal and state – did not understand the threat. Pre-election violence and killings are quite common in Nigeria and the assassination was probably mistaken for the usual acts of political violence that characterize electioneering campaigns in Nigeria.

A conceptual model for insurgency threat assessment (see Figure 15.2) would have considered the implications of the proclamation by Shekau that he is the new leader of BH. As of 2009, Shekau's pedigree as a war-like individual was well known (see Chapter 3 of this book).

Despite the remarkable achievements of the Nigerian military in capturing Camp Zero – the BH headquarters in Sambisa Forest; despite the recapture of all local governments formerly controlled by Boko Haram; despite the reconstruction and rehabilitation effort currently going on in the North East; and despite assurances by government officials that the BH insurgency is now a thing of the past, this author still considers BH to be a significant threat to Nigeria. It is still able to attack targets at will, with deadly accuracy.

On June 16th, 2018, BH used female wolf pack suicide bombers to attack Abbachari village near Damboa LGA, killing 32 people and injuring 84.[2] On May 31st, 2018, five soldiers lost their lives in a BH ambush along the Pridang–Bitta road in Gwoza LGA, Borno State. The insurgents pinned down the troops of 271 Task Force Battalion, Operation Lafiya Dole in a firefight. A pre-planted IED was detonated by the insurgents killing five of the soldiers. The clearance operation continued and the troops fought through the ambush neutralizing (killing) some insurgents

Figure 15.2 Risk mapping process.

Source: Author.

while others fled – some with bullet wounds.[3] On May 28th, 2018, a suicide bomber struck in Kondugha, Borno State, resulting in five deaths
and seven injuries.[4] In another attack on May 20th, 2018, Muslim worshippers in a mosque in Gashua, Gujba LGA of Yobe State were fortunately able to wrestle a female suicide bomber to the ground and prevent
her from detonating the PBIED (suicide bomb) strapped to her body. The
vigilant worshippers observed the woman struggling to detonate her ordnance which apparently malfunctioned and they promptly arrested and
handed her over to security forces.[5]

Let us analyze these four attacks that occurred in the last third of May
2018. In eleven days (May 20th to May 31st, 2018), the insurgents mounted
three attacks – two deadly, one foiled. All the attacks involved the use of
explosive ordnance. Nine people were killed in the three attacks. There
were several injuries. The three attacks occurred within Borno State (2) and
Yobe State (1). The cities/local governments attacked were locations prone
to insurgent attacks – Gwoza LGA, Kondugha and Gujba LGA.

A recent study reported that a large number of women and children
had been abducted by BH and brainwashed to conduct suicide bombing
missions.[6] Their supply of suicide agents seems inexhaustible. Minister

241

of Information Alh. Lai Mohammed has maintained that attacks similar to the ones examined above are signs that BH has been defeated.[7] This author believes that is a mistaken assertion. Terrorists who ambush troops on patrol, pre-plant IEDs that kill five troops and engage in an intense firefight before retreating are hardly defeated. They appear quite lethal and capable. Concluding that reduction in the spate of attacks is a sign of defeat is rather hasty and not supported by facts. BH is a patient and strategic enemy. It bids its time and strikes when it is ready.

The insurgency is a shooting and bombing war. It is not very helpful for the government to engage in psychological dissuasion by giving citizens a narrative that all is well. In 2018, scores of people were killed by the insurgents. In January 2018, the Deputy Secretary General of the United Nations, Hajiya Amina Mohammed, stated that the Boko Haram insurgency in the North East is not over yet and that "more investments are required to help military offensives with equipment."[8] The UN executive told Borno governor Kashim Shettima that the world body was facing a number of challenges in providing humanitarian intervention and assistance to 2.8 million refugees and internally displaced persons (IDPs) in Nigeria.[9]

The displacement theory of crime appears to be unfolding in this insurgency. As the sustained air and ground operations of the Nigerian military defeat the insurgents in their stronghold of the Sambisa Forest (Abubakar Shekau faction) and shores of Lake Chad (Abu Musab Al-Barnawi faction), the insurgents have been displaced and have relocated into villages in Borno and Yobe States.[10] Citizens in communities in Geidam and Gujba LGA in Yobe State[11] and Damboa and Biu LGA of Borno State are perturbed by the increased influx of Boko Haram fighters.[12]

In January 2018, the military recaptured Sambisa Forest from the BH insurgents. The insurgents had retaken the forest during the rainy season. Military offensives in Sabil Huda, Lagara Fulani, Somalia, Parisu I and II and Dar Salam evicted the insurgents from these areas.[13]

Operation Deep Punch is being conducted in the Lake Chad area by the 8 Division of the Nigerian Army. This operation is targeting Abu Musab Al-Barnawi's insurgents. On the southern flank, Operation Deep Punch is being conducted by the 7 Division of the Nigerian Army in the Sambisa Forest area – targeting Shekau's men. The 8 Division Nigerian Army is based in Sokoto. It was created in early 2017 by the Chief of Army Staff, Lt. Gen. Tukur Buratai, but took off in October 2017 with the assumption of duty of its pioneer General Officer Commanding (GOC), Brigadier-General Samuel Olabanji.

In January 2018, the village head of Ndoksa, Lawan Usman Ngari, was quoted as saying that his domain and all other villages in the area are under the control of Boko Haram. He said: "Infact there are no inhabitants in all the villages from Buni Yadi down to those villages under Damboa local council. These include Gogare, Chirala, Munguzon, Kobuk, Gulmas, Dusula, Gorogili and Auma villages."[14]

There is no intention to deny the tremendous achievements of the security forces in the war on terror. These include:

a. The recapture of Camp Zero from Boko Haram.
b. The rescue of over 12,000 Boko Haram hostages including over 1,000 in May 2018.
c. The arrest and trial of Usman Mohammed AKA Khalid Al-Barnawi the leader of the Ansaru terrorist group (a faction of Boko Haram).
d. The arrest and prosecution of Amodu Omale Salifu, leader of an ISIS affiliate group active in North Central Nigeria.

This book recognizes the heroism of the security forces, and urges the political elite to avoid the politicization, psychological dissuasion and incorrect narratives that gave rise to the insurgency in the first place. If the Customs Market Roundabout incident of June 11th, 2009 had been handled differently and competently, the sect members would have been aggrieved, but may not have declared jihad. However, when a chain reaction is set in motion, it is not easy to tell when or how it will end.

SOLUTION OF THE INSURGENCY

An insurgency of this nature is a complex social problem. It does not have a simple solution. The government's military crackdown solution on BH insurgency, which started under President Yar'Adua, has not solved the problem. President Jonathan combated the crisis militarily and the fight has continued under President Buhari. The crisis has survived four Chiefs of Army Staff – namely Lt. Gen. Abdulrahman Dambazzau, Lt. Gen. Azubuike Ihejirika, Lt. Gen. Kenneth Minimah and now Lt. Gen. Tukur Buratai. It is the wish of all Nigerians and the international community to see the end of this crisis under the stewardship of Gen. Buratai. However, it is not likely that that will happen. The BH insurgency is an ill-structured problem with multiple means and objectives. The Nigerian authorities will have to utilize a synthetic, multiple means and objectives problem-solving model to address the challenges.[15]

The government must maintain the military initiative as it has a duty under the Nigerian Constitution and the Westphalian conception of sovereignty to protect citizens within its national borders from being killed by insurgents. However, there are other solutions which the government should employ at the same time in order to defang the insurgency. These include:

a. Risk mapping methodology
b. Intelligence infrastructure
c. Education
d. Court system
e. Bomb prevention initiatives
f. Societal deradicalization.

Let us now consider each proposed solution.

Risk Mapping

The Nigerian government should urgently put in place a mechanism for risk identification, risk analysis, event forecasting, threat assessment and threat mitigation. There is inadequate attention to loss-producing events when they are in their incipient stages. These little fires become huge conflagrations when not attended to in a timely manner.

The authorities at the federal, state and local levels must set up trip-wires for recognizing events that have the potential for causing loss. These events should then be mitigated such that if a loss does occur it is minimal.

We hereby recommend a five-bucket risk mapping process to address risks in developing countries such as Nigeria. The process includes risk identification, risk assessment mitigation planning, countermeasure implementation and evaluation of countermeasure effectiveness.

A. **Risk identification:** The BH insurgency had grave risk written all over it right from when Mohammed Yusuf was converted to radical Islam in 2002. It was a crisis that developed over seven years. Unfortunately, the intelligence services that were supposed to track the events missed them. BH preference for living in communes was to enable them to prepare for jihad outside the glare of prying eyes. The security agencies should keep their eyes on the ball. When an organization begins to amass followers they are building an army. When they acquire weapons then they are getting ready to strike. When the leader makes a threat of armed action, then that is clearly a call to arms for the followers. There are many risks on the horizon in Nigeria. The Islamic Movement of Nigeria's clash with the army has the potential of becoming a large-scale societal risk. The Indigenous Peoples of Biafra (IPOB) matter also has the potential. The government should obey court orders and not give the impression that it is arbitrary and does not obey its courts. The ongoing farmers/herders clashes resulting in fatalities all over Nigeria is another "Boko Haram insurgency" in the making, yet it is not being competently dissected and resolved. This author has described the security problems that the Nigerian authorities need to address urgently as "galaxies of threats."[16] When these risks and threats are not identified and mitigated, the protagonists harden their positions and sometimes take up arms in open rebellion.

B. **Risk assessment:** Once the risk to society has been identified, the government must conduct an assessment of the potential loss event. The impact of the event should be estimated, along with the likelihood of occurrence and the outcome of the event if it were to occur. Neither the federal government nor the Borno State government on June 12th, 2009 correctly assessed the impact of the Customs Market Roundabout killings that occurred the previous day. If they had gazed into an accurate crystal ball and seen the devastation that is now Borno State, they would have gone to appease the BH sect and offered to pay lavish compensation for the 17 sect members killed.

C. **Mitigation planning:** Depending on the types of threat and the criticality of loss, the government can develop risk mitigation measures that will address the risk.

Mitigation measures usually relate to ways the government can either head off the issue or protect threatened populations. If there is a risk of armed attack against a community, the government would typically send in law enforcement assets or the military to address the threat. If it is a bush fire or petroleum pipeline fire, then fire service officials would be sent – each course of action has a cost element.

D. **Countermeasures implementation:** This involves directing resourcing and execution of the course of action (COA) chosen by the executive. Prompt release of funds will make actions move faster. Governments should be aware that when there is crisis, some ethically challenged persons try to cash in and divert funds or other assets for their personal use. There must be adequate physical and procedural controls in place to make it harder for government assets to be stolen and converted to personal use.

E. **Evaluation:** Programs, projects and policy inputs must be evaluated for effectiveness. Are they achieving the designed objectives? What of the overall goals? Are they being displaced? Is there any tweaking required? When policies, programs and projects go into effect, they are usually reshaped by the environment and by the served population. These sensibilities, nuances and cultural factors must be taken into consideration in fine-tuning the policies program and projects for overall effectiveness.

Intelligence

To combat the Boko Haram insurgency, the government of Nigeria must build a robust intelligence infrastructure from the bottom up, which will enable security officials to learn of the plans and terror plots and interrupt them before they become loss events.

Professor Nwolise wrote: "Nigeria's intelligence community could neither penetrate the Boko Haram at the start of the campaign especially between 2011 and 2014, nor gather much information about the sect to be of good use to the military."[17]

Government intelligence efforts must be focused on countering extremism and violence. The attacks on Panshekara police station in Kano, the Sheikh Albani assassination, the jihadi rhetoric of Mohammed Yusuf among others and the militant posture of Shekau from 2002 to 2009 had enough indicators (red flags) to mount a full intelligence operation on the sect before they declared jihad. If the Nigerian authorities had eyes and ears inside the sect, it would have known what it was up against. The intelligence community apparently missed the proverbial elephant in the room. Intelligence includes basic intelligence and current intelligence. The basic intelligence is gathered when there is no conflict. It provides background information on an organization of interest and enables officials to estimate the threat rating of the entity. Current intelligence is that on the insurgency at hand. Before the formation of the Civilian JTF in Maiduguri in May 2013, the JTF-ORO in Borno State was literally fighting with its hands tied behind its back. The operational method was cordon and search of any flash point leading to arrests for screening. However, once the young men were arrested, they became resentful and denied knowledge of any information. There was a psychological wall between the community and the JTF. Even though the military was there to protect them, they did not see it that way.

However, when as a result of enlightened self-interest the youths formed the CJTF to assist in the fight, the military now had an invaluable ally who knew the environment and even knew the terrorists. The CJTF became the key intelligence resource for the military on the ground level.

When the Nigerian government procured air assets and was able to fly intelligence, surveillance and reconnaissance missions everywhere in the North East, the Nigeria Air Force was then able to assist the Army in the battle.

The BH insurgency thrived on the monumental intelligence failure of the Nigerian State – failure to collect intelligence probably due to religious sensibilities. However, conflict and insurgency can arise from any source. The role of intelligence is to identify any thing, any group and/or phenomenon that can potentially harm society (that is risk) and then follow it. The intelligence infrastructure in Nigeria is overdue for a total overhaul and renewal for improved performance and ensuring that Nigeria's national security is not so easily breached.

Education

The government must invest in the education of Nigerian children and youths. The young suicide bombers being used by BH insurgents are not educated. The United Nations Children Fund (UNICEF) reports that Nigeria has the largest number of children, globally, who do not attend school. Out of the 13.5 million out of school children in Nigeria, 60% are girls who live in Northern Nigeria.[18]

The wife of the Chief of Army Staff Mrs. Umma Tukur Buratai declared recently that poor education in the North East region was responsible for the BH insurgency.[19]

In April 2014, then President Goodluck Jonathan said that the lack of education and employment for the youths in the northeast have made the youths into ready tools for terrorists. The President called on governors to take charge of primary and secondary education in the states.[20]

The Borno State government has responded with an initiative called Mega Schools for 70,000 children orphaned by BH insurgency. Twenty-one mega schools have been built in the state. The mega schools would have a special educational curriculum. The schools would have psychologists and guidance counselors to help children who have lost their entire families.[21]

Professor Pat Utomi summed it up this way:

> We must begin to educate the masses of the north so that they can value their lives. Education increases their level of consciousness and when a man has a heightened level of consciousness, he is no longer easily susceptible to manipulation using primordial sentiments.[22]

Court System

The Nigerian Constitution of 1999 provides for an adequate court system in the arraignment and trial of offenders. However, there are several leakages in the system. Justice is painfully slow and the courts give wide latitude to lawyers to ply their strategy of delaying trials endlessly. If someone is accused of a terrorist crime, he should be tried in open court and evidence adduced as to his/her culpability. If the court finds the individual guilty, then they should be punished. However, when trials take on the quality of a witch-hunt, this builds resentment which could lead to unintended consequences.

Most people are law-abiding and see the courts as fair arbiters. The court system must be emphasized in reducing tensions in society. Court orders must also be obeyed by the executive even if the order is not to their liking. When a competent court orders the granting of bail to a suspect the order should be obeyed until the next adjourned date. It is wrong for the government to refuse to release a suspect on bail for a bailable offence when the court has so ruled.

In trying terror suspects, Nigerian courts should grant witness protection to those who will testify in order to avoid reprisals. The Federal High Court sitting in Abuja recently granted protection for witnesses in the trial of BH insurgents.[23]

A 22-year-old commander of Boko Haram, Abba Umar, was sentenced to 60 years in prison in February 2018 for various acts of terrorism by the Federal High Court in Wiwa Cantonment, Kainji, Niger State. Umar told the court during the judicial proceedings that if released he would return to Sambisa Forest to continue terrorist acts. Umar had been in detention since 2014 after a failed VBIED suicide bombing mission to Gombe Secondary School in Gombe.[24] The ordnance failed to explode due to a malfunction and he was captured.

A fair open trial of this nature rekindles hope in all (including insurgents) that the court system works. To combat insurgency, the Nigerian government has set up fast-track special courts in Kainji, Niger State, to speedily try suspects since BH detainees are in excess of 5,000. The Nigerian Bar Association and the National Human Rights Commission observe the proceedings.

Bomb Prevention Initiative

The most terrible weapon in the arsenal of a terrorist is the improvised explosive device (IED). The AK-47 rifle or other assault rifles are a major threat but the IED beats them all. BH insurgents have made IED attacks their weapon of choice. It behooves the governments in all Northern states to put IED prevention initiatives in place.

On April 14th, 2014, after the bombing of the Nyanya transportation center in Abuja which killed over 75 people, this author issued the following template to the government under the auspices of the Association of Industrial Security and Safety Operators of Nigeria (AISSON):[25]

1. Enrollment of citizens by the government into a national bomb prevention initiative would make them into a bulwark of defense against criminal explosions
2. Security awareness program of citizens on IEDs
3. Suspicious objects identification and reporting
4. Suspicious vehicle reporting
5. Report suspicious behavior by terrorists planting IEDs
6. Suspicious behavior of terrorists throwing IEDs
7. Short-code telephone numbers for reporting suspected threats
8. Staffing of call centers with professional, highly trained personnel who can skillfully interact with callers and get relevant information about the threat
9. Dispatch of police EOD personnel to secure the sites
10. Coordination of the National IED Prevention Initiative by the Office of the National Security Advisor
11. Creation of state IED prevention initiatives.

Deradicalization

The Nigerian government currently has a program for the deradicalization of captured Boko Haram fighters and their subsequent release to state governments – particularly Borno State. The deradicalization program should go beyond captured insurgents. It should be a program that addresses the general concern of youth radicalization in the Muslim North. The message of BH has its appeal. Shekau grew up hardened by the hardship and neglect that was his life. However, he found solace in religion, and later he was convinced that jihad was a way to change society. The corruption, debauchery, oppression and other societal ills that Boko Haram preached against remain. One wonders how many 10-year-old children are waiting to pick up a rifle and declare war on the Nigerian state. However, if the government designs and implements a deliberate program of deradicalization of the youth, then in five years' time the benefits will begin to show. Education and jobs must fill the vacuum created. The Almajiri schools set up by President Jonathan in some Northern states must be sustained as a way of propagating Western education among children in the North.

What should a deradicalization program entail?

a. Recruitment of respected and knowledgeable Imams to counter the radical narrative. Nigeria's Boko Haram targets citizens and infrastructure indiscriminately. The Taliban in Afghanistan where Mohammed Alli, and by extension Mohammed Yusuf, were radicalized do not kill people indiscriminately in Afghanistan or destroy infrastructure. Their target is the military or police. The narrative here is that destroying lives and assets is not the answer to societal ills.

b. Use of mass media in propagating the anti-radical message. Radio broadcasts can reach a wider audience. The government should provide AM/FM radios to indigent families.

c. Revival of television viewing centers where counter-radicalization messages will be broadcast. IDP camps will be excellent locations.

d. Printing and distribution of booklets and flyers in Hausa or Kanuri languages to counter the message of hate and extremism.

e. Monitoring of *tafsir* by Imams and dispassionate assessment of *tafsir* that intend to incite violence. Such religious leaders should be invited for questioning by the DSS and released. If they persist in inciting violence then they would have broken the law, and must be promptly arrested and prosecuted.

f. Monitoring of clerics who preach hate and violence – Christian or Muslim.
g. Arrest of politicians who make statements that call for sectarian violence. The government must have zero tolerance for hate speech.

CONCLUSION

A myriad of solutions have been proposed to combat the ongoing BH insurgency in Nigeria. This book views the insurgency from the prism of security. There is no attempt to consider the political or religious implications of the insurgency war.

We argue that a timeline analysis of September to December 2010 provided enough indicators that a major insurgency was afoot in Nigeria. Unfortunately, the authorities missed all the indicators. By June 2011, when the federal government established the Joint Task Force – Operation Restore Order (JTF-ORO) in Maiduguri, the insurgency was already full blown. The next day, June 16th, 2011, the National Police Headquarters was hit with a VBIED in the first suicide bombing attack in Nigerian history. Two months later (August 26th, 2011), the United Nations House was bombed killing 23 and injuring over 100. This internationalized the conflict instantly.

The Nigerian military combated the insurgents for two years without critical local knowledge and intelligence. The youths of Borno State, who were at the receiving end of JTF arrests because they fit the profile of terrorists, decided to join the military in the fight against the insurgents. This was a major break for the military with intelligence. The military now had eyes and ears and could pinpoint the enemy for engagement.

The following recommendations are proffered for countering the BH insurgency in Nigeria. Some of these recommendations may apply elsewhere given local circumstances and factors driving the insurgency.

a. **Risk mapping:** The government must emplace a risk mapping protocol that will enable it to identify risk, assess risk, develop mitigation options, implement countermeasures and evaluate the effectiveness of the countermeasures.
b. **Intelligence:** The government must build a robust infrastructure from the bottom up. Nigeria has a large intelligence community but it must be tasked to produce intelligence on violent extremism.
c. **Education:** This must become the birthright of every Nigerian child. With education comes an ability to reason for oneself and

not just do what an Imam says. State governments must do more in mandating the education of children of primary and secondary school age. One of the Chibok girls who got away recently completed her high school education in the USA.

d. **Court system:** The judicial system must join the fight against insurgency. Suspects must be given fair and expeditious trials. Persons of high standing in society should not be given a pass if they aid terrorists. Court orders against the executive must be obeyed. These conducts reinforce collective belief in the court system and further validation of the judiciary.

e. **Bomb prevention initiative:** The Office of the National Security Advisor should establish a national IED prevention initiative to save lives. If the citizens are enrolled with knowledge, they become a bulwark of the fight against IEDs – the weapon of choice of Nigerian terrorists.

f. **Deradicalization:** There should be a program of action to deradicalize the youths. The present practice of preaching to those in custody does not go far enough. There are many radicals in society waiting for an opportunity to join the fight. They could be dissuaded. Intelligence agents should monitor churches and mosques and question clerics who make hate speeches. If the bad conduct by such clerics persists, then they should be prosecuted. No one is above the law.

It is hoped that with these recommendations and other initiatives, a quick and lasting solution can be found to the Boko Haram insurgency in Nigeria.

NOTES

1. See Katherine H. Pherson and Randolph H. Pherson. **Critical Thinking for Strategic Intelligence**. Los Angeles, CA: CQ Press (2013): Pages 20–21.
2. Michael Olugbode. "32 Killed, 84 Injured in Borno Explosion" *This Day* (June 18th, 2018): Page 1.
3. Blessing Olaifa. "Five Soldiers Killed as Troops Neutralize Boko Haram Fighters" *The Nation* (June 1st, 2018): Page 6.
4. "Boko Haram Suicide Bomb Kills Five, Wounds Seven in Kondugha" *Sahara Reporters* (May 28th, 2018).
5. Editorial Page Comment. "Salute to Heroism" *The Nation* (May 28th, 2018): Page 15.

6. Olajumoke Ayandele. "The Loneliest War: Nigeria's Strategy Against Boko Haram" *The Republic* (June/July 2017).

7. Ayodeji Adegboyega. "Boko Haram Is Defeated – Nigeria Now Facing 'Global Insurgency' – Minister" *Premium Times* (February 7th, 2019).

8. "Boko Haram Insurgency Not Over Yet, Says UN" *The Guardian* (January 12th, 2018): Page 4.

9. Ibid.

10. Hamza Idris and Kabir Matazu. "Fleeing B/Haram Insurgents Lurk in Borno, Yobe Villages" *Daily Trust* (January 30th, 2018): Pages 1, 5.

11. Ibid.

12. Ibid.

13. "Sambisa Forest Go Turn to Road" *BBC News* (January 31st, 2018). https://www.bbc.com/pidgin/tori/42886227

14. See Hamza Idris and Kabir Matazu. "Fleeing B/Haram Insurgents Lurk in Borno, Yobe Villages" *Daily Trust* (January 30th, 2018): Pages 1, 5.

15. The author is referring to the use of a Kantain Inquirer that is capable of solving ill-structured policy problems. See C. West Churchman. **The Design of Inquiring Systems: Basic Concepts of Systems and Organizations**. New York, NY: Basic Books (1971).

16. Dr. Ona Ekhomu. "International and Regional Mechanisms for Counterterrorism and Counterinsurgency (CTCOIN) Operations" Paper Presented at the CTCOIN Lecture at the Armed Forces Command and Staff College, Jaji, Kaduna (June 2018).

17. OBC Nwolise. "Military Intelligence. Military Operations and the War Against Terrorism in Nigeria" in Pius Adejoh and Waziri Adisa (Editors) **Terrorism and Counter Terrorism War in Nigeria**. Lagos, Nigeria: University of Lagos Press (2017): Page 461.

18. Samsom Ezea. "Insurgency and the Disrupted School Calendar in the North" *The Guardian* (November 29th, 2014): Page 49.

19. Luni Sadiq. "Poor Education Responsible for Boko Haram – Mrs. Buratai" *Daily Trust* (May 20th, 2017): Page 9.

20. Nnamdi Felix. "Blame Game Over Insurgency" *The News* (April 14th, 2014).

21. Uthman Abubakar. "Boko Halal: Borno's Mega Schools Renew Hopes of Boko Haram's Orphans" *Daily Trust* (August 19th, 2017): Page 41.

22. Pat Utomi. "Fight Terrorism with Education, Not Guns" *The Punch* (May 17th, 2013): Page 25.

23. Alex Enumah. "Court Grants Protection for Witnesses in Trial of Seven Boko Haram Suspects" *This Day* (April 12th, 2017): Page 53.

24. Ade Adesomoju. "22-year-old B'Haram Commander Jailed 60 Years for Terrorism" *The Punch* (February 14th, 2018): Page 12.

25. Ishola Balogun. "Bomb Prevention Initiative Is Long Overdue – Ekhomu" *Saturday Vanguard* (April 26th, 2014): Page 14.

INDEX

255

For Product Safety Concerns and Information please contact our EU
representative GPSR@taylorandfrancis.com
Taylor & Francis Verlag GmbH, Kaufingerstraße 24, 80331 München, Germany